Csound Power! The Comprehensive Guide

Jim Aikin

Course Technology PTR
A part of Cengage Learning

COURSE TECHNOLOGY
CENGAGE Learning·

Australia • Brazil • Japan • Korea • Mexico • Singapore • Spain • United Kingdom • United States

COURSE TECHNOLOGY
CENGAGE Learning

Csound Power! The Comprehensive Guide
Jim Aikin

Publisher and General Manager, Course Technology PTR: Stacy L. Hiquet

Associate Director of Marketing: Sarah Panella

Manager of Editorial Services: Heather Talbot

Senior Marketing Manager: Mark Hughes

Acquisitions Editor: Orren Merton

Project/Copy Editor: Cathleen D. Small

Technical Reviewer: Andrés Cabrera

Interior Layout Tech: MPS Limited, a Macmillan Company

Cover Designer: Mike Tanamachi

Indexer: Katherine Stimson

Proofreader: Sam Garvey

For product information and technology assistance, contact us at
Cengage Learning Customer & Sales Support, 1-800-354-9706
For permission to use material from this text or product,
submit all requests online at **www.cengage.com/permissions**
Further permissions questions can be emailed to
permissionrequest@cengage.com

All trademarks are the property of their respective owners.

All images © Cengage Learning unless otherwise noted.

Library of Congress Control Number: 2011936043

ISBN-13: 978-1-4354-6004-1

ISBN-10: 1-4354-6004-9

Course Technology, a part of Cengage Learning
20 Channel Center Street
Boston, MA 02210
USA

Cengage Learning is a leading provider of customized learning solutions with office locations around the globe, including Singapore, the United Kingdom, Australia, Mexico, Brazil, and Japan. Locate your local office at:
international.cengage.com/region

Cengage Learning products are represented in Canada by Nelson Education, Ltd.

For your lifelong learning solutions, visit **courseptr.com**

Visit our corporate website at **cengage.com**

Printed in the United States of America
1 2 3 4 5 6 7 14 13 12

Acknowledgments

Heartfelt thanks are due, first of all, to Barry Vercoe for creating Csound, and to Max Mathews for laying the groundwork. Thanks go, in the same breath, to the team of developers and maintainers currently led by John ffitch, who have kept Csound relevant over the course of many years. Thanks to Richard Boulanger for his enthusiastic support of Csound and for his editorship of *The Csound Book,* which introduced many of us to Csound for the first time. Thanks to Andrés Cabrera for his ongoing development of CsoundQt, for his video tutorials, and not least for his work as the technical editor on this book. Thanks to Steven Yi, both for his ongoing development of blue and for his work as editor of *The Csound Journal.* Thanks to the regular contributors to the Csound mailing list, especially Victor Lazzarini and Michael Gogins, for their swift and cogent replies to my many technical questions. Thanks to Joachim Heintz, Iain McCurdy, Rory Walsh, and others for their contributions to the online Floss manual for Csound.

And finally, thanks to Bob Moog and other experts on technology who so generously took the time to educate me on the basics of music technology during my years at *Keyboard.* Without their assistance and support, this book never would have been written.

About the Author

Jim Aikin has written hundreds of articles on music technology for *Keyboard, Electronic Musician, Mix,* and other magazines. He is the author of *Power Tools for Synthesizer Programming, Chords & Harmony, Picture Yourself Playing Cello,* and two out-of-print science fiction novels. His short fiction has appeared in *Asimov's Science Fiction, The Magazine of Fantasy & Science Fiction,* and other magazines. He is also active as a hobbyist computer programmer, having released half a dozen freeware text adventure games. To learn more about his varied activities, visit www.musicwords.net.

Contents

Chapter 3
QuickStart Projects   **33**

Chapter 4
The Structure and Syntax of a .csd File   **55**

Chapter 5
Using the CsoundQt Interface   **65**

Chapter 6
Building Your Own Instruments and Effects   89

Chapter 7
Thirty Opcodes You Must Know   115

Chapter 8
Writing a Csound Score   215

Chapter 9
Front Ends
237

Chapter 10
Using Csound with MIDI, OSC, Pd, Python, and Live Audio
249

Introduction

I'm a big fan of free, do-it-yourself software. For anyone who is willing to dig in and learn a few concepts, the creative possibilities are beyond vast. The same could be said of commercial software, of course, but the market pressures on commercial software companies not infrequently force them to limit the creative options that will be made available to users. With free, open-source software, any sort of visionary idea, no matter how far from the mainstream, can become a reality.

Make no mistake, though: There's always a learning process to trudge through, sometimes a lengthy one. And because free software is developed and maintained primarily by cadres of unpaid volunteers, the functionality sometimes leapfrogs past the documentation.

Some very good free software presents the user with a point-and-click interface, much like commercial software. I use OpenOffice for word processing, GIMP for graphics, and Audacity for audio editing; all three are free and very capable. But sometimes, doing it yourself means actual computer programming—and programming is never simple.

Having debuted in 1985, Csound is quite likely the oldest music software still in active use. It's a highly sophisticated system, capable of doing almost anything you might imagine in the way of audio—and also a great many things you've probably never imagined! All things considered, it's not *that* difficult to learn. Once you've mastered a few basic concepts, using Csound is almost as transparent as plugging patch cords into the jacks on a modular synthesizer. But because of the huge variety of features that have been added over the years by dozens of talented programmers, Csound is one massive mother of a modular. Understanding how to get started and how to move forward is not guaranteed to be easy. Possibly a book would come in handy.

I certainly won't claim to be a Csound virtuoso, but over the years I've dabbled with it quite a bit and have learned enough of the basics to be able to produce musical sounds. (I've also worked very extensively with, and written extensively about, commercial music software.) I was delighted to be offered the opportunity to write *Csound Power!*, first because I love the idea of helping people learn how to use free, do-it-yourself software, and second because writing the book gave me an excuse to really dig in and learn more about Csound.

All of the code in this book has been tested and works correctly with Csound 5.13. There's no guesswork between these covers. Nevertheless, you need to realize that Csound is an ongoing project. As a topic for a book, it's a moving target. Just before this book was sent off to the publisher, version 5.14 was released, and it includes at least one highly desirable new feature that is not covered in these pages. If you're reading this book for the first time two or three years from now, Csound should still work exactly as described here—new versions are fully backward-compatible, unless an error sneaks in and hasn't yet been corrected—but new features that may simplify or enhance some of the tasks described between these covers won't be mentioned.

Note If you find technical errors in this book (there are bound to be one or two), please email the author at midiguru23@sbcglobal.net, so the errors can be noted online and corrected in a later edition of the book, should one be published.

Making music by sitting at a computer and typing lines of code would probably seem quite bizarre to earlier generations of musicians, could they glimpse it. It may also seem bizarre to musicians active today who still practice the time-honored art of making joyful noises by wiggling their fingers. But music is music, however it's produced, and anything that produces musical sounds is a musical instrument, whatever its features. Csound is a musical instrument. But as Richard Boulanger likes to point out, in at least one respect it's no different from any other instrument: If you want to make music with it, you'll have to practice!

An instrument that lives inside a computer is not so complete a break with the past as you might imagine. Luigi Russolo's groundbreaking manifesto, *The Art of Noises,* was published in 1913. Even before that, in the late 1890s, Thaddeus Cahill had been working on a way to generate music and distribute it to listeners using electricity. In the 1930s, concert pianist Percy Grainger championed the use of machinery to produce automated pitch contours. In the 1940s, Conlon Nancarrow began a decades-long exploration of machine-generated music, using player pianos to perform impossibly complex rhythms. By the 1950s, Pierre Schaeffer and other musicians were assembling sequences of tones by snipping apart and painstakingly reassembling segments of analog recording tape. Delia Derbyshire's amazing (and largely unsung) work at the BBC Radiophonic Workshop in the 1960s culminated in her realization of the theme music for the original *Doctor Who* series, which was produced in exactly the same way, by splicing tape.

I've always wondered what marvelous music we would have been treated to if Derbyshire or Nancarrow had been able to realize their musical visions with the aid of Csound.

If you understand what a provocative question that is, welcome home. Csound is quite likely what you've been searching for. It's my sincere hope that this book will help you take your music in whatever directions you can imagine—and maybe in a few directions that you haven't yet imagined. Have fun!

1 The World of Csound

Power, convenience, and low price—choose any two.

In the past 20 years, the personal computer has completely changed the way music is composed, recorded, stored, and shared. Music software for Macintosh, Windows, and Linux is available in (speaking metaphorically) a bewildering variety of shapes and sizes, and music software for handhelds such as the iPad is rapidly gaining in importance. But which software is the right match for your needs?

If you're looking to get involved (or more involved) with computer-based music-making, you probably have a list of things you hope to get from the next program you download or buy. Leading the list will probably be great sound, powerful features, ease of use, and affordability.

Now for the bad news: You can't have it all. Not in a single program, anyway. In selecting a music program that will be the focus of your creative work, you'll have to make some tough choices. Most of today's software is capable of producing high-quality sound, so that's not a factor you'll need to lose sleep over—not unless you're producing albums for platinum-selling pop stars, and maybe not even then. Hit CDs have been and continue to be produced using very modest equipment.

In the end, your options boil down to this:

If you want power and convenience, you can purchase any number of commercial programs: multitrack audio/MIDI recorders, plug-in synthesizers, high-powered audio editors, and more. These programs sound wonderful, they're packed with features, and the user interfaces are usually designed to let you produce finished music quickly, without worrying *too* much about the technical details. But they're not free. A good DAW (digital audio workstation) will cost from $500 to $1,000, and you can easily pay as much or more for a set of software instruments. (The cost is generally far lower if you're running the Linux operating system on your computer, but your software choices in the world of Linux will also be more limited.)

If you want convenience and low price, you can choose from a variety of very friendly entry-level programs, but you'll have to do without the kind of high-end power features that professionals require. DAW software for Windows starts as low as $99, and many of these programs come with both software instruments and a library of loops for building tracks. Macintosh computers

1

come with GarageBand, a free program that does multitrack recording and provides a suite of basic software instruments and recorded loops. Other software instruments are available as free downloads. (Some of them are good, others not so good.)

If, on the other hand, you crave the power of a high-end program, and you also want it at a rock-bottom price, again you have some excellent options—but be prepared to sacrifice convenience. Some of the most powerful music software available today is entirely free. One of the most important of the free power-user music programs is, of course, Csound. (For a quick look at some other options that fit in the same category, see "Alternatives" at the end of this chapter.) Csound is free to download, it runs equally well on Mac, Windows, and Linux, and you just about couldn't find a program with more high-end features for the dedicated computer musician.

Within the last couple of years, Csound has become significantly easier to work with, thanks to "front end" programs such as CsoundQt (formerly called QuteCsound—see Chapter 5, "Using the CsoundQt Interface," to learn to use this program) and blue (see Chapter 9, "Front Ends"), which automate some of the tasks that you formerly had to set up by hand. But "easier" is a relative term. Csound is never going to be point-and-click, and there's an important reason for that. In point-and-click software, the designers of the program have made some musical decisions for you. They have made assumptions about what you'll probably want to do musically. In an entry-level program, for instance, the designers may assume that you'll be recording music in which the same time signature is used throughout a given piece, so you may not be able to switch time signatures within the piece. This is a good assumption for 98 percent of pop music, but it's definitely a limitation. Csound, on the other hand, doesn't assume you'll be using a time signature at all. With Csound, pretty much every musical decision is left entirely up to you—including whether you use Csound to make music or for some other purpose. As a result, you'll have to do some extra work.

Richard Boulanger, who teaches Csound at the Berklee College of Music, likes to say, "With Csound, the only limit is your imagination." I once suggested to him that that slogan should be amended to, "With Csound, the only limit is your patience." It may be true that with Csound (augmented, perhaps, by a fast computer and some good microphones) you can produce literally any music you can imagine, but getting there is not guaranteed to be a stroll in the park.

About This Book

The goal of *Csound Power!* is to help you learn to make music using Csound. I have tried to make as few assumptions as possible about what you already know. Where a new concept is first mentioned, you'll find either an explanation of the concept, a pointer to a later chapter where it is explored in detail, or possibly some links with which to research the topic on the Internet.

Of necessity, I'll assume that you understand how to use your computer—how to launch programs by double-clicking on their icons, how to use menus and keystroke commands, how to

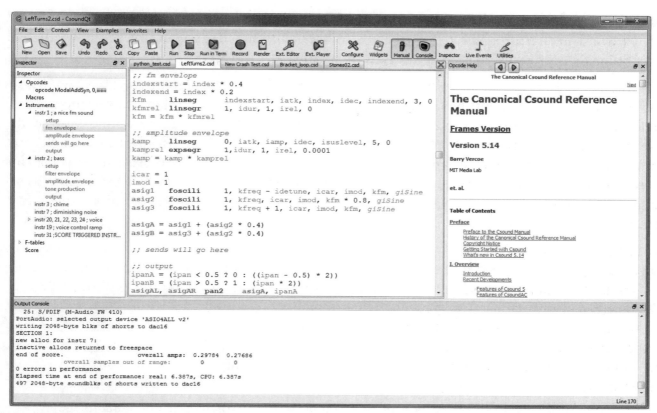

Figure 1.1 Csound's most popular user interface, written in the Qt programming language by Andrés Cabrera, is CsoundQt. CsoundQt is cross-platform-compatible (Windows, Macintosh, Linux) and provides numerous convenience features that make Csound easier to work with. For details on how to use CsoundQt, see Chapter 5. Several other "front end" programs, each providing a different set of features, are also available. For details on the latter, see Chapter 9. **Important note:** Prior to version 0.7, CsoundQt was called QuteCsound. In *Csound Power!,* the program is referred to by its new name.

save and back up your work, and so forth. If you're not at least modestly computer-literate, a system like Csound is just about guaranteed to baffle you.

Because the topics we'll be discussing are complex and interrelated, you may find that a little patience will come in handy. You may find it helpful to make a mental note of any questions that come to mind and trust that the answers will appear in due course. The opening section of this chapter, for instance, mentions "front-end" programs that work with Csound, without explaining exactly what a front end is or how it relates to Csound. For a full explanation of that topic, you'll have to wait for (or jump ahead to) Chapter 9.

In Chapter 2, "Downloading and Installing," you'll learn how to download and install Csound. If you're eager to get started and don't want to spend too much time poring over technical details, after installing Csound you can move on to Chapter 3, "QuickStart Projects," which lays out a few QuickStart projects in hands-on fashion.

Csound is a computer programming language, and Chapter 4, "The Structure and Syntax of a .csd File," explains the precise syntax you'll need to understand while typing your code. Chapter 5 explains how to use the powerful, and fairly friendly, CsoundQt interface. In Chapter 6, "Building Your Own Instruments and Effects," we return to coding with a discussion of Csound's variable types, arithmetic operations, logic statements, and more.

The most important chapter in this book is probably Chapter 7, "Thirty Opcodes You Must Know." Here you'll find detailed discussions of several dozen of Csound's most important opcodes. The opcodes, such as oscillators and filters, are what you'll use to build your own Csound instruments. Chapter 8, "Writing a Csound Score," explains the features you'll use when creating musical scores in Csound. Chapter 9 introduces some alternative front-end programs that can be used with Csound. Chapter 10, "Using Csound with MIDI, OSC, Pd, Python, and Live Audio," discusses using Csound in real time, primarily with MIDI, but also using OSC and for processing live audio.

 MIDI (Musical Instrument Digital Interface) is an industry-wide communications protocol used by music hardware and software for sending control messages. Developed in 1982, MIDI defines a number of message types. For further information, see www.midi.org.

 OSC (Open Sound Control) is a communications protocol for computers, synthesizers, and multimedia devices. OSC overcomes many of the limitations of MIDI but is less widely supported and requires more expert knowledge of the user. For further information, see http://opensoundcontrol.org.

What you won't find in *Csound Power!* is a complete discussion of every feature of Csound. Such a discussion would take several thousand pages! While we'll dig into some fairly sophisticated concepts as we go along, this book is written primarily for new users. It's designed to tell you everything you need to know to get started with Csound and then move forward. As you become a power user, you'll naturally want to draw on other resources. (A list of the main resources can be found at the end of this chapter.)

Nor will you find much discussion of the basics of sound and digital audio. This material has been extensively covered elsewhere—for instance, in *Working with Audio* (Course Technology PTR, 2011) by Stanley R. Alten. Some of the technical terms will be defined in *Csound Power!* when they're first used, but for the big picture, you'll need to consult other resources.

What Is Csound?

Csound is a computer programming language designed specifically for audio synthesis and sound composition. It was initially developed by Barry Vercoe at MIT in 1984–85. The underlying code for Csound is written in the popular C programming language, hence the name—but you don't have to know C in order to use Csound. (If you're entirely new to the idea of computer programming, you should expect to learn some new concepts and processes.)

Vercoe's work was based on the earlier Music-N audio programming languages developed by Max Mathews at Bell Labs, starting with Music-1 in 1957. As such, Csound is perhaps the oldest music programming language still in use. Today, the lead developer for Csound is John ffitch, who has recently retired from his position at the University of Bath in England. Many other developers from around the world actively contribute to Csound, expanding and refining its capabilities on an ongoing basis.

Until the early 1990s, general-purpose computers were too slow to generate complex audio in real time. For a few years prior to that, computers had been able to "stream" previously recorded audio files from their hard drives and send them to an output device (a digital-to-analog converter) so the audio could be listened to, but the mathematical processes required to synthesize new audio signals were too complex for computers' CPUs to attempt them. Special hardware (such as the FM chip in the Yamaha DX7 synthesizer) was required for real-time digital sound synthesis.

For this reason, Csound began as a rendering program. It generated audio files and stored them on the hard drive. Many minutes might be needed to produce only a few seconds of sound. To hear the music you had created, you would play back the previously stored file. Today, thanks to massive increases in computer power, Csound is often used to generate sound, and also to process incoming audio streams, in real time. Messages sent to Csound over MIDI and OSC can be used for control of real-time performances.

However, Csound retains its original form as a text-based programming language, so understanding its origins is useful. As programming languages go, it's fairly straightforward. Csound code is quite easy both to write and to read once you understand a few simple conventions. Nonetheless, in order to use it you'll need to be willing to write (and debug) your own code.

Csound code consists of two discrete elements—an orchestra, which contains user-defined instruments, and a score, which is a list of events that "play" the instruments in the score. Details on how these elements are assembled and work together will be found throughout this book, as well as in *The Canonical Csound Reference Manual*; see the sections of the manual called "Syntax of the Orchestra" and "The Standard Numeric Score."

Using this simple orchestra/score paradigm, you can both design your own sounds (as instruments) and compose music (in the form of a score). If you're familiar with conventional DAW software, you can think of Csound as being roughly equivalent to a virtual rack of software instruments (the orchestra), coupled with a sequencer (the score). However, both of these components are capable of far more sophisticated operation than what you'll find in a typical commercial DAW, even a very good one. Comparing a Csound score to a MIDI event list is like comparing a Lamborghini sports car to a Vespa motor scooter.

Lest anyone be misled, I should make it clear that the word "score" means something quite different in Csound from what orchestral musicians mean when they use the term. Csound is not compatible in any way with conventional music notation. Unless translated into MIDI data by a scanning and notation system such as Avid Sibelius, a notated score can't be used as an input for Csound. Nor will Csound generate a musician-readable score as output.

Included in the Csound distribution are several non-real-time sound analysis tools, which can be used to analyze sampled (recorded) digital sound. The data generated by these tools can then be used to resynthesize the recorded sounds, with or without complex alterations. (See "Analysis and Resynthesis" in Chapter 7.)

For the most part, Csound is backward-compatible. Music written for the very earliest versions, such as Richard Boulanger's "Trapped in Convert" (ported to Csound in 1986 and included in the Examples directory of CsoundQt) can still be compiled and played on the current version, because Csound's older features are never removed (though some are deprecated).

Csound is open-source software. This means that if you know how to program using the C language, you can download the source code for Csound, modify it in whatever way you like, and compile your modified version. This is, in fact, how Csound evolves: An active community of developers makes changes, which are then uploaded to the Csound source code in the Source-Forge repository. At semi-regular intervals, the source code is compiled by Csound's developer team, bundled with other components in installer programs, and made available to ordinary users. Most Csound users, especially if their operating system is Windows or Mac OS, use these pre-compiled *binary* versions rather than building (compiling) their own. A higher percentage of Csound users in the Linux community prefer to compile Csound directly from the source code rather than downloading a pre-compiled version.

Compiling Csound yourself from the source code is beyond the scope of this book, though Linux users will find a few tips in Chapter 2. If you want to try it, you'll probably find yourself asking for help on the Csound email list. (See the "Resources" section at the end of this chapter to learn how to join this list.) One advantage of compiling the code yourself is that you'll be able to take immediate advantage of any bug fixes that have been incorporated since the most recent official release version.

The current version of Csound at this writing is 5.13.

Why Use Csound?

No music software is right for everybody. Although you could certainly use Csound to record a country ballad or a hip-hop track, it's probably not the best tool for the job. Csound is used most often by composers who are interested in exploring the outer reaches of composition and sound design, and by younger musicians (often in college) who are eager to push the boundaries of what can be accomplished artistically using a computer.

Here are some reasons why you might want to use Csound:

■ You have a strong interest in sound design and unusual sonic resources.

■ Your music consists largely of abstract soundscapes (either sampled or synthesized) rather than of phrases and chords made up of groups of notes.

■ You want to interact with your music while it plays, rather than creating a fixed composition that will sound exactly the same every time it is played.

- You want to explore microtonal intervals and pitch relationships.

- You want to explore intricate, mathematically defined polyrhythms.

- You're fascinated by computer-generated algorithmic composition.

- You're frustrated by the limitations of MIDI sequencers.

- You have a background in hardware-based modular synthesis and want to apply your knowledge of patching and modulation to a system that operates in a similar way and provides an essentially unlimited set of modules.

- You have a strong background in computer programming and want to use your skill set to create music (about which you may or may not be as knowledgeable).

- You plan to pursue a career in music software or digital signal processing, and you want to learn how audio software works at a fairly deep level.

- You want the music projects you create today to be fully reproducible (and editable) 10 or 20 years from now, on computer systems not yet invented.

- You've spent every dollar you had on a decent computer and a decent sound system, and you have no money left to invest in commercial music software.

- You have physical limitations that make it difficult for you to use standard types of music technology, such as point-and-click software and keyboard instruments with LCD displays.

Conversely, here are a few reasons why you might *not* want to dive into learning Csound:

- Your main interest is in writing and recording pop music.

- Your main interest is in recording acoustic instruments in a multitrack studio environment.

- You need to produce finished pieces of music quickly, on tight deadlines.

- You're comfortable with, and want to use, standard music notation.

- You're intimidated by the idea of writing computer programming code, complete with mathematical calculations.

 Algorithmic composition is a multifaceted music frontier in which some of the features of a piece of music, such as the precise pitches or rhythms that will be heard, are generated by a computer program rather than directly by the composer.

 Modular synthesis using hardware modules (such as oscillators and filters) began with the voltage-controlled systems developed in the 1960s by Robert Moog and Don Buchla. A typical modular instrument contained a number of specialized modules, which were interconnected by the musician using patch cords.

What You'll Need

The good news is, a fast computer with oodles of RAM is not required to run Csound. Having a fast computer is desirable, of course, and essential if you want to use Csound in real-time performance. Even if you're planning to render your compositions to disk before you listen to them, doing so on a faster computer will be less tedious. But no matter how old and slow your computer may be, if you can get a compatible version of Csound onto your computer's hard drive, you should be able to install and run it. With an older operating system, you might conceivably have to compile Csound yourself using a C compiler, a project that is beyond the scope of this book, and you might find that you need to run Csound from the command line rather than using a front-end program. (For a basic explanation of how to run Csound from the command line, see Chapter 4.)

You'll need some way to listen to your music. That probably means an audio interface and a pair of speakers. The built-in audio output in your computer is usable in a pinch, but you can't expect to get high-quality sound from it. Modestly priced stereo audio interfaces capable of high-quality sound I/O are readily available from various manufacturers. Most will connect to your computer using USB or FireWire. Features such as built-in microphone preamps, headphone jacks, and S/PDIF digital audio connectors are fairly standard, so shop around. I can recommend the M-Audio Fast Track Pro, which retails for about $200.

Speakers are available at all price points, from dirt cheap to solid gold. In general, you should buy the best speakers you can afford. Csound is capable of producing extremely high-quality audio, and you'll want to be able to hear it.

I do not recommend using headphones with Csound—not because of the audio quality, though the quality is questionable, but because of the danger to your ears. A simple typo in a Csound orchestra or score can cause your music to play at the maximum possible volume. Ear damage is not a possibility you want to flirt with!

Tip After making any changes in a Csound code file that I'm not entirely certain are innocuous, I turn down my speaker system the first time I run the file. If you enjoy getting blasted out of your chair by unexpected noise, feel free to ignore this suggestion.

If you can afford to treat your music room using sound-absorbent foam, you'll hear more details and a better representation of the frequency spectrum and stereo imaging than you would in an untreated room. I recently spent $500 on acoustic foam from Auralex and mounted it on the walls. The difference, though subtle, was definitely perceptible.

If you're interested in real-time music-making, a MIDI keyboard with a built-in bank of MIDI sliders would be a good investment. Other types of controller hardware are also available, including controller apps that run on handheld devices.

You'll find audio editing software extremely useful when the time comes to prepare your music for online distribution or CD burning. I recommend Audacity (http://audacity.sourceforge.net), a free cross-platform audio editor. Among its other uses, such as adjusting the dynamic range by applying compression, Audacity can convert your Csound compositions to mp3 format.

 Caution mp3 is a *lossy* compression scheme, which means that the sound quality is degraded when an AIFF or WAV file is converted to it. mp3 files can be created at various bit rates, from 8 kbps (kilobits per second) up through 320 kbps. The quasi-standard rate of 128 kbps works adequately for pop music, but for electronic music, in which sonic detail and clarity of tone are important, I recommend 192 kbps at the very least, and preferably 256 kbps. Better sound quality with equivalent file size can be achieved using the .ogg file format, but not all web browsers can play .ogg files. If you want visitors to your website to be able to hear the music, you may prefer to use mp3 rather than .ogg.

Resources

A great deal of material has been and continues to be written about how to use Csound. Even so, finding the information you need can sometimes be a bit of a chore. One of my goals in writing *Csound Power!* was to put all of the information a newcomer might need in one place, where it's easy to refer to. But this book is certainly not a complete reference manual! In the next few pages, we'll take a quick look at the main resources you may find yourself consulting, and I'll say a few words about how to get the most out of them.

The Canonical Csound Reference Manual

When you download and run the Csound installer, you'll install the current version of *The Canonical Csound Reference Manual* at the same time. In *Csound Power!*, references to "the manual" always refer to this document. The manual is also available as a separate download. The automatically installed version is a large, cross-linked set of HTML pages, which can be read using any web browser. If you prefer to read a PDF version, a Windows Help file version, or a version translated into French, you can download it separately.

To download the manual, go to http://sourceforge.net/projects/csound/files/csound5. Click on the link to the folder of the version of Csound you're using or want to use (for example, csound5.13). You may find the downloads for the manual directly in this folder, or you may need to click on a manual folder within this folder.

I keep a shortcut to the manual on my computer desktop. The shortcut opens up the frames version (it points to the file indexframes.html), which has navigation bars of links across the top and down the left side (see Figure 1.2).

 Caution The HTML version of *The Canonical Manual* for Csound 5.13 is not entirely compatible with the Firefox browser. The information is there, but the links with which the pages are accessed are broken. The manual files are compatible with Opera and Safari, and probably with other browsers as well.

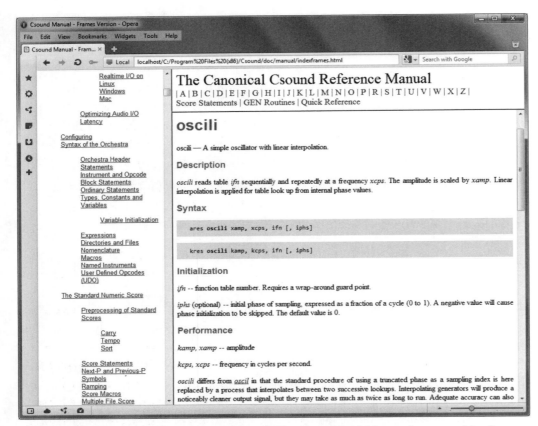

Figure 1.2 The HTML frames version of *The Canonical Manual*, opened in Opera.

Using the Manual

Like Csound itself, the manual is perpetually in a state of flux. It is frequently updated, both to add new information and to correct mistakes. Like Csound, the manual is maintained entirely by unpaid volunteers. (I've rewritten one or two pages myself.) A great deal of vital information is packed into the manual, but its explanations are sometimes terse, and the organization takes some getting used to.

Until you understand the basic syntax of the Csound language and the conventions used in the manual, the manual may prove more frustrating than helpful. To help you understand the organization, we'll take a quick look at one of the pages you'll surely find yourself consulting while learning Csound, the page for the `oscili` opcode. In order to explain what's on this page, I'll need to refer to several technical terms that will be explained later in this book. If the explanation here doesn't make much sense now, please return to it after you've read a bit further in *Csound Power!*

Each opcode in the Csound language has its own page in the manual. (Basically, an opcode is a software component that either generates or processes a signal. For a more complete explanation of what an opcode is, see Chapter 7.) Each opcode page is structured in sections. First is a definition of the opcode. This is followed by a section headed "Description." Below this are the headings "Syntax," "Initialization," "Performance," "Examples," and "See Also."

The definition for `oscili` reads as follows:

oscili—A simple oscillator with linear interpolation.

That's clear enough, provided you know what linear interpolation is. You won't find an explanation of this term on the `oscili` page, however; nor will you find a cross-reference to a page where the term is explained. The description provides a bit more information, but again, you'll need to know what's going on in order to interpret it:

oscili reads table *ifn* sequentially and repeatedly at a frequency *xcps*. The amplitude is scaled by *xamp*. Linear interpolation is applied for table lookup from internal phase values.

The italicized items `ifn`, `xcps`, and `xamp` are references to the two lines in the next section, "Syntax." Here, we're given prototypes that show how to use `oscili` in a Csound instrument:

```
ares oscili xamp, xcps, ifn [, iphs]
kres oscili kamp, kcps, ifn [, iphs]
```

When you're first exposed to Csound, that's enough to make your eyes cross. But in fact there's a lot of information packed into those two lines. The syntax will be explained more fully in Chapter 7. Briefly, there are two lines because the `oscili` opcode can run at audio rate (a-) or control rate (k-). For more on the difference between audio rate and control rate, see Chapter 6. The output of the opcode (the signal that will come from the oscillator) is at the left end of the line, followed by the opcode name itself. Items to the right of the opcode name are inputs to the opcode. Each opcode has its own defined set of inputs.

The x- at the beginning of some of the terms means that those variables can be either audio rate or control rate. Items that begin with i- (such as `ifn`) can only be given inputs at initialization (i-) time and can't be changed while your Csound instrument is running. (Don't worry—if you try to put a variable of the wrong type into an i-time argument, the compiler will complain and force you to change it.) Items that appear at the end of the line, in square brackets, are optional. If you don't supply a value for this variable, Csound will use the default value defined within the opcode.

The "Initialization" section of the page in the manual explains the meaning of the i-rate inputs to the opcode. On the `oscili` page, this section explains the meanings of `ifn` and `iphs`.

The "Performance" section of the manual page explains, briefly, the meanings of k-rate, a-rate, and x-rate inputs. These inputs can be used to modify the output of the opcode while the instrument is running. The "Performance" section may also contain additional information.

Most of the manual pages contain brief examples of Csound code to illustrate how the opcode can be used. You can copy and paste an example into whatever text editor you're using to create Csound files, save the file, and compile (run) it. At this writing, the examples are in the process of being revised to better reflect the way Csound is used today. Older examples may remain in your copy of the manual, however. In some cases, the example may do little more than illustrate the syntax of the opcode as it would be used in an actual Csound file, so copying it and running it may not tell you much. You may learn more by trying it out in your own code, making a few mistakes, revising the code, and so on.

The Csound Website

The Csound website (www.csounds.com—see Figure 1.3) is a hub that provides links to downloads, resources, and so forth. The home page also functions as an announcement area for news of interest to the Csound community.

Figure 1.3 The home page of Csounds.com has numerous links, including links to podcasts of Csound-based music.

The forum on Csounds.com seems to get very little traffic. A better resource for discussion is the Csound mailing list (see below). Other sections of the site, such as the Resources page, are more useful.

The Online Manual

An ongoing, user-written manual can be found at www.flossmanuals.net/csound (see Figure 1.4). The discussions of topics in this manual are generally more thorough and hands-on than in *The Canonical Csound Reference Manual*, and the example code tends to provide more detail as well. Created principally by Alex Hofmann, Iain McCurdy, Joachim Heintz, and Andrés Cabrera, the

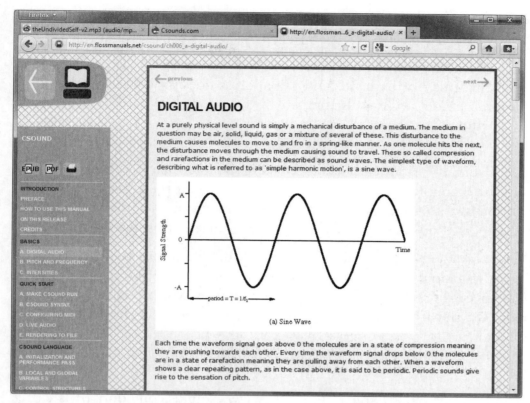

Figure 1.4   The online Floss Manual for Csound (www.flossmanuals.net/csound).

online manual is a work in progress; at this writing, some of its pages are blank. Even in its present state, however, it's very valuable, and as time goes on it should become more comprehensive.

Mailing List

Discussions of various Csound-related topics take place daily on the mailing list. To join this list, send an email to sympa@lists.bath.ac.uk. In the first line of the message, type this:

```
SUBscribe csound <name>
```

Insert your name in place of <name>. You can set up your account to receive new messages via email as they're sent to the list, or as a periodic (once or twice a day) digest.

To browse the recent activity on the mailing list, go to http://csound.1045644.n5.nabble.com/Csound-General-f1093014.html. This page is set up very much like a web-based forum. Lists for developers and for blue (a Csound front end) are also available from this page. In order to post messages to the web page, you will need to register with the mailing list by sending an email, as described earlier.

No question is too basic or too esoteric for the Csound mailing list. As long as you maintain a reasonable standard of politeness and provide details on your problem or quandary, experienced Csound users will be happy to answer any questions you may have. In addition to technical questions, the list provides announcements of computer music conferences and activities, announcements of new music, and so on.

At this writing, the status of the Csound mailing list remains a bit up in the air, due to John ffitch's retirement from the University of Bath. If the email address doesn't work, you should be able to find more current information at Csounds.com.

Code Examples

Assuming you're using the CsoundQt front end, as described in Chapter 5, you'll find a treasure trove of code examples in the Examples menu. It's possible that a few of these may not work in the way you expect. If you're new to Csound, this will be frustrating, but as you start to learn a little more, the examples will give you some easy (or not-so-easy) puzzles to solve.

Other scores, some simple and some bewilderingly complex, can be found on various web pages. Iain McCurdy, for instance, has more than 300 code examples, mostly tutorial in character, on his own website (http://iainmccurdy.org/csound.html). These examples will probably be bundled as Examples within CsoundQt, but if you're using some other front end, you should be able to download them from Iain's site.

The Csound Journal

Published two or three times a year, the *Csound Journal* (www.csounds.com/journal) is a free online magazine devoted to articles about how to use Csound. Some of the articles are highly technical in nature, while others are approachable by relative newcomers. Each issue includes a variety of topics—synthesis, signal processing, integrating Csound with other programming languages, and so on.

Online UDO Library

I'll have more to say about user-defined opcodes (UDOs) in Chapter 7. The code snippets in the online UDO library are created by Csound users. They do various useful or bizarre things. After downloading and pasting into your code, they can be used almost exactly like Csound's built-in opcodes. The main difference is that they're written in the Csound programming language itself, so you can see what's going on in the code and modify it if you need to. The constantly expanding UDO library can be found at http://www.csounds.com/udo.

Books for Further Study

By far the most important reference work for studying Csound is *The Csound Book*, a massive anthology edited by Richard Boulanger and published by MIT Press. If you're serious about mastering Csound, you will definitely want to order a copy of this book. The text is more than 700 pages long—and two CD-ROMs packed with additional material are also included.

Note   The home page for *The Csound Book* at MIT Press can be found at http://mitpress. mit.edu/e-books/csound/frontpage.html. Unfortunately, this page, though its banner proclaims it "The Csound Front Page," is not being actively maintained. At this writing (September 2011), almost all of the links on its sub-pages are broken.

Contributors to the book or CD-ROMs include Barry Vercoe, Richard Boulanger, John ffitch, Michael Gogins, Gabriel Maldonado, Matt Ingalls, Hans Mikelson, Russel Pinkston, and many other luminaries within the Csound firmament. You'll find chapters on FM synthesis, granular synthesis, optimizing your code, designing legato instruments, using delay lines, using the phase vocoder, and many other topics.

Once you move beyond the first 150 pages, you'll find that *The Csound Book* is not really addressed to newcomers. There's not a lot of math in the book, but you'll definitely spot a few equations as you leaf through it. In addition, *The Csound Book* is now more than 10 years old, so it contains no information on the numerous developments that have been added to Csound since the beginning of the new century. For these reasons, I felt that there was a genuine need for a book like *Csound Power!* In no way, however, is *Csound Power!* intended to compete with *The Csound Book*!

Also worth studying or owning, if you can find a copy, is *Virtual Sound*, by Riccardo Bianchini and Alessandro Cipriani. You may be able to order a copy through the Italian publisher, ConTempo, but I have been unable to find a current distributor in the United States. (Not to worry—though written in Italy, it's in English.) *Virtual Sound* is somewhat more beginner-oriented than *The Csound Book,* but like the latter, it's more than 10 years old, so some of the information in it is no longer relevant.

If you're serious about mastering computer music technology, there are several other books to consider. While not dealing specifically with Csound, these will give you a lot of excellent material (some of it quite advanced) on digital synthesis and signal processing. I recommend *Computer Music: Synthesis, Composition, and Performance* (Schirmer, 1997) by Charles Dodge and Thomas A. Jerse and *The Computer Music Tutorial* (MIT Press, 1996) by Curtis Roads.

You

Though it may not seem obvious when you're first introduced to Csound, you yourself are an important resource for Csound development. If you have only a little knowledge, you can help by reporting bugs in Csound itself, in the front-end program(s) you're using, or in any user-defined opcodes that you download. As a knowledgeable Csounder, you'll be able to answer questions from newcomers on the mailing list. As time goes on, you may be able to help with testing by downloading and compiling source code. As Andrés Cabrera commented, "It's the users and their interaction with developers that has kept Csound alive for so long."

Alternatives

The three programs most widely used by computer musicians who favor free, open-source software are Csound, Pd, and SuperCollider. They're about as different from one another as could be imagined, but they have one thing in common: Each of them will require some mental effort to learn.

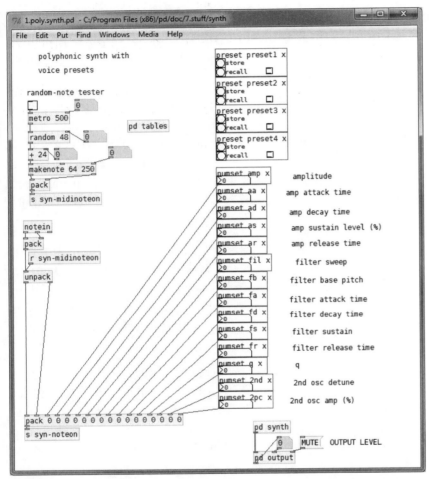

Figure 1.5 Pd, created by Miller Puckette, is a graphical programming system for music. It can be downloaded from http://puredata.info. In Pd, you create and process sounds by patching together on-screen boxes, using the mouse to drag virtual patch cords from one box to another. Pd has a large and active user community and excels at real-time interactive music-making. It also has real-time video processing capabilities.

Each of them is right for some musicians, and each is better than the others at certain musical tasks. Many people use two or even all three of them at different times, and for different purposes. This is not the place for a detailed comparison—nor am I necessarily the best person to make such a comparison. I've used Csound a good deal, Pd from time to time, and SuperCollider hardly at all. Of the three, Csound has both the longest history and arguably the largest set of features. But that hardly matters. What matters is making music, and it's quite possible to make sophisticated music for years without using more than a fraction of Csound's total feature set. In this book I'll have a great deal to say about how to make music with Csound. (We'll also take a quick look, in Chapter 10, about how to use Csound within Pd.)

Before committing to Csound, you might want to download and install the other two and take a quick look at them. Pd is preferred by some musicians because they find its graphic depiction of signal routings intuitively easy to grasp. SuperCollider is, like Csound, a text-based music creation system. It uses a more modern, object-oriented syntax, which is powerful but perhaps not as intuitively obvious as Csound's procedural code, especially to the non-programmer. SuperCollider can be downloaded from http://supercollider.sourceforge.net.

All three systems understand the OSC communications protocol, so if you're willing to take the time to learn more than one system, you can use each of them for its own strengths and combine them into a multifaceted real-time music-making machine.

2 Downloading and Installing

Downloading and installing Csound is not especially difficult, but it may not be quite as easy as downloading and installing some commercial software programs. You'll need to check that you're downloading the correct version. If you're using a front-end program in conjunction with Csound, it will probably be a separate download, and you'll need to make sure that the version of Csound that you're planning to use is compatible with the front end.

Csound downloads are available from SourceForge. You can go to the download page directly (http://sourceforge.net/projects/csound/files) or use the link at www.csounds.com. From the latter site, you can click on the Downloads link in the top menu bar and then click on Csound Page at SourceForge. Either way, you'll arrive at a web page that looks more or less like Figure 2.1.

Most web browsers will sense what operating system your computer uses and provide a quick link to a compatible version in the top line of this page. If you're running Windows, you'll see a link to an .exe file, which is the installer for Csound. If you're running Mac OS, you'll see a link to a .dmg file. Clicking on this link should download the Csound installer. After storing it in some suitable location on your hard drive, you'll be ready to jump ahead to the section on "Running the Installer," later in this chapter.

But as usual with Csound, there's more to the story than that.

Because Csound is maintained by a volunteer community, when a new version is released, the installer for your operating system may not be available for a week to 10 days. Basically, the installer is created when someone has time to create it. Until that happens, the automatic link on the SourceForge page may be to the previous release, not the latest one. The differences between release versions are usually minor, so this is not a big issue; it's just something to be aware of.

Once in a while, you may encounter a bug with the most recent release—something that prevents you from doing the musical work that you want to do. In this situation, you'll need to revert to an earlier version. You can do this by clicking on the name of a folder in the list on the Source-Forge page. Looking at Figure 2.1, you'll find folders for 5.13, 5.12, 5.11, and so on. When you click on one of these, you'll get the complete list of files for that version (see Figure 2.2). This may be a long list, and it's up to you to figure out which file(s) you need. You'll find the software installers (.exe for Windows, .dmg for Mac OS), an archive of source code files (.zip or .tar.gz), and manuals. The manuals may or may not be in their own separate folder.

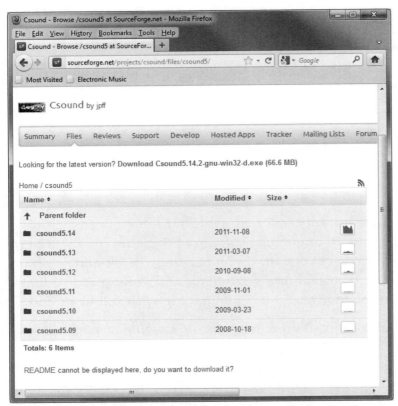

Figure 2.1 The Csound download page at SourceForge, displayed in Firefox.

Compiling Csound Yourself

Source code for older and newer versions of Csound is generally available on SourceForge. If you're a knowledgeable computer programmer and have a C compiler, you can download and compile Csound yourself. The manual provides basic instructions to do this; look for the "Building Csound" page in the Table of Contents.

The process of building Csound is beyond the scope of *Csound Power!* It's a project for an expert. That said, Linux users (who may on average be more computer-literate than Windows and Mac OS users) often compile Csound for their own system. Pre-compiled distributions of Csound are not necessarily available for all varieties of Linux, so Linux users may need to do it themselves. For details, see the "Linux" section, later in this chapter.

A decided advantage of learning to compile Csound is that you'll be able to install bug fixes as soon as they're uploaded to the SourceForge repository. You won't need to wait for the next official release. A second advantage is that, if you're a C programmer, you'll be able to modify Csound—for example, by writing your own opcodes. You don't actually need to do this in order to create opcodes; Csound has its own built-in system for creating user-defined opcodes (UDOs) in the Csound language itself. (See "User-Defined Opcodes" in Chapter 7, "Thirty Opcodes You Must Know," for details.) Nonetheless, user customization is very much a part of the Csound user community, so if you're already a programmer, this is an area you may want to explore.

Figure 2.2   The downloads folder for Csound version 5.12 contains numerous items.

Doubles versus Floats

Csound's developers have a strong interest in giving the program the best possible audio quality. In the early days, Csound worked internally with 16-bit audio. (See "The Orchestra Header" in Chapter 4, "The Structure and Syntax of a .csd File," for more on the implications of this fact.) Versions that used 32-bit floating-point audio came along a few years later. Today, 32-bit versions are being supplanted by 64-bit versions. During the transition period, which lasted for several years, Csound was available for download in both 32-bit floating-point versions (indicated in the filename with "-f") and 64-bit double-precision versions (indicated in the filename with "-d").

To add to the confusion, the question of whether Csound is using 32-bit or 64-bit audio is entirely different from the question of whether it's running on a 32-bit or 64-bit operating system.

At this writing, the Windows version of the installer (compiled by Michael Gogins) has transitioned to 64-bit audio. That is, you'll install the double-precision (-d) version; no -f installer is currently available for Windows. The Mac OS installer (compiled by Victor Lazzarini) installs both the 32-bit and 64-bit versions. If you're running Csound in Mac OS from the Terminal, the command csound will run the 32-bit floating-point version, while the command csound64 will run the double-precision version. However, this may change in the future.

During the transitional period, a few of Csound's capabilities may not have been updated to work with the doubles version. According to Appendix H of the manual for version 5.13, this is the case with the lpanal and cvanal utilities, and there may be a few other items that won't work either. If you encounter this problem and you're using Windows, you may need to revert to an older version of Csound that is available for floats, or alternatively compile a floats version of Csound for yourself from source code.

You may also find that some front-end programs (as described in Chapter 9, "Front Ends") require the doubles or floats version and won't work if you have the wrong version installed.

Running the Installer

It's sometimes useful to keep older versions of Csound on your hard drive. For one thing, if you encounter problems with a new version, it will be easier to revert to the old version if you don't have to install it again. I generally rename the folder containing the older version to something like csound512 before I install the new version. Once I've done this, all I need to do to revert to the old version is rename two folders.

Windows

The Windows installer for Csound operates pretty much like any other Windows installer. You'll be asked to click through a series of screens. Depending on which version of Windows you're running, you may have to begin the process by clicking in a dialog box to confirm that you're allowing the installer program to make alterations in your system. Having done that, you'll be presented with a standard Setup Wizard box.

After clicking the "I Agree" button in the license agreement box (hey, I *always* read license agreements from top to bottom before agreeing with them—don't you?), you'll be asked to choose an install location (see Figure 2.3). There is usually no reason to change this, but if you're installing an older version you might change the folder name in this box so the new installation won't overwrite an existing one.

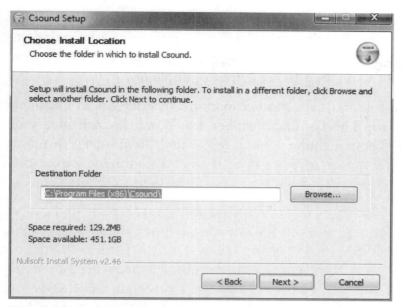

Figure 2.3   Tell the Windows installer where you want to put your Csound installation.

   Note   The user license for Csound is friendlier than some other licenses, as it gives you certain rights explicitly rather than restricting them. For details, you may want to read the license during the installation process.

One or two dialog boxes down the line, you'll reach the Choose Components box (see Figure 2.4). I recommend leaving the checkboxes for the documentation checked. In the Front Ends area, you may want to uncheck CsoundQt, because CsoundQt is updated separately from Csound itself. It's

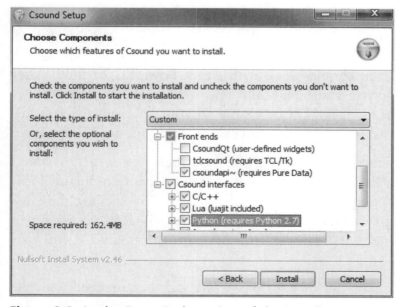

Figure 2.4   In the Front Ends section of the installer, I recommend unchecking CsoundQt (which you can install separately) and checking csoundapi~ (for use with Pd).

sometimes the case that the Csound installer will install an older version of CsoundQt, which is not what you want. On the other hand, the Csound installer might have a newer version of CsoundQt. You might want to rename your CsoundQt folder temporarily, let the Csound installer do its own installation, and then run the two versions of CsoundQt to see if they're different.

If you're thinking you might want to use Csound as a module within Pd, you should click the checkbox for csoundapi~. (I recommend it.) The Csound installer for Windows will give you some choices about optional components. These include:

- C/C++
- Lua
- Python
- Java
- Lisp

These are components for experts. If you don't plan to extend Csound by using any of the other programming languages with which it is compatible, you can save a little space on your disk drive by unchecking these items. I generally activate the Python item. (For more on using Csound with Python, see Chapter 10, "Using Csound with MIDI, OSC, Pd, Python, and Live Audio." Python requires a separate download and installation; it's not bundled with Csound.) After choosing what you want to install, click the Install button, and you should be ready to go.

When you've finished installing in Windows, if you plan to use CsoundQt there's one additional step you may need to take manually. Three of the installed files may need to be removed. For details, see the Tip in the "Syntax Hints and Accessing Opcode Help" section in Chapter 5.

Macintosh

Csound downloads for Mac OS may be available in several versions—for PowerPC and Intel Macs, and also for Mac OS 10.4 or older and 10.5 or newer. The most recent version of the installer is called "-universal," which means it should work with either PowerPC or Intel. After you've chosen and downloaded the package you want, it should open up in a Finder window, as shown in Figure 2.5. The .dmg (disk image) file itself will be visible on your desktop. After installing, you can either drag the .dmg to the trash or store it somewhere in case you need it again.

To install Csound, double-click the .pkg icon. After clicking the Continue button a few times, you'll get to the Installation Type box (see Figure 2.6). Here you can choose a non-default location for the install or customize the list of components that will be installed by clicking the Customize button. Unless you're extremely tight for hard disk space, there's probably no reason to use the Customize list; just leave everything as is. This will install both the floats (32-bit) and doubles (64-bit) versions.

Click the Install button. The computer will ask you for your password and then proceed with the installation.

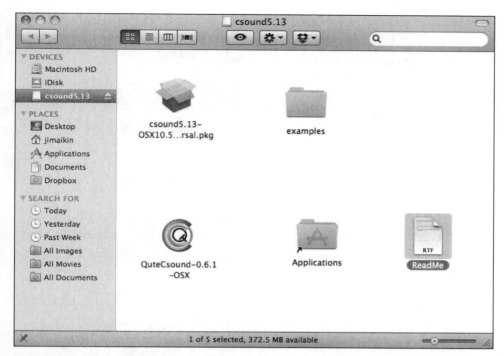

Figure 2.5 A downloaded .dmg file containing Csound for Macintosh.

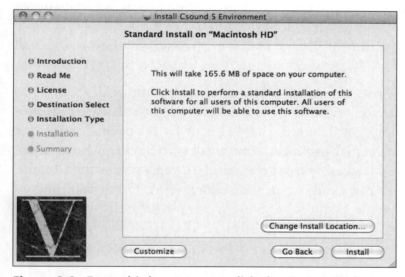

Figure 2.6 From this box, you can click the Customize button to choose the components you want included in the Csound installation.

You can install CsoundQt at the same time, by dragging its icon in the .dmg window onto the Applications folder shortcut in that window. As noted earlier, however, the version of CsoundQt in the Csound installer may not be the most current, so you may prefer to download and install CsoundQt separately.

Drag the Examples folder onto your desktop or into your Documents folder. The Examples folder contains dozens of .csd files that illustrate useful techniques.

Linux

For information on installing Csound in Linux computers, I turned to Linux audio guru Dave Phillips, who generously provided the following information.

The Csound download for Linux is in source code form, as Linux users are quite used to compiling their own software. The download is in the form of a .tar.gz file. Some systems will prompt the user to unpack and uncompress this file, but you can always do it from the command line. A typical command-line invocation would look something like this:

```
tar xzvf foosound.tar.gz
```

The mystery letters are flags. The "z" unzips the package, "x" unpacks the tar'd archive, "v" views the unpacking/uncompression process, and "f" applies the actions to the named file. This will unpack the package in its local directory. You may want to create a directory for all source code packages and unpack it there.

After unpacking, you'll have a new subdirectory in the directory where you unpacked the tarball. If you unpacked it in your home directory, the result would look something like this:

```
/home/jimaikin/foosound
```

Once the tarball is unpacked, Dave suggests, you should inspect its contents using a file manager (or using command-line tools). A tarball may contain a pre-built binary, or only the source code required to build the program, or a combination of binary and source code. The Csound tarball is a source-only package.

"Compiling Csound for Linux isn't really rocket science," Dave reports, "but you do need to know what you're doing. I advise new users to check their Linux distribution's software repositories for a pre-compiled Csound. For example, my Ubuntu 10.04 (Lucid Lynx) package manager lists Csound and a variety of other Csound-related packages, any or all of which can be installed with a few clicks of the mouse." CsoundQt is available from the standard repositories for Ubuntu, Debian, and Arch Linux. At this writing, it's not available in the Fedora or SUSE repositories.

Assuming all of the necessary build tools are installed, here's how you would compile Csound yourself:

```
scons -h
scons WithFoo=1 WithFoobar=0
sudo python install.py
```

The first line runs the Scons build utility and checks for available build options. The second line runs Scons with the selected options, which may include the builds of various front ends. The third line, which requires that Python be already installed in your system, installs Csound. (sudo will prompt you for a password.)

You then need to set some Csound environment variables. Assuming you're using the default installation paths:

```
export OPCODEDIR=/usr/local/lib/csound/plugins/
export OPCODEDIR64=/usr/local/lib/csound/plugins64/
export CSSTRNGS=/usr/local/share/locale
```

The second line is needed only if you're doing a 64-bit build.

"The tools required to build Csound," Dave adds, "are not usually installed for a normal user. Happily, at least for Ubuntu users, there's a way to simplify the process. First we get the basic tool chain components with this command:

```
sudo apt-get build-essential
```

"Next, we get the dependencies required by Csound:

```
sudo apt-get build-dep csound
```

"Now we can go ahead and build Csound locally. Again, the reason to do any of this is to customize a personal build of Csound. If no such customization is required, I suggest that the user install the version of Csound maintained by his or her distribution." Both CsoundQt and blue, Dave points out, have dependencies that may not be met automatically by most major Linux distributions. Qt is usually installed, but Java and Python may need to be added to the system. For CsoundQt you can do:

```
sudo apt-get build-dep qutecsound
```

In Debian and Ubuntu, this will fetch all of CsoundQt's dependencies. (Note that at present, this command still refers to CsoundQt by its old name, QuteCsound. At some point in the future, you may need to change the command to reflect the new name.)

Installing CsoundQt

Before you start exploring Csound, you'll most likely want to install the latest version of the CsoundQt front end. This step is not strictly necessary, as there are other ways to use Csound. But there are two strong reasons to do it. First, CsoundQt provides an excellent environment in which to learn Csound. It has numerous friendly features, but they won't get in the way of your learning the basics of writing Csound code. Second, most of the examples in this book will use CsoundQt, either explicitly or by implication. If you don't install it, you'll have a harder time working your way through the book.

Go to http://sourceforge.net/projects/qutecsound/files. (Note: At present, this directory still refers to CsoundQt by its old name, QuteCsound. At some point in the future, the directory may change to reflect the new name.) The most current pre-compiled version for your OS should be displayed as a link near the top of the window. The installation process is similar to the process for installing Csound itself, so there's no need to go into it here. Also as with Csound itself, the installer might not have been upgraded to the latest version of the program, because CsoundQt is developed and maintained entirely by unpaid volunteers. At this writing, CsoundQt version 0.7 is in testing, and it will probably be released by the time you read this. Most of this book was written, however, using the previous version (which had a different name), QuteCsound 0.6.1 for Mac OS and 0.6.0 for Windows.

Setting Up Your System

The first thing you'll need to do, in order to check whether Csound has been correctly installed, is make sure your audio outputs work. The method you'll use for testing this depends on whether you're using CsoundQt or running Csound directly from the command line.

System Test in CsoundQt

After installing and launching CsoundQt, click on the Configure icon in the toolbar to open the Configuration box. If the toolbar is not visible, you can reach the Configuration box from the Edit menu in the Windows version, or from Preferences in the CsoundQt menu in the Macintosh version.

In the Run tab of the Configuration box, under Realtime Play, PortAudio should be selected in the drop-down menu as the RT Audio Module. Lower down, you'll find the Output Device (-o) field. Click on the three-dot button to the right of this field and choose your audio output from the list. If you're planning to use audio input, choose the input device in the same way. If you're planning to use real-time MIDI input, choose your MIDI interface in the Input Device (-M) field to the right. When you're done, click OK.

Back in the main window, go to the Examples menu. In the Getting Started > Toots submenu, select Toot1, as shown in Figure 2.7. Click the Run button in the toolbar. You should hear a four-second sine wave with a frequency of 440 Hz.

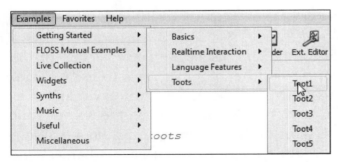

Figure 2.7 To test CsoundQt's audio output, set the output in the Configuration box and then load this file.

The Examples > Getting Started > Basics > Hello World file can be used for testing in the same way. It contains, in addition, a few useful tips in the form of comments, which will appear in the editor window as green text.

Troubleshooting Audio Issues If you don't hear any sound when you run a Csound file, the first things to check are the obvious ones: Is your audio hardware installed correctly in your system? Are your amp and speakers turned on? Have you selected the desired audio driver for Csound's output?

Assuming all of the above are in good order, the next step is to open the CsoundQt Console pane and watch for error messages when you try to run the file. If you're running Csound from the computer's command line, any error messages should show up in the terminal window itself. If you've made a mistake entering your code, for example, you might see Console messages telling you that Csound is operating normally but producing note events with an amplitude of 0.0. That will give you a good indication of what to fix.

System Test in the Terminal

If you're planning to run Csound from the terminal, an audio output test is almost as simple. First, open the terminal. At the prompt, type csound. You should see a long text dump that looks more or less like Figure 2.8. If you don't see this, Csound has not been installed correctly.

Figure 2.8 After entering the csound command in a Windows Command Prompt box, you should see this output.

Open a text editor program (not a word processor). Enter the following code and then save the file to some suitable directory. You should save it with the .csd filename extension—for example, my_test.csd.

```
<CsoundSynthesizer>
<CsOptions>
</CsOptions>
<CsInstruments>

sr = 44100
ksmps = 128
nchnls = 2
0dbfs = 1

instr 1

a1 oscil 0.2, 440, 1
outs a1,  a1

endin

</CsInstruments>
<CsScore>

f 1 0 4096 10 1
i 1 0 4

</CsScore>
</CsoundSynthesizer>
```

This is identical to the Toot1 file loaded from CsoundQt's Examples menu, but without the embedded comments.

In your computer's terminal window, navigate to the directory where you've saved the file. (This is done using the cd command, which is shorthand for "change directory." If you're not familiar with the use of a terminal, you're probably better off using CsoundQt, at least to start.) Assuming you've named the file above my_test.csd, type the following command at the terminal prompt:

```
csound my_test.csd
```

Depending on how your system is set up, you may hear a four-second sine wave at 440 Hz, or you may find that Csound has written a file called my_test.wav to your hard drive. The results will depend on whether the command -odac is present in the file called .csoundrc. This file should be found in your main Csound program directory. See the sidebar for details.

The .csoundrc File   Part of the Csound installation is a small text file called .csoundrc. This file contains a set of default command-line flags. It will be consulted by Csound each time Csound runs, and the flags in the file will be used unless they're overridden by flags in your .csd file or in the command line you're typed at the terminal. In my installation, the .csoundrc file contains the following:

```
-d -m135 -H0 -s -W -o dac - rtaudio=pa -b 128 -B 2048
```

For details on the meanings of these flags, consult the "Csound Command Line" page in *The Canonical Csound Reference Manual.*

In my Windows system the real-time output from the terminal makes crackling noises, because the default audio driver is not low-latency. My ASIO driver (ASIO4ALL v2) shows up in the PortAudio list in the terminal as device 16. To get rid of the crackles, I use a command-line flag, like this:

```
csound -odac16 my_test.csd
```

The flag -odac16 directs Csound to the ASIO driver (as opposed to the default audio driver for my system), and the output is smooth. In your system, the ASIO driver will probably have a different number. Before starting to run, Csound will list all of the audio input and output devices to the terminal, so you can find the correct number easily.

Tip   If you're attempting to run Csound from the command line after writing Csound code in a program that's *not* a front end, you need to take care that you're using a text editor, not a word processor. Word processors insert lots of extra formatting data around the text that you can see on-screen. This extra data will prevent Csound from compiling your code.

Good freeware text editors are available for all of the major computer operating systems. Windows users may want to consider Notepad++ (available from http://notepad-plus-plus.org). On the other hand, why not just do your Csound work in a front end?

3 QuickStart Projects

Some people like to read through lengthy textbooks from start to finish before they try out what they're learning. But they're probably in the minority. Assuming you're not one of them, you may want to just roll up your sleeves, start using Csound, and figure out as you go along what additional bits of information you need or want. So in this chapter we're going to leapfrog straight over the rest of *Csound Power!* I'll show you, step by step, how to create a simple musical project. Two of them, in fact. This chapter will be short on explanations of details (that's what the rest of the book is for) and long on quick results.

By the time you reach the end of this chapter, you'll have a couple of templates that you can use to start making your own music with Csound. One template will show how to play a sequence of musical notes using a conventional synthesizer; the other will show one way to process recorded audio to make a sound design event. As you expand on the code in the templates, you'll be learning the details of Csound techniques.

The only assumptions we'll be making in this chapter are, first, that you've downloaded and installed Csound and CsoundQt, as explained in Chapter 2; and second, that you've gone through the section "Setting Up Your System" in Chapter 2 and verified that CsoundQt can send audio to your speakers.

Sequencing Project

In this project you'll create a Csound synthesizer and write a sequence of notes for it to play. Along the way you'll meet a few essential components, including oscillators and envelope generators.

Launch CsoundQt and Create a New Project

Launch CsoundQt by double-clicking its icon. Depending on how you installed it, the icon may be on the desktop, or you may have to find it in your Applications folder (Mac) or in the Windows Start Menu.

If you've launched CsoundQt before, the main editor window may already have one or more tabs with Csound files. If so, you can create a new project by clicking the New button at the left end of the toolbar. This will create a new, unsaved file called default.csd. If this is the first time you've launched CsoundQt, the default file will be loaded for you; it will be called untitled.csd.

In either case, you should see the following code in the editor window:

```
<CsoundSynthesizer>
<CsOptions>
</CsOptions>
<CsInstruments>

</CsInstruments>
<CsScore>

</CsScore>
</CsoundSynthesizer>
```

If by chance you find yourself looking at an editor window with no code at all (unlikely), type the lines above. For now we're not going to worry about what it all means.

Save the file to some suitable location on your hard drive, such as a Csound Projects folder that you've created.

Create an Instrument and a Score

To start with, we need to give Csound a few general instructions. Position the typing cursor at the end of the line that says <CsInstruments> (*not* the line that says the same thing with a slash character near the beginning), hit Return or Enter a couple of times, and type the following code:

```
sr = 44100
ksmps = 10
nchnls = 2
0dbfs = 1
```

This code tells Csound what sample rate you want your digital audio to use, and a few other things. You'll always need to use a header of this type, but the details may change from one project to another.

In order for Csound to make sound, it needs a waveform. To create a sine wave, position the typing cursor after the line that says, 0dbfs=1, hit Return or Enter a couple of times, and type this code:

```
giSine ftgen 0, 0, 8192, 10, 1
```

Be careful to put commas where shown, and don't capitalize letters that aren't shown as capitals. (Csound is case-sensitive.) If you haven't changed CsoundQt's default settings for syntax coloring, giSine should be in green and ftgen in blue. ftgen is a Csound opcode—a widget that does some work. This particular widget creates a table (a memory space) and puts a digital representation of a sine wave into it. giSine is a value—essentially, a number variable—with which we'll be able to access the sine wave.

Hit Return or Enter a couple more times to leave a blank line below the line you just typed and then add these lines:

```
instr 1
aout oscil 0.6, 220, giSine
outs aout, aout
endin
```

The spacing isn't important—Csound doesn't care whether you indent your lines, and it doesn't care whether you put tab characters between elements or just spaces. What does matter is that each of these instructions has to be on a line by itself. Also, you need to be careful not to leave out a comma or misspell one of the odd-looking words.

Briefly, this code creates an instrument, which we will shortly be referring to by its number—instrument 1. The second line creates an oscillator. The symbol aout is like an audio patch cord; it's the output of the oscil opcode. The third line sends the signal in aout to the stereo output channels, so you can listen to them. And every instrument you create must end with the symbol endin, on a line by itself.

In the line below <CsScore>, add the following code:

```
i1 0 2
```

This instruction tells Csound to play a note. It begins with i1, so instrument 1 will be used. The note will begin at time 0 (the start of the score) and will last for 2 seconds.

Tip   In a Csound score, you can put a space after the i in an instrument event line or omit it. Whether you type i1 or i 1 is entirely a matter of personal taste. The other spaces are necessary, however. If you type i102 in the code shown here, Csound will think you're referring to a nonexistent instrument 102.

Click CsoundQt's Run button. If you've entered the code correctly, you should hear a sine wave at 220 Hz, lasting for two seconds.

If you don't hear the sine wave, of course you should start by checking that your speakers are turned on and so forth. If your system is set up correctly, the most likely culprit is a typo in your code. If CsoundQt's Output Console window is not open at the bottom of the screen, click the Console button in the toolbar to open it. You may see some error messages about illegal characters, or perhaps something like this:

```
error: input arg 'aout' used before defined, line 29:
```

Unfortunately, Csound isn't always correct about counting line numbers. It tends to get confused by multi-line comments and macro statements, for instance. So the fact that the error message mentions line 29 may or may not be helpful. To find the typo, you'll need to go back through your code line by line and check it carefully for mistakes. It can also happen that a single typo will be reported as two or more separate errors. Consider this output, which I copied from the Output Console:

```
instr 1
error: illegal character -, line 321:
asig1 foscli 1, kfreq - idetune, icar, imod, kfm, giSine
                       ^
error: no legal opcode, line 321:
asig1 foscli 1, kfreq - idetune, icar, imod, kfm, giSine
error: input arg 'asig1' used before defined, line 329:
asigA = asig1 + (asig2 * 0.4)
```

There is only one error in this code: I've misspelled the opcode `foscili` as "foscli." Csound first objects to the subtraction symbol (using a caret on the next line to point to it) because it doesn't understand the line at all, then complains (correctly) that there's no legal opcode—and finally, because `asig1` is now undefined, reports a nonexistent error when this symbol is later used.

Sorting through compiler error messages is just part of the fun (??) of writing code.

Note   Not sure what a sine wave is? See the sidebar in the section "Sinusoids with GEN 09, 10, and 11" in Chapter 7, "Thirty Opcodes You Must Know."

Add an Amplitude Envelope

You may have noticed that the sine wave you just played ended with a click. There's a fundamental lesson in this: Unlike commercial music software, Csound doesn't do anything behind the scenes to make sure your music sounds good. When you notice an audio glitch, it's up to you to figure out how to fix it.

In this case, we need to give our instrument an amplitude envelope, so that the sound will fade out smoothly at the end rather than stopping abruptly. Leaving the last two lines of your instrument definition untouched, edit the beginning of the instrument code so that the instrument looks like this:

```
instr 1
iamp = 0.6
kampenv linseg 0, 0.01, iamp, (p3 - 0.01), 0
aout oscil kampenv, 220, gisine
outs aout, aout
endin
```

Here we've added a named value (`iamp`), which will contain the maximum amplitude of the sound. The next line creates an envelope using the `linseg` opcode. `linseg` creates a contour by building it out of linear segments, hence the name. In the `oscil` line, we've replaced 0.6 with the symbol `kampenv`. When you click the Run button, you should hear the sine wave tone start a bit more smoothly and then fade out nicely to silence.

Briefly, `linseg` creates a series of line segments—as many or as few segments as we'd like. The numbers and/or symbols to the right of the `linseg` opcode define, alternately, the levels of the envelope and the times (in seconds) at which those levels are to be reached. By analyzing this line of code, you may be able to see that the envelope starts with a level of zero. Over the next 0.01 second, it rises to the level defined by `iamp`.

The next value being given to `linseg` is, again, a time value. In this case it uses a special symbol, p3. Symbols beginning with "p" and then followed by a number take their values from lines in the score. The "p" is short for "parameter," and you'll sometimes hear numbers in the score referred to as "p-fields." If you look back at the score we created earlier, you'll see that the line beginning with i has three numbers. The first p-field (p1) tells Csound what instrument to use when playing this score line. The second p-field tells Csound when to start the note, 0 being "start playing immediately at the beginning of the score." The third p-field (p3) indicates how long the note is to last.

Our envelope has already used up 0.01 second rising from 0 to the level defined by `iamp`. So the time that it takes to fall back to zero should be set to (p3 – 0.01). This way, if our score contains some longer notes and some shorter ones, the lengths of their envelopes will be adjusted accordingly. Each note will end smoothly.

In the `oscil` line, the fixed value 0.6 has been replaced with the symbol `kampenv`. This symbol is the output coming from the `linseg` opcode. The first value to the right of the `oscil` opcode is used for setting the amplitude of the signal that will come from the oscillator.

As an exercise, you may want to look up `linseg` and `oscil` in *The Canonical Csound Reference Manual*. You'll find that the second input to `oscil` is for the frequency of the wave it will produce. We've set that at 220, so we hear a sine wave at 220 Hz. But what if we want to play different pitches?

Input Pitches from the Score

To play any sort of melody or harmony from the score, we need to tell Csound what pitches (frequencies) we'd like to hear. We can specify these in the score. Add some lines to your score, and add a fourth p-field to each line, so that it looks like this:

```
i1 0 1 250
i1 1 1 225
i1 2 1 200
i1 3 1 225
i1 4 1 250
i1 5 1 250
i1 6 2 250
```

Tip Values entered into a Csound score are not separated by commas, only by spaces (or tabs). The values entered on the line following an opcode in an instrument, however, are separated by commas. (There is no comma between the opcode name and the first item after the name, however.)

The fourth p-field is going to play a melody. Edit your `oscil` line to use p4 as its second argument:

```
aout oscil kampenv, p4, giSine
```

When you click the Run button, you should hear "Mary Had a Little Lamb." Not a very scintillating rendition of it, to be sure, but we're just getting started.

Specifying frequencies using raw numbers can get to be a chore—especially if you're composing music using standard 12-note-per-octave equal temperament, where the frequencies are irrational numbers. (The example above plays the melody in just intonation, not equal temperament.) Fortunately, we don't have to specify the frequencies manually; we can let Csound calculate them for us. Replace the p4 values in your score so that the score looks like this:

```
i1 0 1 8.04
i1 1 1 8.02
i1 2 1 8.00
i1 3 1 8.02
i1 4 1 8.04
i1 5 1 8.04
i1 6 2 8.04
```

Next, add this line to your instrument:

```
ifreq = cpspch(p4)
```

To finish the job, edit your `oscil` line to make use of the value that is now stored in `ifreq`:

```
aout oscil kampenv, ifreq, giSine
```

The `cpspch` opcode calculates the frequencies of notes in 12-note equal temperament. As is often the case in Csound, the name provides a clue about what the opcode does: "cps" refers to cycles per second, which is the frequency, and "pch" refers to the pitch. Musicians tend to consider "pitch" and "frequency" synonymous, but in this case the term "pitch" should be understood as a higher-level musical construct.

The 8 in p4 of the score specifies the octave of the desired pitch, and the decimal part of the number specifies the pitch step within the octave. Now our instrument can play whatever notes we like. We don't need to calculate the pitch values; Csound can do that for us.

Make a Richer Tone Color

Sine waves are among the less interesting tones electronic instruments can produce. (Sometimes, of course, less interesting is good.) Csound gives us many, many ways to produce richer tone colors. To make an analog-style instrument, for instance, we could use the `vco2` opcode. But since our .csd file already has a sine wave, let's use it for a little FM synthesis.

Change the line in your instrument that contains the `oscil` opcode so that it uses `foscil` instead. `foscil` implements two FM operators as a carrier/modulator pair. (If you're not sure what that means, read "FM Synthesis" in Chapter 7 to learn more.) `foscil` has a few additional input parameters. (The technical term for the inputs to an opcode is "arguments.") Edit the `foscil` line so that it looks like this:

```
aout foscil kampenv, ifreq, 1, 1, 3, giSine
```

When you click Run, you'll hear a somewhat warmer sawtooth-like tone. The two 1's in that line control the relative frequencies of the carrier and modulator in the FM process. You can edit these to hear different timbres. Normally you'll want to use integers between 1 and 10, but fractional values such as 1.073 will give you some bizarre and possibly useful sounds.

The 3 in that line controls the amount of FM. The technical term is "FM index." Higher index values will boost the levels of the partials (overtones) in the sound.

As an exercise, you might try adding various values for the carrier, modulator, and index to your score, so that they can be varied from note to note. This is one of the many compositional techniques that are easier to set up in Csound than in a conventional MIDI sequencer. Try adding three more p-fields to each of your score lines, and then use p5, p6, and p7 in place of 1, 1, 3, in the `foscil` line.

Add a Timbre Envelope

The tones produced by many acoustic instruments change, slightly or dramatically, during the course of a single note. To accomplish something similar in Csound, we may want to add a timbre envelope. (Csound gives us many other ways to vary the timbre.) For the instrument we're developing, we'll use this envelope to control the FM index of the `foscil` opcode.

Add these two lines to your instrument:

```
index = 3
kindexenv linseg index, p3, 0
```

Be sure to put them above the `foscil` line. Now replace the 3 in the `foscil` line shown above, which was a fixed value, with `kindexenv`. Your `foscil` line should now look something like this:

```
aout foscil kampenv, ifreq, 1, 1, kindexenv, giSine
```

Thanks to the FM index envelope created using a second `linseg`, the tone becomes more muted as the note decays. If we want the FM sound to have a more definite attack transient, we can edit the index envelope like this:

```
kindexenv linseg index, 0.05, (index * 0.5), (p3 - 0.05), 0
```

This envelope starts at a level set by the index value. Over the course of 0.05 second, it falls to half of that value. It then fades out to 0 during the remainder of the note. So each note will have an attack transient of 0.05 second. Figure 3.1 shows the difference between our first attempt at a timbre envelope and the second version. Much more complex envelopes can be created using this same technique, by adding more envelope segments to `linseg`. Unlike an envelope generator on a hardware synthesizer, `linseg` isn't limited to a fixed number of segments; we can give it as many as we need, by giving it alternate values for level and time—level, time, level, time, level, time, level, and so on, ending with a value for the final level.

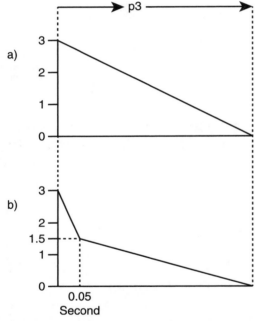

Figure 3.1 An envelope generated by the `linseg` opcode that falls smoothly from an initial level of 3 to a final level of 0 over the duration of a note (a), and an envelope that starts at 3, falls quickly to 1.5, and then falls more slowly to 0 (b). This diagram assumes that the total length of the note (p3, a value taken from the score) is considerably longer than 0.05 second. If the note is shorter, the decay to 0 will be more abrupt. In fact, if the entire note is shorter than 0.05 second, the output of `linseg` will drop abruptly to 0 at the moment when the note ends. There will be no smooth decay at all.

While we're adding features to the instrument, let's improve the tone color a little by adding a second `foscil` and detuning it from the first one. Using two detuned oscillators is a standard technique in synthesis: It produces a sort of chorusing quality due to the interference patterns between the two tones. Here's the new code for the oscillators:

```
idetune = 0.7
aout foscil kampenv, ifreq - idetune, 1, 1, kindexenv, giSine
```

```
aout2 foscil kampenv, ifreq + idetune, 1, 1, kindexenv, giSine
aout = aout + aout2
```

You can adjust the value of `idetune` to produce a smoother or more active tone. The last line above mixes the two signals (`aout` and `aout2`) and puts the result back into the `aout` "patch cord."

When you add the second oscillator and play the project, you may hear digital distortion. Open CsoundQt's Console window, if it isn't open already. Even if the audio sounds okay, as it plays you'll see messages indicating that some samples are out of range. This is not good. Samples that are out of range cause clipping distortion, which is nasty stuff. The reason the sound is distorting is because we're adding two waveforms together, so the total amplitude level is higher than before.

One solution is to reduce the value of `iamp` to 0.4 or thereabouts. After doing this, replay the project to check whether the out-of-range samples have gone away. Another solution is to pan the two oscillators so that one is feeding the left output channel and the other the right. To do this, delete the line in which `aout` and `aout2` are summed and then edit the `outs` line as follows:

```
outs   aout, aout2
```

This adds a stereo chorusing quality to the sound.

Summing Up What We've Done So Far

Let's pause to review the code we've developed so far in this tutorial. If you've been entering it as you read, the instrument should now look something like this:

```
instr 1

; setup:
iamp = 0.6
ifreq = cpspch(p4)
idetune = 0.7
index = 3

; envelopes:
kindexenv linseg index, 0.05, (index * 0.5), (p3 - 0.05), 0
kampenv linseg 0, 0.01, iamp, (p3 - 0.01), 0

; tone generators:
aout foscil kampenv, ifreq - idetune, 1, 1, kindexenv, giSine
aout2 foscil kampenv, ifreq + idetune, 1, 1, kindexenv, giSine

; output:
outs aout, aout2

endin
```

If you're new to writing code, you might find it easier to understand this if it's presented graphically. Figure 3.2 shows the same instrument as it would appear if we diagrammed it.

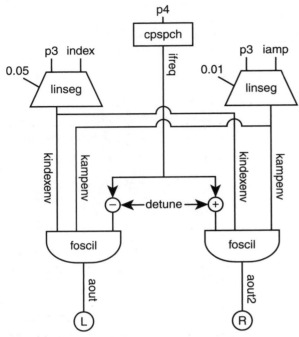

Figure 3.2 Diagrams can often help make the signal flow in a software instrument easier to understand. The signals move from the top of the diagram toward the bottom. Modules' inputs are at the top, and the "patch cord" lines are labeled with the names of the variables used in the code.

Add Rhythms, Chords, and Dynamics to the Score

The meanings of the first three p-fields in a Csound score are fixed: They refer to the instrument number, the start time of the note, and the note's length. (The meaning of the word "note" is somewhat arbitrary. "Event" might be a better term, as a single score line in Csound can generate a very complex sound event, perhaps consisting of hundreds of discrete notes. For more on the techniques with which you might do that, see "Creating Score Events during Performance" in Chapter 7.)

The meanings of any other p-fields that you add to a score line are defined by the user and may be different from one instrument to another. In the score events we've looked at so far in this chapter, p4 has been used to control the pitch of the note. But it's more usual (though not required) to use p4 to control the amplitude of the note and p5 for the pitch. To see this in action, we'll have to edit both the instrument and the score. First the instrument. Edit these two lines as shown:

```
iamp = p4 * 0.6
ifreq = cpspch(p5)
```

Then insert new values for p4 into your score, pushing the pitch values back to p5, like this:

```
i1 0 1 0.6 8.04
i1 1 1 0.5 8.02
i1 2 1 0.4 8.00
```

```
i1 3 1 0.5 8.02
i1 4 1 0.6 8.04
i1 5 1 0.7 8.04
i1 6 2 0.8 8.04
```

The second and third notes will get softer, and the last four will get progressively louder.

So far, the values in p2 and p3 have been some number of seconds, so our rendition of "Mary Had a Little Lamb" has been proceeding at a stately, if not lugubrious, tempo. Before we start adding some rhythmic spice to it, let's speed it up by adding a t statement to the score. The t is an abbreviation for "tempo." Add this line before the first i statement:

```
t 0 120
```

When you play the example again, the tempo will be twice as fast. If there's no t statement in a score, Csound defaults to a t value of 60—60 beats per minute. In other words, the values in p2 and p3 are interpreted as seconds. Now we're running at 120 bpm, so Csound will produce notes that move twice as quickly and are half as long.

To add rhythmic interest to a Csound score, we need to edit the start times (p2) and probably the lengths (p3) of various events. Below is a slightly elaborated version of the tune. It uses eighth notes (p2 values that increase by 0.5) and triplets (p2 values that increase by 0.33). I've also bumped the melody up by an octave (replacing the 8's in p5 with 9's) to make room for the harmony we're about to add.

```
i1 0      0.5    0.7    9.04
i1 0.5    0.5    0.5    9.02
i1 1      0.5    0.6    9.04
i1 1.5    0.5    0.4    9.02
i1 2      1      0.7    9.04
i1 3      1      0.5    9.02
i1 4      0.3    0.6    9.00
i1 4.33   0.3    0.5    9.02
i1 4.67   0.3    0.4    8.11
i1 5      0.3    0.6    9.00
i1 5.33   0.3    0.5    9.02
i1 5.67   0.3    0.4    8.11
i1 6      1      0.5    9.00
i1 7      1      0.6    9.02
i1 8      0.7    0.6    9.04
i1 8.67   0.7    0.5    9.05
i1 9.33   0.7    0.4    9.03
i1 10     0.7    0.6    9.04
```

```
i1 10.67 0.7  0.5  9.05
i1 11.33 1.7  0.7  9.04
```

Using tab characters to line up the columns will make your score easier to read.

Now let's add some chords to the music. There are two main ways to organize a Csound score when you want several notes to sound at once. You can list the notes in strict chronological order by start time, or you can list the events for each part in a multi-part texture in their own set of lines. This can be easier to read.

Before performing your score, Csound will sort the score lines, so it doesn't matter what order you put the lines in. (In more complex score situations, it may matter a great deal, for reasons that would take several paragraphs to explain. The score we're working with is simple enough that we don't need to get into that.) All that matters is the start times of the notes. Two notes that have the same start time will, indeed, start at the same time.

Leaving the melody above as is, let's add a harmony below it. Copy these lines into your score below the lines that are creating the melody.

```
i1 0 2 0.3 7.00
i1 0 2 0.3 7.07
i1 2 2 0.3 7.05
i1 2 2 0.3 7.09
i1 4 2 0.3 7.04
i1 4 2 0.3 7.07
i1 6 2 0.3 7.05
i1 6 2 0.3 7.09
i1 8 2 0.2 7.02
i1 8 2 0.2 7.05
i1 8 2 0.2 7.09
i1 10 1.3 0.3 7.07
i1 10 1.3 0.3 7.11
i1 11.33 1.7 0.3 7.00
i1 11.33 1.7 0.3 7.07
```

As when we added a second oscillator, adding more voices may cause clipping distortion in the output. If you see the "samples out of range" message in the Console window—and if you've been entering the code exactly as shown, you will—it's time to lower the output level again.

There are at least three ways to do this. First, we could edit all of the p4 values in our score. This would be very time-consuming and also error-prone. Second, we could change the orchestra header to indicate that 0dbfs=1.5. This will fix the problem in our sample score, but in a project that has several different instruments playing (as opposed to several instances of the same instrument, which is what we have here), all of the instruments would get quieter, which may not be desirable musically.

A good compromise would be to edit instrument 1 to reduce its amplitude. This has the same effect as lowering the fader on a mixer channel. Leaving `0dbfs=1`, edit the `iamp` line of the `instr` code to reduce its value as needed:

```
iamp = p4 * 0.3
```

Now the level of this instrument will be half as loud as before, while any other instruments that are playing will be unaffected.

Control the Instrument Panning from the Score

We're almost ready to send "Mary Had a Little Lamb" out to pasture (and none too soon!), but first let's look at a couple of other techniques that are extremely useful.

This project runs in stereo, because the header says `nchnls=2`. In case it isn't obvious, that's a cryptic abbreviation for "number of channels." When Csound is operating in stereo, any instrument that we want to hear will use the `outs` opcode, which takes two input signals, one for the left channel and the other for the right channel. So far, those signals have been identical, so our music was functionally monaural.

Let's add a new p-field to our score, to control panning. The values for p6 can be anywhere from 0.0 (hard left) to 1.0 (hard right). At the end of instrument 1, add a new line using the `pan2` opcode, and edit the `outs` line, like this:

```
aL, aR pan2 aout, p6
outs aL, aR
```

The `pan2` opcode has two outputs, which appear at the left end of the line. We'll name these outputs `aL` and `aR`. These signals are now the inputs for the `outs` opcode. To use panning, we'll add p6 to the score lines.

 Tip Csound is a *case-sensitive* programming language, so the symbols `ar` and `aR` are not the same.

While doing so, we'll introduce one of a number of convenience features that make building Csound scores easier. When p-fields are at the end of the line, if they don't change we can skip them. Csound will infer that the same value should be used again, until it sees a different value. So we can type a p6 value of 0.5 (for center panning) only on the first line of the melody. This value will be used until a different one appears. For example:

```
i1 0   0.5 0.7 9.04 0.5
i1 0.5 0.5 0.5 9.02
i1 1   0.5 0.6 9.04
i1 1.5 0.5 0.4 9.02
```

For the accompaniment, we'd like to spread the chord notes to the left and right. You can enter 0.1 and 0.9 alternately on these score lines. (One of the chords in the accompaniment shown above has three notes, not two, so give one of the notes a p6 value of 0.5.) Now our ensemble is nicely spread out, with the melody in the center and the accompaniment voices at left and right. As a side benefit, this will lower the level of the signal being sent to each of the outputs, so we can increase the overall amplitude of our instrument:

```
iamp = p4 * 0.5
```

Process the Sound through a Reverb

To conclude our first QuickStart tutorial, we're going to add a reverb. This will be in a separate "instrument." We'll send the signal from instrument 1 to the reverb instrument using a stereo bus. To create the bus, add these two lines to the orchestra header, just below the ftgen line that creates the sine wave and above the first instrument definition:

```
gaRevInL init 0
gaRevInR init 0
```

After the endin for instr 1, leave one or two blank lines and create a new instrument, like this:

```
instr 100
aInL = gaRevInL
aInR = gaRevInR
gaRevInL = 0
gaRevInR = 0
aoutL, aoutR reverbsc aInL, aInR, 0.8, 10000
iamp = p4
kdeclick linseg iamp, (p3 - 0.05), iamp, 0.05, 0
aoutL = aoutL * kdeclick
aoutR = aoutR * kdeclick
outs aoutL, aoutR
endin
```

This instrument starts by reading the audio signals in the stereo bus and assigning them to local variables. It then zeroes out the input bus. This is important, as we'll see in a moment. Next, the reverbsc opcode processes the signals. Its outputs are adjusted by a "declick" envelope, which ensures that the output of the reverb falls to zero as it's being shut off. This envelope also adjusts the output level of the reverb by taking an amplitude value from the score using p4. The enveloped signals are sent to outs.

The code in the reverb instrument above is written for clarity (because we're in the middle of a tutorial). We could reduce it from twelve lines to six by rewriting it like this:

```
instr 100
aoutL, aoutR reverbsc gaRevInL, gaRevInR, 0.8, 10000
```

```
clear gaRevInL, gaRevInR
kdeclick linseg p4, (p3 - 0.05), p4, 0.05, 0
outs aoutL * kdeclick, aoutR * kdeclick
endin
```

We've used the global audio variables directly as inputs to `reverbsc`, introduced the `clear` opcode, which can zero out a number of audio variables in a single line, used `p4` directly as an argument to `linseg`, and multiplied the output variables by the declick envelope directly in the call to `outs`. The result will be exactly the same as before. As this example illustrates, Csound code can be written in various ways. Some methods will be more concise, while others may be easier to read.

We need to do two more things in order to hear the reverb. First, we need to send a signal to it. Add these two lines before the `outs` line for instrument 1:

```
gaRevInL = gaRevInL + aL
gaRevInR = gaRevInR + aR
```

These lines add the signals from `aL` and `aR` to whatever is in the reverb send bus already. We have to use addition here, because several instances of instrument 1 are running at the same time. There will quite likely be a signal in the bus already, and we want to mix the new signal with it. The reverb itself will clear out the bus by setting the signals to 0. If it didn't do this, the signal would quickly build up to an astronomical level. For this reason, we want to give the reverb instrument a higher number than the number(s) of any instruments that are sending signals to it.

Finally, we have to turn on the reverb instrument in the score. It needs only a single "note" event, which will run for as long as the rest of the score, and a couple of seconds extra at the end, to let the reverb tail die away. Looking at our score, we can see that the last note ends at beat 13, so we need a 17-beat reverb event. Add this line near the end of your score, directly above the `</CsScore>` line:

```
i100 0 17 0.2
```

When you play the file, you should hear a pleasant wash of reverb behind the notes. If you want more reverb, you can increase the `p4` value for the `i100` line from 0.2 to 0.4 or thereabouts. When you do this, however, you'll quite likely hear output distortion again, because the reverb signal is being mixed with the original, dry signal coming from instrument 1. One solution is to go back to instrument 1 and lower the value of `iamp`. By adjusting the amplitudes of instruments 1 and 100, you can get whatever wet/dry reverb mix you'd like.

Sound Design Project

In this project, we'll load a recorded sound file into Csound and then process it in various ways. Rather than generate notes, we'll look at a few of Csound's many sound design techniques.

Load a Sound File into a Table

Create a new file in CsoundQt and add the same header used in the first tutorial in this chapter. Your starter file should look like this:

```
<CsoundSynthesizer>
<CsOptions>
</CsOptions>
<CsInstruments>

sr = 44100
ksmps = 4
nchnls = 2
0dbfs = 1
</CsInstruments>
<CsScore>

</CsScore>
</CsoundSynthesizer>
```

Csound will look for an audio file to load in the directory you've specified using the environment variable SSDIR or SFDIR. These variables can and should be set in the Environment tab of CsoundQt's Configuration box. Set them to the directory where you have your audio source files stored.

Note   In the version 0.6 release (called QuteCsound), the Configurations fields for SSDIR and SFDIR don't work. If you're using this version, you'll have to specify the entire path to the sound file within your .csd code. In CsoundQt 0.7, this bug has been fixed.

This time, instead of using a `ftgen` opcode, we'll create a table using Csound's original method, using an f-statement in the score. These two methods are entirely equivalent and interchangeable. To load the file into a Csound table (a RAM memory area), add the following line to the start of the score (after `<CsScore>`), substituting your filename for `olive.aiff`:

```
f 1 0 0 1 "olive.aiff" 0 4 0
```

If you're using version 0.6, or if for some reason Csound is unable to find the settings for SSDIR and SFDIR, you can specify the entire directory structure, from the root of the hard drive, like this:

```
f 1 0 0 1 "C:/Users/Jim Aikin/Documents/csound
scores/samples/olive.aiff" 0 4 0
```

This f-statement uses a Csound routine called GEN 01 to load the audio data. For more information on the parameters you might need to change, look up GEN 01 in *The Canonical Csound Reference Manual*.

Create an Instrument and a Score

The easiest way to play a sampled sound is with Csound's `loscil` opcode. Here is a basic instrument:

```
instr 1
audio loscil p4, 1, 1, 1
outs audio, audio
endin
```

The third input to `loscil` is the number of the table we want to use. We created this in the score with `f 1`, so we use a 1 here to access the table. In complex Csound scores, we might pass different f-table numbers to the instrument using p-fields, in which case a single audio playback instrument could make many different sounds, just like any other sample playback module.

The output of `loscil` can have any name we like, as long as it begins with the letter a-. Here I've used "audio" as it makes the code easier to read. My file is mono, so I gave `loscil` only one output. If the file were stereo, the left end of the `loscil` line would need to say something like aL, aR, and these same values would be used with `outs`.

In order to play the instrument, we need to add an event to the score. But how long should the event be? That depends on how long your source file is. Mine is a little more than 16 seconds, so my score event looks like this:

```
i1 0 17 0.5
```

The value in the third field (p3) is the length of the note, and p4 is used by the instrument to control the amplitude. The length of the note has no direct relation to the length of the audio file; the two are independent. If you only want to hear the beginning of the file, create a short note.

 Caution   In versions 5.13 and older of Csound, `loscil` is limited to files of less than a minute in length. The exact maximum length depends on whether the file is stereo or mono, on the sampling rate, and on other factors. If your code seems to be correct, but `loscil` produces no sound when trying to play a longish file, you'll need to use `poscil` or `tablei` instead.

Change the Playback Speed

The second argument to `loscil` is the sample playback speed. Instead of setting this to a fixed value of 1, as above, we might want to create a ramp so that the playback speed starts slow and then speeds up. Replace the `loscil` line with these two lines:

```
kramp line 0.5, p3, 1.5
audio loscil p4, kramp, 1, 1
```

The `line` opcode creates a ramp signal. Here, it starts at 0.5, and during the duration of the note (p3) it increases to 1.5. The output of `line`, which I've named `kramp`, is sent to `loscil`. Play the file to hear the result.

Here's another possibility. Before entering the code into your project, see if you can guess what the sound will do.

```
klfo lfo 0.2, 7, 1
audio loscil p4, klfo + 1, 1, 1
```

The `lfo` opcode is set to play a triangle wave at 7 Hz, with a fairly shallow amplitude of ±0.2. We add this to the playback speed parameter of `loscil` to produce a warbling effect.

These audio effects are fairly trivial, though. Let's try something more interesting.

Add Ring Modulation

Get rid of the LFO and add an ordinary `oscil`. The new instrument should look like this:

```
instr 1
audio loscil p4, 1, 1, 1
asine oscil 1, 200, 2
audio = audio * asine
outs audio, audio
endin
```

In order to use this instrument, we need a second table containing audio data. We'll create the same sine wave as in the first tutorial, but this time we'll do it in the score:

```
f2 0 8192 10 1
```

This is f-table number 2, so we use 2 as the final input to the `oscil`.

Ring modulation is a very simple, yet exotic-sounding effect. It's created by multiplying one audio signal by another. The only danger to be aware of is that we don't want the two signals to have an amplitude greater than 1. If each of them hits a peak level of 2, for instance, at any point in the waveform, the output will have peak levels of 4. Assuming that your orchestra header specifies `0dbfs=1`, a peak level of 4 will certainly cause drastic clipping. That's why the sine wave above is created with an amplitude of 1.

Play this instrument and listen to the sound quality. I find ring modulation especially useful with vocal samples. Try different values for the frequency of the `oscil` by replacing 200 with a higher or lower number.

Instead of using a fixed frequency for the sine wave, we can restore the ramp generator we were using before and modulate the frequency of the sine wave with it. Replace the `oscil` line with these two lines:

```
kramp line 200, p3, 1000
asine oscil 1, kramp, 2
```

Now the frequency of the modulating oscillator will rise from 200 Hz to 1000 Hz during the course of the event.

Modulate the Playback Speed

In order to play with the audio source file more flexibly, we need to replace `loscil` with a `phasor` and a `table`. In place of the `loscil` line, insert these four lines:

```
aphas phasor 1/p3
ifilelength = 709288
aphas = aphas * ifilelength
audio table aphas, 1
```

You should use the actual length of your source file in samples as `ifilelength`. In addition, you'll need to make a minor change in the score. We created table f1 with a length of 0. Obviously, the length of the sound file isn't 0; using 0 for this parameter is simply a way of letting Csound set the length of the table based on the actual length of the file. But this strategy isn't compatible with the `table` opcode. We need to create a table whose length is a power of 2—the next power of 2 greater than the size of the audio file we're using. The exact value you use will depend on your source file.

```
f1 0 1048576 1 "olive.aiff" 0 4 0
```

The instrument should sound pretty much the way it did before. The advantage of using `phasor` is that we can mess with its output, thereby scanning the sound file in various ways. We can make it back up, for instance. Add an LFO to the input of the `phasor`, like this:

```
klfo lfo 1, 0.25, 1
aphas phasor (klfo + 0.1)/p3
```

Depending on your source material, you might want to adjust any of these values. Here's a slightly more complex instrument, in which the audio file is being scanned by two `table` opcodes, each under the control of its own `phasor`. The outputs are sent to the left and right speakers.

```
instr 1
kphasramp line 0.1, p3, 1.5
klfo lfo 1, (0.1 + kphasramp), 2
aphas phasor (klfo - kphasramp)/20
aphas2 phasor (klfo + kphasramp)/20
ifilelength = 709288
aphas = aphas * ifilelength
aphas2 = aphas2 * ifilelength
audioL table aphas, 1
audioR table aphas2, 1
outs audioL, audioR
endin
```

The `lfo` opcode is set to produce a square wave (the 2 at the end of the line), so the sound plays forward and backward alternately.

Add a Delay

To make the sound a little more complex and interesting, we'll finish this tutorial by adding a stereo delay. As with the first tutorial in this chapter, we'll start by creating a stereo send bus in the orchestra header area (directly below the line `0dbfs=1`):

```
gaDelaySendL init 0
gaDelaySendR init 0
```

Next, we send the left and right signals from the sample player to this bus. Let's reverse the sends, sending the right channel to the left bus and vice versa. Put this code near the end of instrument 1, just before the line with the `outs` opcode:

```
gaDelaySendL = audioR
gaDelaySendR = audioL
```

Because we're using only one instance of the sample playback instrument, we don't need to add `audioL` and `audioR` to whatever signal is in the bus; we can just copy them into the bus using the equals sign.

One odd thing about Csound's implementation of delay lines is that we have to read from the output of the delay before we write (send a signal) to it. For our delay instrument, we'll create two delay lines, one each for the left and right channels, and we'll use cross-feedback. Because we're going to send the signal in `adeloutR` to the input of the left delay line, we have to create this signal using the `init` opcode before using it. Here is the complete instrument:

```
instr 100
ilevel = p4
ifeedback = p5
itimeL = p6
itimeR = p7
ainL = gaDelaySendL
ainR = gaDelaySendR
gaDelaySendL = 0
gaDelaySendR = 0
adeloutR init 0
adeloutL   delayr itimeL
           delayw ainL + (adeloutR * ifeedback)
adeloutL dcblock2 adeloutL
adeloutR   delayr itimeR
           delayw ainR + (adeloutL * ifeedback)
adeloutR dcblock2 adeloutR
```

```
adeloutL = adeloutL * ilevel
adeloutR = adeloutR * ilevel
outs adeloutL, adeloutR
endin
```

Note the use of `dcblock2` here. This is a safety precaution, to prevent the possible buildup of DC (direct current) offset in the delay line's feedback loop. Another safety precaution is setting the level of the send bus signals back to zero after the signals have been received by the delay line.

This instrument will need seven p-fields in the score—for duration, output level, feedback level, and the left and right delay times. Here are the two events in my final score:

```
i1 0 26
i100 0 30 0.5 0.3 0.5 0.75
```

The exact numerical values you choose for the parameters sent to instruments of this sort will depend heavily on your source material. The best way to discover what sounds good is usually to try out a bunch of things until you start to develop a feel for what works.

A Basic Vocoder

To round out this chapter, let's use a vocoder to process the audio file. Go back to the beginning of the Sound Design Project, if you need to, and resurrect this instrument. This time, rather than receiving an amplitude value from the score, we'll just put 0.5 into the `loscil` directly:

```
instr 1
audio loscil 0.5, 1, 1, 1
outs audio, audio
endin
```

We're going to use a vocoder opcode created by Victor Lazzarini as a user-defined opcode (UDO). Go to www.csounds.com/udo and scroll down to the Filters section. There you'll find a link for the `Vocoder` opcode. (The other UDOs on this page are well worth exploring.) You can download the `Vocoder` code to your hard drive, or just copy and paste the text into your .csd file. Put it in the orchestra header section directly above `instr 1`—below the `0dbfs=1` line and below any global declarations, such as the delay send busses you created earlier in this chapter.

A vocoder needs two audio inputs—a carrier signal and a modulator (speech) signal. The modulator is the "voiced" source, so use the same vocal sample you've been using so far in this chapter. Any sound that is rich in harmonics can be used for the carrier; let's try out Csound's `vco2` opcode, which defaults to a sawtooth wave. These four lines will create a major triad played by sawtooth waves. Put them into instrument 1:

```
acar1 vco2 0.3, 200
acar2 vco2 0.3, 250
```

```
acar3 vco2 0.3, 300
acarrier = acar1 + acar2 + acar3
```

Below these lines and below the `loscil` line playing the vocal sample, insert a line sending your signals to the `Vocoder` UDO. To make the structure a bit clearer, we'll also change the name of the signal being sent to `outs`:

```
aout Vocoder acarrier, audio, 200, 10000, 20, 25
outs aout, aout
```

Your vocal sample should now be imprinted onto the major triad. The values chosen for the arguments to `Vocoder` may require a bit of fiddling to get the best sonic result; this is normal for Csound. The code for the `Vocoder` UDO documents the meanings of the inputs, but the meaning of the `kq` parameter (filter Q) may not be obvious. A higher Q value gives the filters in the vocoder a narrower bandwidth. If this value is either too low or too high, the speech-like signal emerging from the vocoder will be less intelligible. A value of 20, as shown in the code above, seems to be about right.

You'll also find that the output of the vocoder drops to a lower level when the Q is higher. You may need to boost the level of the speech input (the amplitude of the `loscil` opcode, which is set to 0.5 in the code above) in order to produce an optimal output level.

As an experiment, you might try assigning the frequencies of the three `vco2` opcodes to `p5`, `p6`, and `p7` in your score, so that each note in your score can play different harmonies. Here are the edits for the `vco2` lines:

```
acar1 vco2 0.2, p5
acar2 vco2 0.2, p6
acar3 vco2 0.2, p7
```

And here is a possible score:

```
i1 0 4 1.0 200 250 300
i1 4 4 1.0 225 300 360
i1 8 4 1.0 250 300 400
```

You could instead create a vocoder implementation that would accept chords played in real time on a MIDI keyboard, but this project would take us well beyond the bounds of a QuickStart tutorial. If you'd like to give it a try, turn to Chapter 10, "Using Csound with MIDI, OSC, Pd, Python, and Live Audio," where the basics of real-time MIDI instruments are introduced.

4 The Structure and Syntax of a .csd File

If you've gone through the tutorials in the previous chapter, you will already be acquainted with some of the main elements of a Csound file. In this chapter we'll explore this important topic in more detail.

 Tip Because Csound is a computer programming language, precision in typing is a must. Even a single misplaced comma will stop Csound dead in its tracks. Some of the syntax for code has optional features or elements, which you can include or omit depending on your needs; other syntax has to be followed more strictly.

The Command Line

Csound was originally designed to be run from the command line. The command line was a normal user interface element in computers in the 1970s and early 1980s, before the graphical user interface came to dominate the world of computing. The command line is still available in modern computers: In the Mac OS, you can use the command line (for Csound or for many other purposes) by going to Applications:Utilities and opening the Terminal program. In Windows, the Command Prompt is found in the All Programs/Accessories folder in the Start Menu. The command line is used more often in Linux systems, though Linux distributions also have graphical user interfaces.

This heritage is important for several reasons. For one thing, you can still run Csound from a command line if you want or need to. Here is an example of a command line invoking Csound, as given in *The Canonical Csound Reference Manual*:

```
csound -n -m 3 orchname -x xfilename -S scorename
```

Some of the symbols (such as -n, -m, and -S) are called command-line flags. They tell Csound how you would like it to operate. A complete list of command-line flags is included in the manual, and you can also display it by opening a Command Prompt (Windows) or Terminal (Mac OS) and typing csound. If Csound is properly installed, most of the available command-line flags will be displayed in response to this command. In addition to zero or more command-line flags, the Csound command expects to see three filenames—one for an orchestra, one for a score, and one for the output audio file that is to be written to the computer's hard drive. However, in place of an output filename you can use the -odac flag with a number that tells Csound what real-time output port you would like the audio sent to.

In early versions of Csound, the orchestra (the code defining one or more instruments) would be stored in a file with the filename extension .orc, while the score (the code listing the events that were to be played using the instruments) would be in a file with the filename extension .sco. These filenames would be supplied separately on the command line (as orchname and scorename in the line above). Today, a single .csd file usually contains both the orchestra and the score, so this one filename can be given on the command line.

The complete list of command-line flags can be a bit intimidating. Among the more useful items are:

-odac sets the real-time audio output.

-M sets the MIDI input device.

--displays causes the contents of f-tables to be displayed as they're being created. (If you're using CsoundQt, you'll need to create a Graph widget to display the data.) Note that --displays is the default, but the code in the .csoundrc file installed in Windows systems overrides it.

-B sets the number of audio samples in the real-time output hardware buffer.

-b sets the number of audio samples in the real-time output software buffer.

All of these flags except --displays must be followed by numerical arguments. If you're using CsoundQt, you'll normally set the values in the Configuration box rather than in the <CsOptions> area.

Tags in the .csd File

The system of separate .orc and .sco files was later supplanted by a single-file format with the filename extension .csd. Most Csound music written today is in the form of .csd files. A .csd file has a very specific structure, which is delineated by a few tags. These look like HTML markup tags, but they have nothing directly to do with HTML. The bare template for a .csd file looks like this:

```
<CsoundSynthesizer>
<CsOptions>
</CsOptions>
<CsInstruments>

</CsInstruments>
<CsScore>

</CsScore>
</CsoundSynthesizer>
```

In HTML markup, as here, tags are surrounded by angle brackets: < and >. Each section begins with a tag that has a special name and ends with a tag that has the same name preceded by a slash character (/). Sections can be embedded within other sections. Looking at this code, then, we can see that the outermost section is surrounded by <CsoundSynthesizer> tags. Within this are three subsections—<CsOptions>, <CsInstruments>, and <CsScore>, each of which has its own start and end tags.

Between the <CsInstruments> tags, you'll create instruments. An instrument is basically just a chunk of code that carries out one well-defined task. It does something. (Usually it will generate audio signals, but it might do something else instead.) Between the <CsScore> tags, you'll create an event list. Each event in the score will start an instrument and tell it to do whatever it does. The score may contain a few lines that do other things instead, as explained in Chapter 8, "Writing a Csound Score," but if you think of the score as a list of instructions that you're giving to Csound, telling it when to start a note on a given instrument and how long that note should last, you won't go far wrong.

The relevance of Csound's history may become apparent if you think about this structure for a moment. Within the <CsOptions> area, we can place whatever command-line flags we need (and also the name of the output file to write to disk). When we put the flags here, we don't have to type them at the command line each time we want to run Csound. The <CsInstruments> section replaces the old .orc file and contains the instruments that will be used in the project. The <CsScore> section contains the same elements that would have been placed in a .sco file.

We can invoke Csound from the command line, as in the early days, and give it the name of a .csd file containing all the information it needs to run. (The older .orc/.sco file format can still be used as well.) More often, Csound users write their music in a front-end program. (See Chapter 9, "Front Ends," for more on front ends.) *Csound Power!* was written using the CsoundQt front end, which is described in detail in Chapter 5, "Using the CsoundQt Interface."

One of the many services that front ends generally provide is that they replace the command-line flags with settings in a dialog box. The functionality of such a dialog box will be largely or entirely the same as the functionality of a set of command-line flags, but modern computer users are more accustomed to dialog boxes.

Because CsoundQt has a Configuration dialog box, the <CsOptions> section of the .csd files can normally be left blank. In fact, these tags can be omitted altogether if there's nothing between them. You can do all of your work in the other two areas, creating instruments in the <CsInstruments> section and score events in the <CsScore> section.

If you open, in a normal text editor, a .csd file that was created in CsoundQt, you'll see some other tags, including things like <MacOptions>, <MacGUI>, <bsbPanel>, and <EventPanel>. These sections contain code generated by CsoundQt for its own internal use. Normally this code is hidden from the user by CsoundQt, and it shouldn't interfere with Csound's operation if you invoke the .csd from the command line. In the next chapter, we'll look at the features of CsoundQt that these elements control.

The Orchestra Header

At the top of the `<CsInstruments>` area of the .csd file (or at the beginning of an .orc file, if you're using Csound the old-fashioned way), you need to include a header. The code in the orchestra header gives Csound some vital information, without which it can't run. The header will look something like this:

```
sr = 44100
ksmps = 10
nchnls = 2
0dbfs = 1
```

The first line sets the sample rate (`sr`) of the output file or the real-time data stream being sent to your audio interface. A value of 44100 is standard, because it's the sampling rate used by audio CDs, but depending on your needs and the capabilities of your hardware, you may want to use a higher number or possibly (though it's unlikely) a lower one. Csound can produce audio with any sample rate, but your audio hardware will probably only be able to use a few standard rates, such as 44100, 48000, 88200, and 96000.

The next line sets the number of samples in each k-cycle. The precise meaning of this setting will be explained in Chapter 6, "Building Your Own Instruments and Effects," in the section "i- versus k- versus a-." For now, all you need be concerned about are two things. First, `ksmps` should usually be an integer factor of the value you've set for the hardware buffer (which is determined by the `-B` command-line flag). Generally the value of `-B` will be a power of 2, such as 512, so values for `ksmps` of 1, 2, 4, 8, 16, and so on should work. Second, a higher value of `ksmps` will save on CPU power but will also reduce the audio quality—perhaps imperceptibly, but perhaps very perceptibly, depending on how your instruments are designed. Some Csound users set `ksmps` to 128 while developing their music, because more complex orchestras can play in real time when this value is higher, but they change it to 1 when rendering the finished piece to the hard drive, as that doesn't need to be a real-time process.

Tip If you're using Csound live, a higher setting for `ksmps` will put less load on your CPU, so you'll be less likely to hear the sound break up.

The `nchnls` setting tells Csound how many output channels you want. Normally this will be set to 2 (for stereo sound) or 1 (for monaural). But if you have a multi-channel audio interface or want to use Csound for quadrophonic or surround sound applications, you'll need a higher setting for `nchnls`. The details of how to set up your system for multi-channel operation are beyond the scope of this book.

The `0dbfs` setting tells Csound what numerical value will be the maximum for the audio signals your .csd will create. In the early days, Csound's maximum output level was set at 32,768, because the output was 16-bit audio. The largest number that can be expressed with 16 binary digits (bits) is 65,536—and if you want to include both positive and negative numbers, as you'll need to do in order to describe audio waveforms, half of the values will be below zero, so you'll be left with a maximum value of plus or minus 32,768.

Modern digital audio systems, however, are capable of much better sound quality than this. If you look at the General tab in CsoundQt's Configuration box, you'll see that Csound can create files in 16-bit, 24-bit, or 32-bit floating-point format. The numbers used in these formats can get far larger than 32,768, so using them in your orchestra code would be impractical. The `0dbfs` setting bypasses that issue. After setting `0dbfs` to 1.0, you can deal with all of your audio levels as decimal point values between 0.0 and 1.0. This is very convenient and is the preferred method, but older .csd files used as examples in some texts have no setting for `0dbfs`. If this value is not set in the orchestra header, Csound defaults to the original value, `0dbfs=32768`.

If your code produces audio values higher than the setting for `0dbfs`, the output will clip. If only a few samples exceed this level, you may not hear the clipping, but if you listen closely, the crackling distortion may be audible. When larger numbers of samples clip, the results will be nasty.

One quick way to get rid of clipping distortion on the output is to increase the value of `0dbfs`. When you increase the value, the output level of your sound will fall, so the distortion will go away. However, writing good code will become harder, because each time you add or edit an instrument, you'll need to remember what value you've set for `0dbfs`. It's a better procedure to get rid of clipping by editing the instrument code.

Other Items in the Header

The code in the instrument header is run when Csound starts. Because of this, you'll often use it to set up global variables and data structures of various kinds. The code for user-defined opcodes (UDOs) is included in the header area; we'll have more to say about UDOs in Chapter 7, "Thirty Opcodes You Must Know." Macros can be defined in the header; these are discussed later in this chapter.

In *The Canonical Csound Reference Manual* you'll find a page listing a number of global reserved symbols that can be used in the header. In addition to the items we've already looked at, the list includes `ctrlinit`, `ftgen`, `kr`, `massign`, `pgmassign`, `pset`, `seed`, and `strset`. We'll look at `ctrlinit`, `massign`, `pgmassign`, and `pset` in Chapter 10, "Using Csound with MIDI, OSC, Pd, Python, and Live Audio," when we explore using Csound with MIDI. `kr` used to be required, but it's now optional and redundant; if you use it, it should always be set so that `kr * ksmps = sr`.

`ftgen` is used for creating data tables and is more or less equivalent to f-statements included in the score. We'll have more to say about it in Chapter 7.

`seed` is used for seeding Csound's random number generators, including the noise sources. Setting `seed = 0` will seed the random number generators from the computer's system clock, in which case different random numbers will be generated each time the music is played. Any other value for `seed` will cause the random number generators to operate predictably—that is, they'll generate the same series of quasi-random output values each time the piece is played. This can be useful both for testing purposes and in computer-assisted composition: You can keep changing the value of seed until you hear a pattern of notes that you like.

The header is also the place where you'll create global variables. These begin with the letter g; Csound's system for naming variables is explained in Chapter 6, "Building Your Own Instruments and Effects." In the tutorial in Chapter 3, we've already used global audio-rate variables and global initialization-pass variables. Control-rate variables can also be put in the header. Here's a quick example:

```
giBaseFrequency = 33
gkControlBus init 0
gaAudioBus init 0
```

Note the use of the init opcode here. giBaseFrequency is an i-time variable, so its value can be set using the equals sign. But the data in gkControlBus and gaAudioBus will almost certainly change while the music is playing, so an equals sign wouldn't make sense. (In fact, it will generate a compiler error, so your file won't run.) The init opcode tells Csound the initial (starting) value of the signal, which should usually be zero.

If you're using Csound's zak patching system to send signals from one instrument to another, you'll need to put the zakinit opcode in the header. You can read about zakinit and the other zak opcodes in *The Canonical Csound Reference Manual*.

Last but not least, any user-defined opcodes should be placed in the orchestra header, after everything else and before the beginning of your instrument code.

Adding Comments to Your Code

It's always a good idea to add comments to your code while you're developing a piece in Csound (or a program in any other programming language, for that matter). Comments will be ignored by the Csound compiler. Comments are useful first and foremost because you may open up a file two years from now and have no memory of what your code does. Comments will also be immensely useful if your code is read by someone else. For a good example of how helpful copious comments can be, go to CsoundQt's Examples menu, look in the Music submenu, and open up "Kung-Xanadu." (This piece also provides an inspiring example of a few of the sound colors you can create with Csound.)

Csound provides three ways to add comments. First, anything on a line that follows a semicolon is a comment. This is the original format for Csound comments:

```
instr 1 ; a plucked FM sound
; first, read the p-fields into the instrument:
idur = p3
iamp = p4
; etc....
```

Here, Csound will "see" the symbols `instr 1`—they're active code. But the rest of the line, `; a plucked FM sound`, is strictly for the benefit of anyone who happens to be reading the code. Likewise, the lines with `idur` and `iamp` will be read by the Csound compiler, but the lines immediately above and below them are comments and will be ignored.

More recently, a comment syntax borrowed from the C programming language has been added to Csound. If you want to type a longish block of text and not have to put a semicolon at the beginning of every line, you can start and end your comment text like this:

```
/*
This is also a comment.
*/
```

The symbol `/*` starts the comment, and the symbol `*/` ends it.

Finally, anything you type into your file before the `<CsoundSynthesizer>` tag or after the `</CsoundSynthesizer>` ending tag will be ignored by Csound.

Spacing and Parentheses

Csound code is written with one statement (an instruction to the compiler) per line. The carriage-return character ends a statement. Other than that, Csound is fairly tolerant of how you enter your code. You don't need to indent the lines within an if/then/endif block. You can use tab characters to align columns in order to make them easier to read, but this is purely a convenience; to Csound, any string of one or more space or tab characters is the same.

When entering formulas, you can use or not use spaces around the symbols—again, it's up to you. The three lines below are entirely equivalent as far as Csound is concerned:

```
if(ivalue=5)then
; ... is functionally the same as:
if (ivalue = 5) then
; ... and, for that matter, the same as:
if ivalue=5 then
```

Parentheses are required only when you need to change the order of precedence of two or more operators. For example, the multiplication operator (*) has higher precedence than the addition operator (+). So these two statements are identical:

```
ivalueX = ivalue1 + ivalue2 * ivalue3
ivalueX = ivalue1 + (ivalue2 * ivalue3)
```

...but they're not the same as this:

```
ivalueX = (ivalue1 + ivalue2) * ivalue3
```

In the first two lines, `ivalue2` will be multiplied by `ivalue3`, and then `ivalue1` will be added to the result. In the third line, the parentheses ensure that `ivalue1` and `ivalue2` will be added first, and then the result of the addition will be multiplied by `ivalue3`.

If you're not sure of the precedence of two operators, using extra parentheses is an easy way to make sure your code does what you want it to. Adding superfluous parentheses also helps group complex expressions so as to make them easier to read.

Parentheses are required around the arguments to a few opcodes, such as `sqrt`, even when the expression being used as an argument is simple. These opcodes are often referred to as functions, because their syntax is identical to the syntax used in other programming languages to call functions:

```
ivalueX = sqrt(ivalue)    ; this compiles ...
ivalueX sqrt ivalue       ; ... but this doesn't
```

Spaces are required only in a few places, such as around the names of opcodes and between numerical values (p-fields) in the score.

Macros

Macros can be used in Csound, both in the orchestra and in the score, to define text that will be inserted into your code by the preprocessor, before the code is compiled. This functionality is well explained in *The Canonical Csound Reference Manual*. Here is the example used in the manual to illustrate the `#define` command:

```
#define VOLUME #5000#
#define FREQ #440#
#define TABLE #1#


instr 1
; This will be expanded to "a1 oscil 5000, 440, 1".
a1 oscil $VOLUME, $FREQ, $TABLE
```

A macro is defined using a `#define` statement, followed by the name of the macro, followed by the text content of the macro surrounded by # symbols. To refer to the macro in your orchestra, use its name preceded by a dollar sign. When the preprocessor is preparing your .csd file for performance or rendering, it simply replaces the dollar sign and the macro name with whatever text you have specified in the macro definition.

Macros can be defined with up to five variable arguments. The variable arguments are separated by apostrophes (`'`). The prototype for a macro with arguments looks like this:

```
#define NAME(a'b'c') #replacement text#
```

Here is the example code given in the manual:

```
#define OSCMACRO(VOLUME'FREQ'TABLE) #oscil $VOLUME, $FREQ, $TABLE#

instr 1
; This will be expanded to "a1 oscil 5000, 440, 1".
a1 $OSCMACRO(5000'440'1)
```

Note the use of dollar signs within the definition to refer to the places where the variables will be inserted when the macro is being "unpacked" by the Csound compiler. The example above is rather trivial, in that it won't actually save you any typing. The point of the example is to illustrate the syntax in a clear way.

What the manual doesn't mention explicitly is that the values used as the variable arguments needn't be constants. In the example above, if the output of an LFO has been created using the symbol klfo, then this code will work:

```
a1 $OSCMACRO(5000'klfo'1)
```

We'll look further at the uses of macros in Chapter 8, "Writing a Csound Score."

5 Using the CsoundQt Interface

As explained in Chapter 4, Csound can be run from your computer's command line (Terminal in Mac OS or the Command Prompt in Windows). But most users today, with the possible exception of some folks who use the Linux operating system, prefer to run Csound from within a front-end program. Generally speaking, front ends don't do anything to extend the actual functionality of Csound as a synthesis and composition language. They do, however, make Csound much easier to use, and some append or mingle their own specialized code with your code in order to integrate new features of the user interface. The friendly features differ widely from one front end to another.

 Note Prior to the 0.7 release, CsoundQt was called QuteCsound. The name change was being made as *Csound Power!* was going to press. There's no need for confusion: The two programs are the same entity. However, certain aspects of the download and install instructions may still refer to the program under its previous name.

CsoundQt is a very capable front end for Csound; it was written (and is being maintained and updated) by Andrés Cabrera. It was chosen as the primary point of reference in *Csound Power!* for two reasons. First, it's a fairly "vanilla" front end. You don't have to learn how to utilize a lot of esoteric features found only in the front end in order to make music with the Csound/ CsoundQt duo, though as you get deeper into CsoundQt, you'll find that it has some very useful features. To get started, you can just write and run straight Csound code within CsoundQt—and that fact will make the learning process easier. Second, CsoundQt is currently bundled with the Csound distributions for Mac OS and Windows, so if you've installed Csound, you probably already have it, and it should run without any major glitches.

In this chapter we'll explore the CsoundQt user interface in detail. The main elements we'll be concerned with are the Editor window, the Inspector, Live Events, the Configuration box, and Widgets. At this writing, CsoundQt 0.7 is still in testing. Its features will be referred to where appropriate, but a few details of the version installed in your computer may differ.

The Toolbar and Menus

The toolbar in CsoundQt (see Figure 5.1) is fairly self-explanatory. At the left end is a set of buttons that are found on many computer application toolbars—New, Open, Save, Undo, Redo,

Cut, Copy, and Paste. These commands duplicate the standard functions in the File and Edit menus and hardly need explaining. The buttons in the center part of the toolbar—Run, Stop, Run in Term, Record, Render, Ext. Editor, and Ext. Player—invoke commands that cause Csound itself to do things. The buttons on the right end of the Toolbar—Configure, Widgets, Manual, Console, Inspector, Live Events, and Utilities—are commands that open and close panels in the CsoundQt workspace.

If the main window is too narrow to display all of the tool buttons, you'll see a right-pointing arrow at the right end of the toolbar. Clicking this will display the hidden tool buttons.

Figure 5.1 The CsoundQt menu (in Windows) and toolbar.

The Run button causes the currently active .csd file (the one visible in the multi-tabbed Editor window) to do whatever it does. Most likely, it will produce sound. If it's set up for real-time MIDI input from an external source such as a keyboard, it may start silently and then wait for you to start sending it MIDI messages. The sound output will be sent to whatever audio device you have selected in the Configuration box (as explained later in this chapter). The Stop button will stop the output immediately.

 Note By default, clicking the Run button saves the currently active .csd file (the one you see in the Editor pane) before compiling and running it. This behavior can be switched off in the Editor pane of the Configuration box.

If the Run button fails to work, it won't be highlighted. In that case, open up the Output Console window by clicking the Console button in the toolbar, if it isn't open already. In the Output Console, you'll see the text output that Csound produces while running or attempting to run. Various useful messages, including error messages, will appear here. If the Run button doesn't work, it's probably because your code has one or more bugs. These will be listed in the Console. After fixing the bugs, try clicking the Run button again.

Csound will also fail to run if your MIDI or audio setup has changed. To remedy this situation, open the Configuration box, choose the Run tab, and select inputs and outputs from the drop-down menu.

The Run in Term button bypasses the CsoundQt framework. This button runs Csound in your computer's Terminal (Mac OS) or Command Prompt (Windows) rather than via the CsoundQt interface. This can be useful for diagnosing problems. If CsoundQt crashes when you try to run a file, for instance, your first stop, after re-launching CsoundQt, should be the Run in Term button. If the .csd file runs as expected in the Terminal/Command Prompt, then it's possible you've uncovered a CsoundQt bug. In that case, you should report it to the Csound mailing list or the CsoundQt mailing list.

Note   When you use the Run in Term button, you may need or want to make changes in the command-line arguments in the `<CsOptions>` area of your .csd file. In addition, Run in Term can fail (in QuteCsound 0.6 for Windows) if the file paths to SSDIR and SFDIR, as set in the Environment tab of the Configuration box, aren't enclosed in double-quotes and there are spaces in any of the folder or file names. These text strings will be passed directly to Csound as command-line arguments when Csound is run in the terminal, and enclosing them in quotes will ensure that they're interpreted properly. This bug has been fixed in CsoundQt 0.7.

The Render button will save the output audio from Csound to a file on your hard drive rather than playing it through your audio interface and speakers. If you've checked the Ask for Filename Every Time checkbox in the Run tab of the Configuration box, you'll be prompted for a filename; the default name will be whatever you've specified in the Configuration box in the Output Filename field. If you uncheck Ask for Filename Every Time, CsoundQt will simply use whatever filename you've provided in that field without asking you to confirm. This could conceivably overwrite an audio file that you want to keep, so leaving Ask for Filename Every Time checked is probably a good idea.

Rendering is a non-real-time process. Unless your orchestra and score are uncommonly dense or your computer is uncommonly slow, rendering will be faster than real time, perhaps much faster. A piece that lasts for several minutes may render in 10 or 15 seconds. You won't hear any audio output while the rendering is taking place. But this fact raises a question: What if you want to interact with Csound in real time while the music is playing (perhaps by sending it MIDI messages or live audio), but you also want to capture the audio to your hard drive? For that purpose, CsoundQt provides the Record button. This button will both play the file in real time and capture the audio to your hard drive, into the same file folder where the .csd file itself is located.

In version 0.6, the Record button fails to work in the Windows version, though it works in the Mac version. This problem is fixed in 0.7. You won't be prompted for a filename, but not to worry: CsoundQt won't overwrite your file if you do several takes. Each file will be given a name that corresponds to the .csd file, with "000.wav", "001.wav", and so forth appended. They will be recorded to the same directory where the .csd file itself is located.

The Ext. Editor button will launch whatever external audio editor you've specified in the Configuration box under External Programs/Wave Editor. The most recently recorded or rendered audio file should be loaded into the wave editor program, ready to edit. Whatever edits you make won't be reflected in Csound or CsoundQt, because you're editing the audio data itself, so this is strictly a convenience feature. You might, for instance, want to normalize the gain of your final rendered file and then export it as an mp3 or .ogg compressed audio file before uploading it to a website.

The Ext. Player button works in a similar way: It should launch whatever external player (such as iTunes) you've specific in the Configuration box under External Programs/Wave Player.

Note These features are not quite functional in the 0.6.0 (Win) and 0.6.1 (Mac OS) releases. The Ext. Editor button works in Windows but not in the Mac. Ext. Player works on neither platform. This is no more than a minor inconvenience, as you can still launch your favorite apps in the normal way, such as by dragging and dropping the audio file onto their desktop icons. These buttons seem to be working in version 0.7.0.

The buttons on the right side of the toolbar open windows or boxes within the CsoundQt user interface. They will be alluded to in the sections later in this chapter that deal with these windows and boxes.

Menus

While inspecting the commands in CsoundQt's menus, take note of the keyboard equivalents. In many cases they're real time-savers. These shortcuts are not, in every case, identical between the Mac and Windows versions.

Windows users who are vision-impaired may want to be alerted that the standard Windows menu shortcuts, which use the Alt key to open menus, are not implemented in CsoundQt. Once a menu has been opened with the mouse, however, the cursor keys can be used to navigate it. Menu navigation from the cursor keys works both in Mac OS and in Windows.

The File Menu

Most of the items in the File menu will be familiar to anyone who has ever worked with modern computer software, so there's no need to go into the specifics here. A couple of items are worth special mention, however.

The File Information command opens a little read-only box (see Figure 5.2) that gives some useful information about the current .csd file. The Export without Widgets command allows you to save your .csd file in a "vanilla" form, without the extra code used by CsoundQt to construct graphic controls. This code is normally invisible within CsoundQt itself, but you can view it by opening your .csd file in a text editor program.

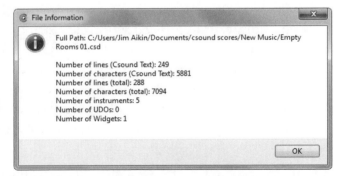

Figure 5.2 The File Information box, which is launched from the File menu, provides some statistics as well as a reminder of the full path to the file.

The Edit Menu

The top few items in the Edit menu (Undo, Redo, Cut, Copy, Paste, Find) will, again, be familiar to almost all computer users. Other commands here are more specific to CsoundQt.

To use the Autocomplete command, position your text cursor on an empty line, type the name of a Csound opcode, such as oscil, and then hit the keystroke equivalent of the command (Alt+C on Windows, Option+C in Mac OS). CsoundQt will replace your text with the entire prototype of the opcode, including its output type(s) and input arguments. This feature can save you hours of looking up opcodes in the manual. At first, the meanings of the symbols in the prototype may not be clear—and you'll need to understand them in order to replace them with actual values suitable for your code. For details, see Chapter 7, "Thirty Opcodes You Must Know." Some opcodes can be used in two or more forms; with these, Autocomplete will choose the first form it finds in the manual, which may not be what you want.

After selecting one or more lines of your code, or placing the text cursor anywhere within a single line, you can use the Comment or Uncomment command. In Windows, commenting and uncommenting uses Ctrl+/. On the Mac, Cmd+/ is used. Commenting out sections of code temporarily is a great way to save time and track down bugs. These commands are very useful.

The Indent and Unindent commands are also handy. Csound code does not require that lines be indented, but indentation (such as of a block of code that begins with an if...then statement and ends with an endif) can make the code easier to read.

The Kill Line (Ctrl+K, Cmd+K) and Kill to End of Line (Ctrl+Shift+K, Cmd+Shift+K) commands are an idea carried over from full-featured text editors. Using these commands is faster than selecting text with the mouse and then hitting the Delete key.

After loading an .orc file and an .sco file (Csound's original file formats for instrument code and score code), you can use the Join orc/sco command to combine them in a new .csd file. This is a bit easier than copying and pasting all of the code. If you open an .orc file and an .sco file at the same time from the File Open dialog box, CsoundQt can invoke this command automatically if you've checked the appropriate checkbox in the Editor pane of the Configuration box. CsoundQt will create a new file that combines the two and invite you to save it. Alternatively, you can invoke the command from the Edit menu after opening only one of the two files. CsoundQt will look for a matching file in the same directory.

The Invalue->chnget and Chnget->invalue commands are complementary. Csound provides two more or less equivalent ways to send and receive external real-time commands—the invalue and chnget opcodes. These two menu commands can be handy if you've acquired a file from someone else and need to convert dozens of opcodes at once. The commands also swap outvalue and chnset. (Note, however, that chnset and chnget can be used internally to transmit values between Csound instruments. outvalue and invalue are used to communicate with external objects, such as widgets.)

The Insert/Update CsLadspa Text item adds a new pair of tags (<csLADSPA> and </csLADSPA>) near the top of the current .csd file and places some default text between them. This feature is for developing LADSPA plug-ins in Csound. LADSPA plug-ins run in some Linux audio applications. Developing such plug-ins is beyond the scope of this book; for more information, consult the LADSPA home page (www.ladspa.org) or the *Csound Journal* article on this topic (www.csounds.com/journal/issue6/csLADSPA.html).

The Widget Edit Mode command (Ctrl+E or Cmd+E) switches the Widgets panel in and out of edit mode. For more information, see the "Widgets" section later in this chapter.

The Set Keyboard Shortcuts command opens a dialog box (see Figure 5.3) in which you can configure some aspects of CsoundQt's operation to be more to your liking. The list of commands available from this box may be slightly different in the Mac versus Windows versions of the program, but in both, the Restore Defaults button can be used to get rid of the items you don't like.

To create a new shortcut, click in the right-hand column beside the entry you want to change and then type your desired shortcut. If the shortcut you type is already being used, you won't be allowed to give it a new meaning. (There seems currently to be no way to delete an existing shortcut.)

Figure 5.3 In the Set Keyboard Shortcuts box, you can set up quick keyboard access to important commands.

The Control and View Menus

The Control and View menus duplicate functions found in the toolbar. To save screen space, you can turn off the toolbar from the Editor tab of the Configuration box by unchecking the Show Toolbars option. Note, however, that if you turn off the toolbar and want to turn it back on, you won't find the command for opening the Configuration box in the Control or View menu. In Windows, that command is in the Edit menu; on the Mac, it's in the CsoundQt menu, where it appears as Preferences.

If you activate Split View in the View menu, the main editor area will be split horizontally, with the score portion of the .csd file displayed in the lower pane in spreadsheet form.

The View Code Graph command in the View menu requires the installation of Graphviz (www.graphviz.org). This tool is a way of translating your code into a visual form.

The Examples and Favorites Menus

From the Examples menu, you can load a wide variety of examples of Csound code. A lot can be learned by studying these examples, as they demonstrate many useful techniques. There are far too many to discuss in these pages, however, and more are added from time to time. Most of the examples contain comments that will help you understand what's going on, but even so, a bit of study and experimentation may be required. If you've edited a file, you'll have to use Save As to save it out to your own Csound Scores directory, because the examples can't be saved back into their own repository. They're not stored on the hard drive as separate files; they're embedded within the CsoundQt program itself.

It's possible that one or two of the examples may not work perfectly. As with many things in the world of Csound, they were put together by volunteers, and errors are only fixed if they're reported and if the person who is maintaining the code has time to fix the problem. If you spot an error, please report it.

Especially worth note are the examples in the Floss Manual subdirectory. These are taken directly from the online Floss Manual. If you're studying this document, you won't need to do any typing in order to run the examples found therein.

In version 0.6 for Windows, Favorites is a sub-menu under Examples. In version 0.7, however, it's a top-level menu in both Mac and Windows. In the Environment tab of the Configuration box, you can set a directory for your Favorites. Once you have set this directory, the items in it, including both .csd files and sub-folders, will show up in the Favorites menu.

The Help Menu

The first command in the Help menu, Show Opcode Entry (Shift+F1), is very useful. Park the text cursor on the line with an opcode and use this command, and you'll see why. It opens the Manual pane and displays the page for that opcode.

The Show Opcode Entry in External Browser command works well in Mac OS with Safari, but not necessarily with other browsers. In my Windows system it doesn't currently work well with either Firefox or Opera, but I've reported the bug, and it should be fixed by the time you read this. In any case, it's not a big deal, because it's easy enough to make the Csound manual your home page in your browser and then put a shortcut to the browser on the desktop. Once you've done this, looking up an opcode in the external browser (which will have a bigger display than CsoundQt's own Manual pane) is easy.

The Help Forward and Help Back commands duplicate the functionality of the green triangle buttons at the top of the Manual pane, stepping you forward and backward through multiple pages of the manual.

The next four items in the Help menu open alternate pages in the built-in Manual pane. Below these is the Open Quick Reference Guide command. At this writing, CsoundQt has no manual; this item opens a PDF document that provides a little guidance in how to use CsoundQt, but the PDF covers only version 0.4. To use the menu command, you may need to go to the External Programs tab in the Configuration box and select a PDF viewer program.

Before using the Reset Preferences command, you should be sure to write down all of the settings in the Configurations box, including the directories where CsoundQt is to look for things such as the Csound manual. All of that information will be erased by this command, which is designed to be used only in cases where the Preferences have become corrupted.

The Main Window

The main window of CsoundQt is divided into several panes, as shown in Figure 5.4. Below the menu bar and tool button bar, which run across the top of the window, are four areas. The Inspector runs down the left side and the Console across the bottom. The multi-tabbed text editor occupies the central area. On the right is a dual-purpose pane, which can show the Widgets, the Csound manual, or both at once. Each of these areas, except the editor, can be closed by clicking the X button in its upper-right corner. They can be resized by clicking and dragging on the border between two areas; the mouse cursor will turn into a double line with arrows when you're in the right spot to resize the panes. Note, however, that each pane has a minimum size, beyond which it can't be reduced. Some details of how this works are operating-system-specific. In the Mac OS version, the Editor pane can be narrowed further after you've closed some of the open files, because the file tabs across the top of the Editor pane have a minimum width.

The panes can be turned into floating windows by clicking on the dual-window icon in the top bar of the pane. While floating, they can be docked back into the main window by double-clicking the title bar of the floating window or by dragging the floating window into position. The latter process may prove a bit finicky. (If the Inspector docks across the top of the main window rather than along the left edge, try narrowing its window while it's floating, and then dock it.) Double-clicking the title bar is more reliable, at least in my Windows 7 system.

In the next few pages, we'll look at each of these areas in turn.

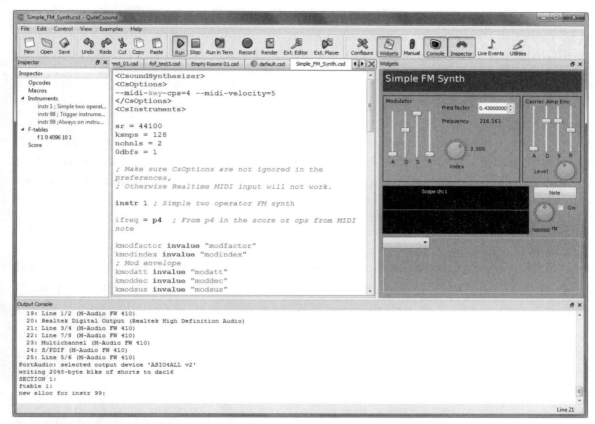

Figure 5.4   The main window of CsoundQt, showing the Inspector pane (left), the Widgets pane (right), the Output Console (bottom), and the text editor (center). When Csound is running, it sends messages to the user, which appear in the Output Console. Widgets are user-defined interface items. The Inspector provides shortcuts for navigating through long files.

The Editor

CsoundQt's Text Editor pane is not fancy, although it has one very cool feature—the Split View command in the View menu. (See below for more on this.) Numerous files can be open at the same time; their names will be displayed across the top of the editor in a multi-tabbed interface. Clicking on a tab will take you to that file. If the file has not been saved since your most recent editing, you'll see a green button beside the filename.

The editor understands quite a bit about Csound code. It uses syntax highlighting (colored text) to indicate what type of Csound element you've just typed. This can be quite useful. Opcodes appear in blue, comments in light green italic, audio variable names in heavy (boldface) green, p-field variable names in heavy black, reserved words such as `ksmps` in dark red, double-quoted strings in lighter red, light gray for unrecognized elements, and so forth.

At present, the choice of syntax colors is not user-configurable, but I've found the built-in system easy to read. You can, however, change the font and size of the text in the editor window, using the Editor pane in the Configuration box.

CsoundQt gets its information about which words are opcodes by consulting the installed copy of the manual. In extremely rare cases, an opcode might be undocumented. In that case, it may run properly, but CsoundQt may fail to display its name in blue.

To close one of the open files, select it by clicking its tab at the top of the Editor pane and then click the red X button in the upper-right corner of the pane. In the Windows version, file tabs display the complete name of the file, and more files can be open than there is room for on the row of tabs. In this situation, left and right scroll arrows will appear to the left of the red X button, so that you can navigate to tabs that are not visible. The Macintosh version lacks this functionality: On the Mac, file tabs have a fixed minimum width and can't be hidden. If you open more files than there is room for in the Editor pane, CsoundQt's main window will widen to accommodate the tabs. On my MacBook Pro laptop, it's practical to keep about a dozen files open at any given time.

The width of the text tab character (not to be confused with file tabs) can be set in the Editor tab of the Configuration box. The number doesn't correspond to the number of fixed-width characters in the indent; it seems to be a value in pixels. Using Tabs will help keep your code readable; it's highly recommended.

In this area of Configurations, you can also switch auto-wrapping on or off by checking or unchecking the Wrap Lines box. Auto-wrapping of long lines is for display purposes only and will have no effect on how Csound interprets your code. If auto-wrapping is switched off, when your code contains a line that is too long for the display area you'll see a scrollbar at the bottom of the Editor window. Auto-wrapping can make code with lots of long lines harder to read, but if you only have a few long lines, it's convenient.

The Editor pane can be split into Orchestra and Score panes using the Split View command in the View Menu. The score will then be displayed in spreadsheet form. You'll probably find this display very useful, especially with larger scores. The p-fields will automatically be aligned, and you can move the input cursor among them using the arrow keys or the Tab key. In addition, the right-click menu used in the Live Events implementation is available for making quick edits of the p-fields. For more, see "Live Events," later in this chapter.

Syntax Hints and Accessing Opcode Help

When you put the text cursor on the same line as an opcode, the prototype of the opcode will be displayed along the bottom of the main window. If you need more help, press Shift+F1 (function key 1, at the top of your QWERTY keyboard). This will open the Manual pane on the right side of the main window, with the page for that opcode displayed. For more information, see "The Help Menu," earlier in this chapter, and "The Manual Pane," later in this chapter.

 Caution In Windows systems, you may find that the standard Cut, Copy, and Paste commands don't work in the CsoundQt editor. This problem, which should be resolved in the 0.7 release, is due to a conflict caused by three files in the plugins64 directory. If you encounter this problem, find the plugins64 directory in the directory where you've installed Csound and remove the following three files: fluidOpcodes.dll, virtual.dll, and widgets.dll. (You may want to save them to a separate directory that you might name "removed plugins".) Once they're gone, launch CsoundQt, and you should find that Cut, Copy, and Paste work normally.

The Inspector

As your .csd files grow longer, you'll find the Inspector extremely useful for navigating quickly through the text in the Editor pane. The information in the Inspector is assembled on the fly by CsoundQt.

Clicking on a visible item in the Inspector causes the Editor to jump up or down so that that line is at the top of the visible area.

The main headings used by the Inspector are Opcodes, Macros, Instruments, F-tables, and Score. When there are sub-items to be displayed in any of these categories, they can be shown or hidden by clicking the gray triangles along the left edge. The Inspector operates, in other words, rather like a standard file browser.

Certain items will be displayed automatically. If your file contains any user-defined opcodes, they'll show up under Opcodes, because CsoundQt sees the `opcode` opcode and grabs that line of text to put into the Inspector. Likewise any line of text that begins with `instr`. The F-tables display is a little slicker: It displays both f-tables created in the orchestra header using `ftgen` and f-tables created in the score using f-statements.

In addition, the Inspector looks for lines that begin with two semicolons. Only one semicolon is needed to set off a comment, but if you use two, the Inspector will understand that this comment is a tag that you would like to be able to navigate to. For instance, in an instrument, you might have comments like this:

```
;; first oscillator
;; second oscillator
;; filter envelopes
```

The Inspector will place a gray open/close triangle next to the instrument line so that you can find these tags or hide them.

The Output Console

When Csound is invoked and is running (or fails to run), its messages will appear in the Output Console, which can be displayed or hidden using the tool in the toolbar. The text generated by the printing opcodes, for example, will appear in this window.

If you're new to Csound, you'll find it useful to keep an eye on the output level data in the Output Console pane. Each time a new i-statement is encountered in the score or a real-time MIDI message starts a note, you'll see the maximum output level for the preceding period of time. When Csound finishes playing and stops, you'll see this line:

```
overall samples out of range: 0 0
```

These two numbers correspond to the left and right output channels. If either of them is greater than zero, some of your samples have clipped, so you'll need to reduce the output level in some way. By scrolling back through the series of events and looking at their output values, you may be able to figure out which event or events caused the clipping.

When Csound can't compile your file, you'll see an error message. The line numbers pointed to by error messages in the Output Console generally fail to correspond to the text display in the main CsoundQt Editor pane. This is an area of the program that will probably be improved in the future. But the text of the error message will quote the offending line of code, so if you know what's going on in your own code, you should be able to find the bug without too much effort.

Another useful aspect of Csound's output text is the list of MIDI and audio ports. You don't need this information as long as you're using CsoundQt, because you can set the ports using the Configuration box. But if you want to run Csound directly from the terminal, you'll need to know which values to set using the -i, -o, and -M command-line flags. The numbers you use will of course depend on your computer's system devices, and you'll find the list in the Output Console.

The Manual Pane

Pleasantly little needs to be said about the Manual pane. Like the other panes, it can be detached so that it will float on the screen. Assuming you've used the field in the Environment tab of the Configuration box to tell CsoundQt where to find the HTML version of the Csound manual, it will be displayed in the Manual pane. You can click the links in the manual to navigate through the pages. The link for the frames version doesn't work in the Manual pane, however. The green arrow buttons at the top of the Manual pane can be used exactly like the back and forward buttons in your web browser.

The Configuration Box

Many of the features of the Configuration box have been discussed earlier in this chapter. In this section we'll go through the details, tab by tab.

The Run Tab

Possibly the most important settings in CsoundQt are the Buffer Size and HW (hardware) Buffer Size, which appear at the top of the Run tab. You should normally leave these checkboxes checked. The numerical values you enter in the two fields will determine the latency of your system, which is not crucial if all you're doing is playing back a standard score. If you're playing Csound live, however, you want these values to be as small as possible.

The values are the number of samples in the buffers. For instance, with my system I normally set -b to 256 and -B to 512. With a sample rate of 44,100, a buffer size of 512 produces an

11-millisecond delay, which I feel is acceptable. If I try to dial back to 128 and 256, the real-time audio output breaks up badly. The safe way to enter data in these fields is in powers of 2.

 Latency is often a concern in computer audio systems when the computer is being asked to generate sound in real time in response to user input. Latency is the time that passes between when you send a command, such as a MIDI note-on message, into the computer and when you hear the output. Usually latency is measured in **milliseconds**. (A millisecond, abbreviated ms, is .001 second.) For reference, it's useful to realize that sound travels about one foot per millisecond in air. A latency of 10ms, then, is equivalent to plucking a guitar string and hearing the sound from an amplifier positioned 10 feet from you. An electric guitar player on a large stage may easily be standing more than 10 feet from his or her amp, without ever noticing the latency. Amounts above 20ms, however, tend to make a computer audio system feel sluggish.

The checkbox and field for additional command-line flags can be used to add flags (as listed in *The Canonical Csound Reference Manual*). One useful flag, for instance, is --displays. This does nothing if you're running your .csd within CsoundQt unless a Graph widget is being used in the Widgets panel. With a Graph widget, --displays is needed to cause the widget to display any f-tables in your score. In addition, if you use the Run in Term button, when Csound runs you'll see a graphic display of the f-tables if the --displays flag is used. This can be helpful if the data in an f-table isn't doing what you think it ought to. You can also enter command-line flags in the <CsOptions> area of your .csd file, but in that case they'll only operate within one file. Entering the flags in the Configuration box will make them active for all of your Csound files.

Normally, you should leave Use CsoundQt Options checked in both the File and Realtime Play areas of the Run tab. Unchecking this box will cause other options in the Configuration box, such as the buffer size settings, to be ignored. Unless your .csd file includes some equivalent flags in the <CsOptions> area, Csound won't know what to do.

Quite a number of options are available in the File Type and Sample Format drop-downs in the File (offline render) area. Some of these may not work with your computer's other audio applications, so you should probably choose either .WAV or .AIFF as the File Type and either 16-bit or 24-bit as the Sample Format.

I suggest checking the Ask for Filename Every Time box, as this will enable you to avoid accidentally overwriting a file during offline rendering.

In the Realtime Play area, you'll need to select your input and output devices for audio and MIDI. Click on the "..." button, and you'll see a list of the available devices. From time to time the devices in your system may change—for example, if you haven't switched on a MIDI keyboard, causing its USB driver to be inactive. In this case, .csd files will refuse to run, and an error message will appear in the Output Console, until you select an active device or choose

Disabled or None from the menu. If you never use MIDI devices, you can leave the MIDI fields blank.

The General Tab

The Run Utilities Using area has two radio buttons—Csound API and External Shell. If you invoke a file analysis utility from CsoundQt's Utilities box, the former choice will cause messages to appear within CsoundQt's Console pane. The latter choice will open up an external shell (Command Prompt in Windows, Terminal in Mac OS), and messages will appear there.

The Performance Tweaks area is useful if you're pushing your CPU's ability to generate sound. The Disable Python Callback checkbox will be grayed out unless you have built PythonQt and have CsoundQt built with PythonQt support.

The settings in the Console area are self-explanatory. They're used in the Console pane of the main window.

The Record file can be set to a different bit depth than the offline render from the Record area of the General Tab.

The `sensekey` opcode is used for real-time input from the QWERTY keyboard. If this checkbox is checked, holding down a key will cause repeated events. If it's not checked, you'll get only a single event, when the key is first pressed.

The Allow Simultaneous Play checkbox lets you run several files at once. This process is not guaranteed to be error-free, however. It depends on whether the code to be run is re-entrant. Some Csound modules, such as portmidi, are not re-entrant, so using portmidi while attempting to run simultaneous files will cause crashes.

The Widgets Tab

The checkboxes in the Widgets tab are fairly self-explanatory. The widgets can transmit and receive using either `invalue` and `outvalue` or `chnset` and `chnget`, depending on what you choose in the drop-down menu. (The choice makes very little functional difference.) Normally you should leave Save Widgets in csd File checked. If you don't, your widgets will be lost.

You may find that there are conflicts between CsoundQt and the FLTK opcodes, which generate graphic control panels rather like CsoundQt's widgets. If you're planning to use FLTK or have downloaded a Csound file that uses FLTK, you may be well advised to run Csound from the command line rather than within CsoundQt. If you want to try running an FLTK .csd file within CsoundQt, you need to enable FLTK using the checkbox in this tab.

If screen space is at a premium, you may prefer to check Widgets Are an Independent Window, as this generates a pop-up window where the widgets are displayed and can be interacted with. This option can also be handy if you have multiple computer screens, and it will allow you to minimize CsoundQt while leaving the Widgets panel open.

The Editor Tab

Again, the items in this tab are easy to understand. You can choose the font and size for text in the editor window and the format for line ends. (Leave this set to the value that matches your computer operating system.)

If you have Autocomplete Menu While Typing checked, CsoundQt will sense when you're typing the name of an opcode and will offer a pop-up menu. You can move up and down through this menu using the arrow keys, select the item you want, and hit Return. This will put the prototype of the opcode into the text. I prefer to leave this box unchecked and consult the hint text at the bottom of the Editor window. This text contains the same information and doesn't require that I replace text items with my own constants or variables. The feature is provided for those who prefer to work this way.

The Environment Tab

Use the buttons in this pane to select directories on your hard drive. In the Html Doc Directory tab, you want to find the /manual directory of your Csound installation. This will enable CsoundQt to display the manual.

The next five fields are explained on the "Csound Environment Variables" page in the manual. SADIR is the default directory for analysis files, which are created using the utilities in the Utilities box. SFDIR is the default directory for output audio files, and SSDIR is the default directory for input files, including both audio and MIDI files. INCDIR is the include directory and is the default location for files that are referenced by #include statements.

The External Programs Tab

In the External Programs tab, you can tell CsoundQt where to find other programs. In Windows, the Terminal field will normally have:

```
cmd.exe
```

In the Macintosh version, you'll find:

```
/Applications/Utilities/Terminal.app
```

The Wave Editor, Wave Player, Browser, and PDF Viewer fields are used for telling CsoundQt where to look when you click the Ext. Editor or Ext. Player icon in the toolbar, or the Show Opcode Entry in External Browser or Open Quick Reference Guide command in the Help menu.

The Template Tab

When you start a new .csd file by clicking the New button in the toolbar or using the File > New menu command, CsoundQt will copy whatever text you've defined in the Template tab into the new file. By default, this text contains only the main tags, <CsoundSynthesizer> and so forth. You might want to add your preferred orchestra header to the template, as doing so saves a bit of typing.

Widgets

Clicking on the Widgets icon in the toolbar opens the Widgets panel. Widgets give you the ability to control Csound with a graphic panel that you design yourself. You can use the knobs and sliders you create in the Widgets panel either to set the starting values of sound parameters or to interact with Csound's instruments while they're playing. What you can't do quite so easily is record your real-time knob and slider movements on one pass and then have them play back on subsequent passes. It's possible to do this, but you'll need to do a fair amount of programming in order to accomplish it, because CsoundQt won't do it right out of the box. (Cecilia 4.2 has this capability; see Chapter 9, "Front Ends," for more on Cecilia.)

The best way to learn to use widgets may be to open up and study the example .csd files that illustrate their use. The Examples > Widgets menu provides access to more than 15 example files, which you can freely edit. You can't save the files in the Examples folder back to their original locations, however. You have to use Save As to save them in your own location. This ensures that the examples will remain intact.

In this section, rather than walk through the examples, we'll explore how to create and use widgets. The general process is as follows:

1. Open the Widgets panel.

2. Right-click (Mac: Control-click) in the panel and create a widget, using one of the choices in the pop-up menu (see Figure 5.5).

3. The Properties box for the new widget will open automatically. In the Properties box, give the widget a unique and easy-to-remember channel name.

4. In your code, use the `invalue` opcode to receive k-rate data from that channel.

The pop-up menu will give you a choice of 14 different types—Slider, Label, Display, ScrollNumber, LineEdit, SpinBox, Button, Knob, Checkbox, Menu, Controller, Console, Graph, and Scope. The Slider and Knob types should be easy to understand. The Label type is strictly for adding useful text to your panel: It doesn't transmit values to Csound. And the Console widget appears not yet to do anything at all. The other types are more complex, so we'll look at them in more detail.

All of the Properties boxes for widgets let you set their X and Y positions and the width and height for the widget. However, not all of these parameters affect all widgets. Changing the width or height of a checkbox, for instance, does nothing, because a checkbox has a fixed size. The X (horizontal) and Y (vertical) positions will be calculated in pixels from the upper-left corner of the Widgets panel. (If you remember Cartesian coordinates from trigonometry, you'll understand that the Y value is actually -Y in Cartesian coordinates, because larger Y values will move the object further down on the panel. This is fairly standard in computer graphics.)

With sliders and knobs, setting the minimum and maximum values that will be needed by your code is a good idea. At present, the knobs and sliders have no minimum resolution value. That is, they output a different value for each pixel through which they move. You can produce a

Create Slider
Create Label
Create Display
Create ScrollNumber
Create LineEdit
Create SpinBox
Create Button
Create Knob
Create Checkbox
Create Menu
Create Controller
Create Console
Create Graph
Create Scope

Cut
Copy
Paste
Select all widgets
Duplicate Selected
Delete Selected
Clear all widgets

Properties

Store Preset
Recall Preset
New Preset

Figure 5.5 The pop-up menu for creating widgets. Also in this menu are some useful editing commands and the ability to store and recall presets for the current widget configuration.

more coarse resolution in the Csound code if you need to, but if you need finer resolution the way to get it is to make the widget larger. If you only need a few values, such as 1.00, 2.00, 4.00, and 8.00, you'll probably find that a row of buttons or checkboxes will give you a better interface. (See below for how to do this.)

The LineEdit widget may be of limited value. The example file in the Examples directory illustrates two ideas. One simply echoes the text you type back to a Display widget. The other allows you to play tones from the QWERTY keyboard by typing single characters into a LineEdit, which is immediately cleared. You could also use this widget to enter a filename before running your .csd file, after which an instrument would load an audio file from disk; but there would most likely be more graceful ways to accomplish the same thing.

The SpinBox widget lets you type numerical input values and also select them using up and down arrows. This widget is sometimes convenient, because the up and down arrows have a resolution (which is set in the Properties box using, obviously, the Resolution parameter). In version 0.6, typing values into a SpinBox doesn't work too well, but the problem has been resolved in version 0.7.

The Menu widget lets you create a named list of options (such as, perhaps, "saw," "square," "triangle," and "sine" for a waveform selector menu), which will appear on a drop-down menu. These will be transmitted to the `invalue` opcode as integers 0, 1, and so on, in the order in which you list them in the Items field in the Properties box. Items should be separated by commas, but without spaces:

```
saw,square,triangle,sine
```

Button widgets can transmit either a value (via `outvalue`) or a score event. The value to be transmitted is set in the Value box (see Figure 5.6). If the Latch checkbox is checked, the button acts as a toggle: Clicking it once will send the value, and clicking it a second time will send a value of zero. If the checkbox is not checked, the mouse-down event when you click will transmit the value, and the mouse-up event will transmit zero.

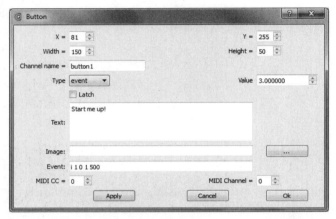

Figure 5.6 The Properties box for CsoundQt's Button widget. Choose the type of button you want by using the Type drop-down menu.

If you choose the event type for a button, you should type a score event in the Event field. This event will be transmitted to Csound each time the button is clicked. (The Latch box is ignored with events.) The value for p2 in the event will normally be zero, in which case the event will start immediately—but if you enter a non-zero value for p2, the event will be delayed.

Controller widgets are visually attractive and come in several types, as illustrated in the demo in the Examples menu. They can operate like vertical or horizontal sliders, or they can be configured as X/Y mouse control surfaces. The latter can display either crosshairs or a point. The background of these widgets is always black, but the foreground color can be edited. You can choose the type of Controller you want (fill, llif, line, crosshair, or point) from the Type drop-down in the Properties box. Both the fill and llif types create solid bars of color that you can drag across the black background with the mouse; the difference is whether the background is to the left/bottom or to the right/top. The horizontal or vertical movement of the fill depends entirely on the Width and Height parameters of the Controller. Whichever is larger will determine the direction of active movement.

To use the Graph widget, you need to enter the command --displays in the Additional Command Line Flags field in the Run tab of the Configuration box and check the associated checkbox. If you do this, a graph widget will display the f-tables generated by a running .csd file. You can use the drop-down menu in the widget to choose a table to display.

Channel names don't strictly need to be unique. If you create two sliders with the same channel name, for instance, you'll find that you can grab and move either of them with the mouse, and that each of them will follow the movements of the other. There's probably no reason to do this. You might imagine that it would be useful to create a bank of buttons, as mentioned above, give each button its own output value, and give all of the buttons the same channel name. Unfortunately, this technique doesn't yet work. If you try it, you'll find that the output value received by Csound's invalue opcode will always be the value set in the Properties box for the first-created button, no matter which button you click. This behavior may change in the next release. In the meantime, the way to get the desired result is to create four buttons with different channel names and then write Csound code that will adjust the desired variable to the desired value.

As a way of illustrating how to get data out of widgets, let's look at an example that does that. Create four buttons. In their Properties boxes, give them display text of 1.0, 2.0, 4.0, and 8.0, the corresponding output values, and the channel names button1, button2, button4, and button8. Then create this instrument:

```
instr 1
kcurrentbutton init 1
kbutton1 invalue "button1"
kbutton2 invalue "button2"
kbutton4 invalue "button4"
kbutton8 invalue "button8"

if kbutton1 != 0 then
  kcurrentbutton = kbutton1
endif
if kbutton2 != 0 then
  kcurrentbutton = kbutton2
endif
if kbutton4 != 0 then
  kcurrentbutton = kbutton4
endif

if kbutton8 != 0 then
  kcurrentbutton = kbutton8
endif
asig oscil 0.25, 200 * kcurrentbutton, 1
outs asig, asig
endin
```

Only one button can output a non-zero value at a time, because you have only one mouse. (This code may fail with future versions of Csound designed for multi-touch devices.) The buttons will let you choose the octave of the tone.

Designing a Widgets Panel

The point of origin of a newly created widget will be wherever you right-clicked to create it. When you create a widget, its Properties box will open automatically; in this box you can edit both the point of origin and the X and Y dimensions. You can also make changes in the size and position by entering widget edit mode (using Ctrl+E or the command in the Edit menu) and moving or resizing the objects graphically. The size of widgets can be controlled by clicking and dragging on the red handle in the lower-right corner, and the position of the widget can be changed by clicking on it and dragging.

Right-click menu options in the Widgets panel offer further editing possibilities. If one widget partially or completely obscures another, you can use the Send to Back command. The Align, Distribute, and Center commands in this menu can be used after selecting several objects to tidy up a layout.

Live Events

Live Events are one of the more interesting features of CsoundQt. In its original form, Csound was designed to compile your orchestra and score code before producing output. Real-time input, for example from a MIDI keyboard, is now quite practical, as explained in Chapter 10—but MIDI places some limitations on how notes can be defined. Specifically, each note is associated with only two control parameters: its note number and velocity. The note events in your score, in contrast, can have many p-fields, but they must be compiled before Csound starts to play.

Live Events give you a simple, flexible way to type, edit, and trigger score events, in standard i-statement format, while Csound is running. Andrés Cabrera has uploaded three videos to YouTube that give an introduction to using Live Events. You can easily find them by using the YouTube search box and searching for QuteCsound (yes, under that name—at this writing, the YouTube videos haven't been re-tagged with the new name), or go directly to www.youtube.com/watch?v=O9WU7DzdUmE.

In *Csound Power!* we'll take a slightly more detailed look at the features of Live Events.

Live Events have two main uses. First, you can use Live Events as part of an improvised live performance. Second, they're good for prototyping score sections. You can create a list containing an arbitrary number of note events and then edit the list while it plays back over and over in a loop. When you get to a phrase that has the characteristics you want, you can copy the events into your actual score (and perhaps adjust the p2 times as needed).

The main limitation to be aware of, before you get too excited about using Live Events live, is that at present Live Events have no way to sync loops to one another or to a master clock. (CsoundQt is not, let's admit, going to compete with Ableton Live in the synced loops department. At least, not until you do quite a lot of coding by hand. A future version of CsoundQt may take this feature much further, however.) But if your music makes use of sustained sheets of sound or scattered sounds whose precise rhythmic relations are not crucial, using Live Events onstage might be an area that's well worth exploring.

To start your experiments with Live Events, you might want to create a .csd file something like the one below. (As in other examples in this book, the outer tags and the standard orchestra header have been omitted.)

```
giSine ftgen 0, 0, 8192, 10, 1

instr 1
idur = p3
iamp = p4
ifreq cpsxpch p5, 19, 2.0, 27.5
iatk = p6
irel = 0.1
isus = idur - iatk
index = p7
ipan = p8

kamp linsegr 0, iatk, iamp, isus, iamp, irel, 0
kindex linsegr 0, iatk, index, isus, index * 0.2, irel, 0
asig foscil kamp, ifreq, 1, 1, kindex, giSine
aoutL, aoutR pan2 asig, ipan
outs aoutL, aoutR
endin

</CsInstruments>
<CsScore>
e 3600
```

This instrument gives us several p-fields (duration, amplitude, frequency in octave/pitch-class format, attack time, FM index, and pan position) with which to experiment using Live Events. I chose to use `cpsxpch` to create 19-tone equal temperament simply because this is an interesting scale to play with. The last line is the only line in the score. An e-statement with a p-field value will cause Csound to run for that number of seconds—in this case, for an hour, which should be plenty.

When you click the Live Events icon in the toolbar, the LE Controller window will open (see Figure 5.7). Initially the list in this window will be empty. To create a new Live Events score sheet, click the New button. A score sheet that looks somewhat like the one in Figure 5.8 will appear. You can give the sheet a name by clicking in the Name field in the LE Controller window or by choosing Rename from the Menu in the Live Events score sheet window itself.

The empty score sheet will have one line and columns for five p-fields, so your first order of business will be to add a few lines and, if you're using something like the instrument used in the code

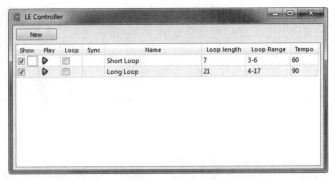

Figure 5.7 The LE Controller window displays an interactive list of your Live Events score sheets.

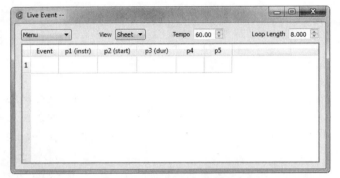

Figure 5.8 A new Live Events score sheet, in which you can create Events by typing.

above, more columns for p-fields. To do this, right-click (Mac: Control-click) in the empty area of the box. From the pop-up menu, choose Add Columns, type **3** in the dialog box, and hit Return or Enter. Do the same thing to create some event rows.

Add some values to your Live Events sheet—perhaps something like the events shown in Figure 5.9. After doing this, click the Run button in the main CsoundQt window. If you

	Event	p1 (instr)	p2 (start)	p3 (dur)	p4	p5	p6	p7	p8
1	i	1	0	1	0.5	4.00	0.01	0.8	0.2
2	i	1	1	1	0.5	4.03	0.01	0.8	0.2
3	i	1	2	1	0.5	4.06	0.01	0.8	0.2
4	i	1	3	1	0.5	4.08	0.01	0.8	0.2
5	i	1	4	1	0.5	4.11	0.01	0.8	0.2
6	i	1	5	0.3	0.5	4.05	0.01	0.8	0.2
7	i	1	5.5	0.3	0.5	4.11	0.01	0.8	0.2
8	i	1	6	1.5	0.5	4.02	0.01	0.8	0.2

Figure 5.9 A Live Events score sheet with data entered in a number of columns and rows.

remembered to include a suitable p-field as part of the e-statement in your score, CsoundQt will begin running silently. In the LE Controller window, click the small green triangle (the Play button) on the line where your Live Events sheet is displayed. The events you've entered should play back. When you click the Play button again, the events will play again. In fact, you can click it several times quickly, and several iterations of the data in your score sheet will play, overlapping one another.

Tip   A Live Events list starts playing not when you click on the Play button or Loop checkbox for the Events score sheet but when you *release* the mouse button. With a little practice, you can achieve reasonable (though not perfect) synchronization between rhythmic loops by pressing the mouse or trackpad button a little early and then lifting your finger at the right moment.

Editing Live Events

The right-click menu for a Live Events sheet contains a number of commands with which you can edit groups of values all at once, very much as if they were in cells in a spreadsheet program. You can select a column of cells by clicking on its header (p4, p5, and so on) or select a range of cells within a column or row by dragging across it with the mouse. Having done this, you can add, subtract, multiply, divide, randomize, rotate, reverse, or shuffle the values in the cells, or fill the cells with an arbitrary value.

In the example in Figure 5.9, for instance, you could select the p5 column, right-click on a cell in the column (not on the column header), choose Add from the menu, type **1**, and hit Enter or Return. Because this p-field uses Csound's octave/pitch-class format for the data, adding 1 would transpose the notes upward by an octave.

The dialog box for the Fill Cells command has a Mode field. A mode of 1 creates a linear fill between the first and last values you enter. Modes higher than 1 create progressively more exponential (that is, concave) curves, while modes between 0 and 1 create logarithmic (that is, convex) curves. This is an extremely useful feature.

As you'll find while exploring loop playback, edits that you make using these commands will not be heard until the next time the loop starts playing. Essentially, this is because CsoundQt is sending the entire contents of a given Live Events list to Csound at the same time. Once the list has started playing, it can no longer be interrupted.

Events in a Live Events list can also be viewed as text, by choosing Text instead of Sheet in the little window's View menu.

The Menu header in the upper-left corner has commands for New Frame (which creates a new, empty list, duplicating the function of the New button in the LE Controller window), Clone Frame, Delete Frame, Rename, and Mark Loop. The Delete Frame command in this menu is currently the only way to get rid of a list that you no longer want; it can't be deleted from the LE

Controller window. The Mark Loop command can be used after dragging across one or more rows with the mouse. You can also edit the loop range in the LE Controller window.

The Clone Frame command creates a copy of the entire score sheet—very handy for making alternate versions of a Live Events list. (You can also copy and paste events from one sheet to another.)

Playback and Looping of Live Events

While Csound is running, you can trigger Live Events sheets, edit their tempo, change their data values, and—if a phrase is looping—change the loop length and loop range. Changes will be heard only on the next repetition of the phrase.

The loop length, which is in beats based on the tempo set for the Live Events sheet, is independent of the durations and timings of the events in the loop. If an event list lasts for 16 beats, for instance, you could set a loop length of only 5 beats, 11 beats, or whatever. The new iteration of the loop will start before the last one finishes. Conversely, if the event list ends before the loop finishes, there will be some silence before the new iteration of the loop starts playing. The loop length does not have to be an integer.

6 Building Your Own Instruments and Effects

I f you've read the QuickStart tutorials in Chapter 3, you will already have encountered many of the fundamental coding techniques that we'll be looking at in Chapter 6. However, the time has come to discuss them in a more orderly and systematic way. Chapters 4, 6, 7, and 8 are the heart of *Csound Power!* Until you master the concepts in these chapters, or at least become familiar enough with them that you know where to look when you're uncertain about something, using Csound will remain beyond your grasp.

In this chapter we'll be looking at a grab bag of essential techniques—basically, everything important that didn't fit into those other chapters. A few opcodes will be discussed in this chapter, but most of the details on opcodes will be found in Chapter 7, "Thirty Opcodes You Must Know."

instr and endin

Every Csound project must contain at least one defined instrument. If there's no instrument, Csound will have nothing to do. The instruments you define make up the Csound "orchestra." The code with which you create instruments will go between the <CsInstruments> and </CsInstruments> tags in the .csd file and will follow the orchestra header. For more on what goes in the orchestra header, see Chapter 4.

Instrument definitions begin with instr, followed by a unique instrument number. Instrument definitions always end with the symbol endin, on a line by itself. endin is short for "end instrument." These and other abbreviations in Csound date back to the early days of computing, when filenames and almost everything else had to be kept short because operating systems were simple and computer memory was expensive.

Here is a fairly generic instrument definition. It uses instr to create an instrument numbered 1. It has a few other features that will be covered later in this chapter.

```
instr 1
idur = p3
iamp = p4
ifreq = p5
iatk = p6
```

```
idec = p7
ipan = p8
asig         oscili iamp, ifreq, giSine
aout         linen asig, iatk, idur, idec
aoutL, aoutR pan2 aout, ipan
             outs aoutL, aoutR
endin
```

An instrument can be given several different numbers. This is legal:

```
instr 1, 2, 3
```

At first glance, this might seem fairly pointless. The i-statements in the score will call this instrument, so why would you want to have a choice of numbers? Wouldn't that just make your score more confusing? Perhaps—but when you're writing the score, the value of the first p-field is available within the instrument code. You can get it by using the symbol p1. As a result, you could, if so inclined, define the above instrument with numbers 1, 2, and 3, and then do something like this:

```
ifreq = p5
if p1 == 2 then
   ifreq = ifreq * 2
elseif p1 == 3 then
   ifreq = ifreq * 3
endif
```

This is a trivial example, but it illustrates how defining an instrument with several numbers might be useful. Most of the code could be the same whether the instrument is referred to in the score as i1, i2, or i3. But there could be a few salient differences, and you could easily switch among them by changing one digit in an i-statement.

If the syntax in the preceding example doesn't make sense to you, see the section on "Logic and Flow Control" later in this chapter.

A fairly new feature of Csound is the ability to give an instrument a name instead of a number. If you use a name, Csound will give the instrument a number internally, for its own purposes. In fact, you can give an instrument both one or more numbers and one or more names. The name, in double quotes, can then be used in the score in the position of p1:

```
i "SineTone" 0 1 0.4 220 0.1 0.1 0.3
```

The advantage of this approach is that the score is more human-readable. The downside is that you can't test in the code whether p1 = "SineTone", so mixing names and numbers is likely to be of limited utility.

As explained on the page of the manual that discusses named instruments, "An instrument name may consist of any number of letters, digits, and the underscore (_) character. However, the first character must not be a digit. Optionally, the instrument name may be prefixed with the '+' character." The point of preceding the name with '+' is that when Csound is running, generating sound, it processes the instruments in numerical order. Instruments that perform audio processing on the signals coming from other instruments (that is, effects) should usually be given a higher number than the instruments whose signals they're processing. If you fail to follow this guideline, the output of the effect will always be delayed by one k-period, because the input to a low-numbered effect will be the signal created by the source instruments during the preceding k-period. As noted above, when you give your instruments names, Csound internally assigns them numbers. When a named instrument is given a name preceded by '+', Csound gives it a higher number than any of the numbered and named instruments that don't have a '+'.

i- versus k- versus a-

As you've probably noticed, the names of most Csound variables begin with the letters i-, k-, or a-. The time has come to explain what those letters mean. The meanings are simple enough, but in order to make their implications clear, we'll have to look at what happens when Csound is running.

 Note The symbol *i* in the score has a completely different meaning from the i- variable prefix in instrument code.

When an i-statement in the score starts an instrument (or when the instrument is started from another instrument using an opcode such as `event`), Csound pauses for a moment to *initialize* the instrument. During the initialization process, the instrument is set up so that it's ready to play. This is called the initialization pass, or "i-time" for short. The details of the process are a bit complicated internally. At the user level, what you mainly need to know is that Csound goes through the instrument code, looking for variables that begin with i-. When it finds them, it substitutes actual numerical values. For example, consider these three lines:

```
idur = p3
iamp = p4
kampenv  linen iamp, 0.01, idur, 0.01
```

As the instrument is being initialized, Csound finds the numerical value in the score for this event's p3 and p4. These are constants; that is, they're not going to change during the event. We'll suppose that p3 is 2.0 and p4 is 0.5. In that case, the `linen` opcode is initialized like this:

```
kampenv   linen   0.5, 0.01, 2.0, 0.01
```

Notice that the value 0.5 has been substituted for `iamp` and 2.0 for `idur`.

Unless the instrument is later reinitialized from its own code using the `reinit` opcode (as explained in the "Instrument Control" section in Chapter 7), the initialization pass happens only once—when the instrument is loaded by Csound and made ready to play a given event. This happens not just once for the instrument, but separately for each event that uses the instrument, because the values in the p-fields may be different for each event.

The important thing to understand is that i-time variables cannot change their values while the instrument is playing a given event. They can only be set to a value at the very beginning of the event (or when the instrument is being reinitialized by reinit.)

This might be considered something of a limitation, but it has an important positive consequence in terms of efficiency. If you're trying to reduce the CPU load on your computer in order to get Csound to run better in a live performance situation, you should use an i-time variable when possible, in preference to a k-rate variable, because as far as Csound is concerned, i-time variables are "set it and forget it" values. k-rate values, on the other hand, can change continuously while an instrument is playing, so Csound will need to evaluate them during every k-period, even if the value hasn't changed.

Used before Defined One of the more common error messages encountered by newcomers to Csound is the statement that a variable was used before being defined. Several different syntax errors can cause this:

- A comma inserted or omitted at the wrong point in a line that should be defining the variable.

- A variable defined in the orchestra header, but without the g- prefix (for instance, giBaseFrequency) that causes it to be available for use in all instruments.

- A typo in the name of the variable.

The basic rule is that a variable must first appear at the left end of a line. Only after it has appeared at the left end of an earlier line can it later be used on the right side of an opcode or equals sign.

k- is an abbreviation for "control," and a- is an abbreviation for "audio." Variables that are used to control the sound, such as, perhaps, kampenv, will typically begin with a k-, while audio variables, such as asignal, begin with an a-. In order to understand the distinction, you need to know a bit about how Csound produces sound.

Once an instrument has been initialized and starts playing, Csound runs through all of the instrument's code once during each k-period. The instrument's code is processed over and over, hundreds or thousands of times per second, for as long as the event lasts.

Let's suppose your orchestra header says this:

```
sr = 44100
ksmps = 100
```

The value for sr means that the sample rate is 44,100 samples per second—the CD audio standard. The value for ksmps means that in each k-period, 100 samples of audio will be generated. This concept is absolutely key. Csound audio signals are not, generally speaking, computed one at a time. Instead, during a k-period, Csound computes an entire *vector* of audio. (If you think of a vector as a chunk of data, you won't be far wrong.) Given the orchestra header above, on every pass through every instrument that is currently playing, Csound will compute a vector containing 100 samples.

Given that 44,100 samples have to be computed for each second of audio, it's easy to see that given the settings above, Csound will need to run through the instrument's code 441 times in every second. This value is the k-rate, or kr. In older versions of Csound, you would also have had to state the value for kr, which is the control rate, explicitly in the orchestra header. kr still exists as a system variable, but today Csound computes it automatically using the formula:

```
kr = sr / ksmps
```

What this means is that the control rate (in repetitions per second, or Hz) is equal to the sampling rate (also in repetitions per second) divided by the number of samples in each k-period. When ksmps=100 and sr=44100, as above, kr=441.

The reason Csound operates this way is because it's efficient in terms of usage of the computer's CPU. The larger the value of ksmps, the fewer k-time passes Csound will have to make through your instrument code during each second.

The value of a k-rate variable can change only once per k-period. Depending on how the instrument is designed, this can sometimes have an effect on the audio quality. Given a value of 100 for ksmps, as above, the output of an amplitude envelope like this:

```
kampenv  linseg 0, 0.1, 1, p3 - 0.2, 1, 0.1, 0
```

will be computed 441 times per second. Because its attack time (the first time value in the arguments to linseg) is 0.1 second, there will be only 44 different values computed and stored in the variable kampenv while the output rises from a level of 0 to a level of 1 during the attack ramp of the envelope. If you know a little about digital audio, you may suspect that this is less than ideal. Depending on how an envelope like this is used, you may possibly hear *zipper noise*, a sort of grainy quality, as the envelope signal rises from 0 to 1.

How do you avoid zipper noise? Lower the value of ksmps. Many Csound users set ksmps rather high while developing a piece, because they gain a tiny bit in the time required to produce an audio output, but when they're ready to render a finished piece to an audio file, they reset ksmps to 1 for the smoothest possible sound.

When ksmps is 1, kr=sr. The k-rate is the same as the sampling rate. Consequently (though this fact is not generally too important to the user), the size of an audio vector will be one sample.

Some opcodes require input arguments in a particular form—i-time arguments, or k-rate arguments, or a-rate arguments. (The term "a-rate" is somewhat misleading, because everything in

Csound happens at k-rate.) With other opcodes, you may have a choice of what type of argument to use. In the latter case, the prototype will show a variable whose name has the x- prefix. An x- variable can't be used in your own code, because Csound always needs to know whether a given value is to be computed at i-time, at k-rate, or as an audio vector. This prefix is used only in prototypes in the manual.

The same thing is true of output variable types. Some opcodes always output a-rate values, some k-rate values, and some can output at either rate depending on the type of output variable you specify.

The init Opcode

Like many other computer programming languages, Csound insists that variables be declared before they're used. If you try to use a variable as an input argument for an opcode before it has been defined in the instrument, your orchestra will fail to compile, and you'll see an error message. (You can use a new variable as an output for an opcode, however. That usage, in effect, declares it.)

This fact could give rise to a problem of circularity, however. Suppose we want to create two LFOs and have each of them modulate the frequency of the other. (This is a patch I used to use a lot on an analog modular synthesizer.) This won't work:

```
klfo1 lfo 3, klfo2
klfo2 lfo 3, klfo1
```

It won't work because the value klfo2 is being used before it's defined. Let's suppose we want the frequency of LFO 1 to begin at 2 Hz when the instrument starts. We might first think to do this:

```
klfo2 = 2
klfo1 lfo 3, klfo2
klfo2 lfo 3, klfo1
```

But this won't work either. Can you see why? On every k-rate pass through the instrument's code, the value of klfo2 will be set to 2. It won't matter what value is created for that variable by the second LFO, because the value will always be reset to 2 on the next pass.

The solution is the init opcode. init is unique in that it operates on k-rate (and a-rate) variables, but runs at i-time, during the initialization pass. The correct way to set up our two cross-modulating LFOs is to use init like this:

```
klfo2 init 2
klfo1 lfo 3, klfo2
klfo2 lfo 3, klfo1
```

Now the variable klfo2 has been properly declared, so it can be used as an argument to the first LFO, but it will be given a value of 2 by init only on the first k-rate pass. After that, it will have whatever value is output by the second LFO.

As a footnote, here's a simple instrument that uses this type of patch to produce an animated burbling tone. The two LFOs are used to control amplitude, pitch, FM index, and panning.

```
klfo2 init 1
klfo1 lfo 2, klfo2, 1
klfo1 = klfo1 + 1.2
klfo2 lfo 2, klfo1, 1
klfo2 = klfo2 + 1.1
asig foscil 0.1 + (klfo2 * 0.2), 220 + (55 * klfo1), 1, 1, \
   klfo1 - klfo2, giSine
aoutL, aoutR pan2 asig, klfo2 - klfo1
outs aoutL, aoutR
```

Caution   To make a long line of Csound code easier to view, you can break it up into two or more short lines by ending each line (except the last one) with a backslash character (\). This method is used in the code examples in *Csound Power!* Note, however, that the backslash character is not currently supported by CsoundQt. If you're using CsoundQt as a front end to enter the examples in this book, you must type backslash-interrupted lines as single long lines.

Converting from a- to k-

Occasionally you may need to convert an audio signal to k-rate. This is necessary, for instance, if you want to use the signal as an argument to an opcode that won't accept an a-rate input. The tool for this is downsamp. The downsamp opcode down-samples the audio signal, producing one value in every k-period. It takes an optional argument specifying the number of audio samples to be averaged in producing the k-rate output. Especially with high-frequency audio signals, averaging is useful, because it smooths out the signal.

Converting in the other direction is easy:

```
asig = ksig
```

However, the manual suggests that the upsamp opcode performs the process a little more efficiently. This conversion produces an audio signal that repeats the most recent value of ksig for an entire k-period. With high values of ksmps, the audio signal created by up-sampling will be very distorted. The interp opcode performs linear interpolation while up-sampling, so it's a better choice than upsamp when the value of ksmps is higher than 4 or thereabouts.

S- and Other Variable Prefixes

Three other variable prefixes are occasionally used in Csound instruments. The S- prefix denotes a text string variable. The w- and f- prefixes are used with spectral data types. Spectral processing is beyond the scope of *Csound Power!* An introduction can be found in *The Canonical Csound Reference Manual*, on the "Tools for Real-Time Spectral Processing" and "Non-Standard Spectral Processing" pages.

Both S- and f- variables have global versions (gS- and gf-, respectively).

Global Variables

Variable names beginning with i-, k-, and a- are local to a particular instrument. You can reuse a name (such as asig) in any number of instruments without causing Csound to get confused. These variable types have global equivalents, which begin with gi-, gk-, and ga-. Variable names preceded by g- are exactly the same as their non-g- counterparts: Values defined with gi- are constant, those defined by gk- operate at control rate, and those defined by ga- contain audio vector data.

Normally, global variables should be declared (and given an initial value) in the orchestra header. They can be declared in an instrument instead, but in this case they won't be available in any other instrument until the instrument in which they're declared starts running, either because of an event in the score or because of an alwayson opcode in the header.

Mathematical Operations

The symbols used in most computer programming languages for performing basic mathematical operations work as you'd expect in Csound.

To begin with, the equals sign (=) is used as the *assignment operator*. Whatever variable appears on the left side of the equals sign is assigned the result of the arithmetic operation on the right side. Programmers refer to the variable on the left side of the equals sign as an *l-value* ("l" being an abbreviation for "left"). The l-value must be a variable; it can't be a constant or an expression. This is legal:

```
kampsum = kenv1 + kenv2
```

But this isn't:

```
5 = kenv1 + kenv2
```

And this isn't either:

```
kenv1 + kenv2 = 5
```

These statements would be meaningless, because no computer programming language would know what you meant to do with them. This may look more sensible:

```
5 = kenv1
```

But it's also defective and won't compile. The way to assign a value of 5 to the variable `kenv1` is to make the variable the l-value:

```
kenv1 = 5
```

On the right side of the equals sign we can put whatever formula we need, using the standard set of symbols: +, -, *, /, ^, and %. Some of these may be less familiar to you than others, so let's look at them all.

Most of these symbols are used to perform an operation on two values. For instance, the plus symbol (+) is used for addition. You probably knew that already. We might write:

```
iresult = ivalA + ivalB
```

This tells Csound to take whatever number is currently stored in `ivalA`, add it to the number stored in `ivalB`, and put the result in the variable named `iresult`. Variables are basically just named storage locations in computer memory. Csound will keep track of the actual storage location; you will always refer to it by name. (Csound has no equivalent of the *pointer* data type used in general-purpose programming languages such as C to refer to memory locations.)

The minus symbol (-) is a little different, however. It has two uses: It can subtract one value from another, or it can be used to negate a value. That is, it's shorthand for multiplying the value by –1. If `ivalA` is 6, then `-ivalA` is –6—and conversely: If `ivalA` is –6, then `-ivalA` is 6.

Multiplication is performed using the asterisk (*):

```
iresult = ivalA * ivalB
```

Division uses the slash symbol (/):

```
kresult = kvalA / kvalB
```

Division has to be used with care, however. As you may have learned in algebra class, it's not possible to divide by zero. In the statement above, if the value of `kvalB` is ever zero, there may be a run-time error, causing Csound to crash. (The crash may not be immediate. The result of the operation will be stored as NaN—not a number. If this result is then fed into an opcode that chokes on it, a crash is the likely result.) Since signals in Csound are normally in the form of floating-point numbers, an actual value of zero is not too likely. To be safe, though, you would be well advised to use a workaround—the `divz` opcode. This divides two numbers, but if the divisor is ever zero it outputs a substitute value instead. Details can be found in the manual.

The modulus operator (%) performs a division and outputs the remainder. For example:

```
ivalA = 7
ivalB = 3
ivalC = ivalA % ivalB
```

Here, `ivalC` will be 1. When we perform the division, 3 goes into 7 twice (3 * 2 = 6), and the remainder after the division is 7 – 6, or 1.

The caret symbol (^) is the power-of operator. For example:

```
ival = 2^8
```

Here, `ival` is 2 to the 8th power, which is 256.

> **Note**   Unlike some computer programming languages, Csound does not include the `+=` and `-=` operators. This is illegal:
>
> ```
> ival += 1
> ```
>
> In other languages, this statement would add 1 to whatever value was stored in `ival`. In Csound, the addition must be performed explicitly:
>
> ```
> ival = ival + 1
> ```
>
> Nor does Csound have any pre/post-increment/decrement operators, so this type of thing is not possible:
>
> ```
> kdata    table    kindex++, giDataTable
> ```

Using Parentheses

When computer programmers talk about *precedence,* they're referring to the fact that when a complex mathematical formula is written into code, some operations are performed before others. Generally (and this is true in Csound, though not in all programming languages), multiplication and division are performed before addition and subtraction. For example, if you write:

```
iresult = 7 - 3 * 2
```

the value of `iresult` will be 1, not 8. The multiplication (3 * 2) will be performed first, and then the subtraction (7 – 6). If you want the other result, the way to do it is by grouping the terms in the statement with parentheses:

```
iresult = (7 - 3) * 2
```

The operations inside of parentheses will always be performed before operations outside of them. Parentheses can be nested, if desired:

```
iresult = ((7 - 3) * 2) / 9
```

If you aren't sure whether parentheses are needed in a statement in order to get the result that you want, it's always okay to add them as a safety precaution. This can also make the code easier to read. These two statements are exactly equivalent:

```
iresult = (ival1 * ival2) - (ival3 * ival4) + (ival5 / ival6)
iresult = ival1 * ival2 - ival3 * ival4 + ival5 / ival6
```

But the first one is easier to read and is less likely to contain an inadvertent error.

If two operators have equal precedence (as is the case with + and -, and with * and /), Csound will perform the operations in left-to-right order.

I was unable to find any information in *The Canonical Csound Reference Manual* about the precedence of the % and ^ operators. In my tests, it appears that % has the same precedence as * and /, while ^ has a higher precedence than any of the others. Raising a number to a power, in other words, always happens before other operations are performed. The manual does warn, however, that ^ should be used "with caution as precedence may not work correctly." A safer approach is to use the pow opcode. Also worth note: In the formula (a ^ b), b cannot be an audio-rate variable. This is because the value in an audio-rate variable is not a single number; it's a vector of numbers. However, pow can be used safely with audio-rate variables:

```
Acubed   pow asig, 3
```

Care must be taken, however. If the value of the audio signal ever rises past 1.0, taking the signal to a higher power can increase the output level rather drastically. On the other hand, pow with an odd integer for the exponent is a quick way of adding a few overtones to a sine wave. An even number will rectify the wave (no peak will drop below 0) and transpose it up by an octave. Non-integer exponents and negative exponents should be avoided with pow.

Other Useful Mathematical Operations

Csound provides a good basic suite of other mathematical operations. These are generally in the form of opcodes rather than operators. The "Mathematical Functions" and "Trigonometric Functions" pages in the manual (which appear under the header "Mathematical Operations" in the left-side index) give lists. For more complex mathematical processes, you may want to resort to incorporating Python code in your Csound instrument. (For more on using Python, see Chapter 10, "Using Csound with MIDI, OSC, Pd, Python, and Live Audio.")

Also on the "Mathematical Functions" page is powershape. This opcode is more useful for DSP than for math: It continuously raises an audio signal to an arbitrary power. powershape is probably best used when `0dbfs=1.0`, because raising signals greater than 1.0 to a power greater than 1 can easily result in astronomical audio levels.

Here are the most useful math functions:

- `abs` Returns the absolute value of a number. (If the number is negative, `abs` makes it positive.) Useful for transforming negative p3 values, among other purposes.
- `ceil` Returns the smallest integer not less than x. (Compare to `floor`.)
- `cos`, `cosh`, `cosinv` Cosine functions.
- `exp` Returns e to the power of x. (The example in the manual is fun to play with.)
- `floor` Returns the greatest integer not greater than x.
- `frac` Returns the portion of a decimal number to the right of the decimal point. For instance, `frac(2.3) = 0.3`.
- `int` The opposite of `frac`. Returns the integer portion of a number. `frac(2.3) = 2.0`.
- `log`, `log10`, `logbtwo` For calculating natural, base 10, and base 2 logarithms.
- `max` Returns the greatest of two or more values.
- `maxabs` Takes the absolute values of two or more inputs and returns the largest. (The output is always non-negative.)
- `min` Returns the smallest of two or more values.
- `minabs` Takes the absolute values of two more inputs and returns the smallest. (The output is always non-negative.)
- `pow` Returns the value of one number to the power of another number. (Similar to the ^ operator, but may be safer.)
- `round` Returns the integer value nearest to x. (As the manual notes, if the fractional part of x is exactly 0.5, the behavior of round is undefined. This probably means it could return either the higher integer or the lower one.)
- `sin`, `sinh`, `sininv` Sine functions.
- `sqrt` Returns the square root of x.
- `tan`, `tanh`, `taninv`, `taninv2` Tangent functions.

p-fields and p-values

When Csound prepares to play an event in the score, it stores the data in the score line for the event in a series of variables. The values in the score can be accessed within the instrument using the symbols p1, p2, p3, and so forth. These symbols are unique and local to each event.

It's legal to use these symbols directly in arguments to opcodes, like this:

```
kampenv  linen p4, 0.01, p3, 0.1
```

However, your code will be more readable, especially as you add more p-fields to your events, if you initialize named variables with the values in the p-fields, like this:

```
idur = p3
iamp = p4
kampenv   linen iamp, 0.01, idur, 0.1
```

If you accidentally use too many or too few p-fields in a score event, Csound will issue a warning message during playback. If you use a symbol, such as p5, for which no p-field exists in the score, Csound will initialize the value to 0.

> **Note**   Unlike an error message, a warning message from the Csound compiler will not prevent playback from starting and continuing. Warning messages can, however, tell you why you're getting unexpected results from your score, so it's a good idea to keep an eye on the Output Console while developing a piece.

The meanings of p1, p2, and p3 are fixed. p1 is the number of the instrument, p2 is the start time of the event (with reference to the current section of the score), and p3 is the duration of the event. Any subsequent p-fields have meanings that will be determined by your code.

The symbols beginning with p are variables, so their values can be changed by your instrument code while the instrument is playing. For most p-fields, this is a fairly trivial feature. However, changing the value of p3 in an instrument is meaningful: If you change p3, Csound will change the length of the event when it is being initialized.

This feature has a couple of possible uses. First, if you set a value for p3 in the instrument, the number you use will be an actual number of seconds, irrespective of the tempo defined by the score. Thus you can override the tempo within the instrument if you need an instrument to always play an event of a given length, irrespective of the current tempo. Second, the lengths of notes can be controlled interactively in performance (with a MIDI slider, for instance). Here's a simple example that uses a global variable to set note length interactively:

```
giSine ftgen 0, 0, 8192, 10, 1
gkLength init 0.2

instr 1
gkLength line 0.2, p3, 2
endin

instr 11
p3 = i(gkLength)
asig oscil p4, p5, giSine
outs asig, asig
endin
```

```
</CsInstruments>
<CsScore>

i1 0 5
i11 0 1 0.2 220
i11 + . . 330
i11 + . . 440
i11 + . . 550
i11 + . . 660
```

Although the five notes to be played by instr 11 are all the same length in the score, each note will be longer than the preceding note when the score is played, because the value of p3 is being read from the variable gkLength, which is being ramped upward in instr 1.

A text string (surrounded by double-quotes) can be used in a p-field in the score. This feature can be used, for instance, to tell an instrument which sample to load from your hard drive into its own internal table. As of Csound 5.13, only one p-field can contain a string.

Logic and Flow Control

The code for many of your Csound instruments will be structured in a fairly straightforward way. During each k-period, Csound will run through the instrument code from top to bottom, one line at a time, cycling through the code over and over for as long as the instrument is active. The sound may change radically while this is going on, but the process of running through the code from top to bottom will always be the same.

With some instruments, however, you'll undoubtedly want the order in which the lines of code are executed to change depending on some condition or other. This is a very standard requirement for computer programming languages—to test whether a certain condition is true or false, and to do something different when it's true than when it's false. In effect, the code *branches*. If the condition is true, Csound will execute the code in branch A. If the condition is false, it will execute the code in branch B.

Testing whether a condition is true or false requires a special set of symbols, as we'll see below.

At the beginning of a new score event, the code in an instrument is run through in an initialization pass. Then the instrument starts playing, and the code is executed repeatedly, once in each k-period. As a consequence of this design, you'll need to consider whether you want the conditional branching to occur during initialization, during each k-period, or both.

Because Csound's ancestry dates back to an earlier period in computer science, its original branching mechanism would be considered rather primitive by today's programmers. Yes, Csound lets you use the goto command, which was common in BASIC and other languages of the same era but is generally frowned on today. A slightly more modern form of flow control is also available and allows us to write more concise, readable code without using goto. But

Csound is not well equipped with more advanced mechanisms for logic-based branching. In particular, Csound has no switch statement.

Switch statements are used in computer programming languages to set up parallel sets of branches. For instance, the code might say, "If x is 1, do these operations; if x is 2, do these other operations; if x is 3, do a different set of operations..." and so on, ending with, "if x is none of the above, here's what to do." A long list of conditions can be set up using very concise syntax. You can create an equivalent structure in Csound, but it will use ordinary logic and flow control statements, not a switch statement *per se*.

In recent years, a form of the `for` loop, another type of flow control structure familiar to computer programmers, has been added to Csound using the `loop_ge`, `loop_gt`, `loop_le`, and `loop_lt` opcodes. These are discussed below. Again, it's possible to create loops in Csound using basic logic tests and the `goto` statement, but these opcodes allow us to avoid the embarrassment of having our computer-science-major friends snicker when they look at our code.

Testing Values

For testing whether a condition is true or false, Csound provides the operators ==, >, >=, <, <=, and !=. These operators can be used with both i-time and k-rate values (and with constants), but not with a-rate variables, because a-rate variables are vectors, not single numerical values. More complex logical tests can be constructed using the && and || operators.

The meanings of these symbols are easy to understand:

== "is equal to"

!= "is not equal to"

> "is greater than"

>= "is greater than or equal to"

< "is less than"

<= "is less than or equal to"

&& "and" (if both of the expressions are true, the result is true)

|| "or" (if either of the expressions is true, the result is true)

To use any of these symbols, you'll need to write a statement using the `if` opcode. There are two ways to structure this, as indicated in the following sections of this chapter. No matter which form you use, the statement will begin something like this:

```
if kfreq > 300
```

This statement will evaluate as either true (if the current value of `kfreq` is greater than 300) or false (if `kfreq` is 300 or less).

> **Note** One of the most common mistakes in computer programming is to type the assignment operator (=) when you meant to type the equality operator (==). In Csound, this mistake is harmless, because Csound doesn't allow assignments to be made within `if` statements. All the same, it's wise to be in the habit of typing ==.

When you write a simple logical test, Csound doesn't care whether you use parentheses. These two lines are exactly equivalent:

```
if kfreq > 300 then
if (kfreq > 300) then
```

Sometimes, more complex logical tests are needed. In this situation, it will sometimes be necessary to use parentheses. Complex logical tests use the && (and) and || (or) operators. When two expressions are connected by &&, they must both be true for the compound statement to evaluate as true. For example:

```
iValA = 2
iValB = 3
iValC = 2
if (iValA < iValB) && (iValA == iValC) then
```

The compound expression in this `if` statement will evaluate as true, because both the first part and the second part are true. But what happens if we change the less-than operator to a greater-than operator?

```
if (iValA > iValB) && (iValA == iValC) then
```

In this case, the compound statement evaluates to false, because only the second condition is true. The first condition is false, because iValA is *not* greater than iValB. The && operator causes the compound expression to evaluate as true only if *both* parts are true. This next compound statement, however, evaluates as true:

```
if (iValA > iValB) || (iValA == iValC) then
```

Here, we've replaced the "and" operator with an "or" operator. A compound expression using "or" evaluates as true if *either* of the component expressions is true. If this seems confusing, try reading the line out loud: "If iValA is greater than iValB *or* iValA is equal to iValC, then...."

Using if/goto

Csound provides three forms of the traditional `goto` instruction: `igoto` is valid only during the i-time pass, `kgoto` only during k-rate passes, and `goto` itself combines the two, operating both at i-time and at k-rate. These can used in an `if` statement or on a line by themselves. In either case, they direct Csound to jump to a named label. In some cases it may be safer to use `if/ igoto` or `if/kgoto` rather than `if/then`, because with `igoto` and `kgoto` you know exactly when the branching will or will not take place. With `if/then`, Csound will make its own decision about whether to branch. That said, branching with `if/then/else`, as explained in the section following this one, is usually safe.

A label is any word that isn't a variable name, a reserved word, or an opcode. A label should be placed on a line by itself. Here's a simple example:

```
if (ifreq > 200) igoto hifreq
   ilforate = 6.0
   igoto done
hifreq:
   ilforate = 7.0
done:
```

The indentation is purely to make the code easier to read; it has no effect on the logic. This block of code, which will run only during the initialization pass because everything in it relates to i-time, tests whether the value of `ifreq` is greater than 200. If so, Csound jumps past the next two lines without even looking at them. It jumps directly to the label `hifreq`. At that point, the value of `ilforate` is set to 7.0. However, if the value of `ifreq` is 200 or less, the expression (`ifreq > 200`) evaluates to false, so the first `igoto` is not obeyed. Instead, Csound proceeds as it normally would, to the next line, where `ilforate` is set to 6.0. On the third line, Csound is instructed unequivocally to jump to the label `done`, so it skips the line where `ilforate` would be set to 7.0. The result, assuming `ifreq` sets the frequency of the note and `ilforate` is used to set the rate of an LFO, is that higher-frequency notes will have an LFO rate of 7 Hz, while lower-frequency notes will have an LFO rate of only 6 Hz.

This type of branching code is extremely useful for making an instrument respond more flexibly to the data in p-fields and to other variables. If we know that we want the LFO rate to be directly contingent on the note frequency, we don't need to create a separate p-field in the score for LFO rate. Instead, we set it on the fly using an `if` statement and `igoto`.

Using if/then/else

Because the `goto` instruction is not much favored these days by computer programmers, Csound was enhanced a number of years ago to enable a more standard type of if/then/else syntax to be used. We can rewrite the code in the preceding section like this:

```
if (ifreq > 200) then
  ilforate = 7.0
else
  ilforate = 6.0
endif
```

Again, the indentation is purely cosmetic. It's ignored by the Csound compiler; it's strictly there to make the code easier to read. In this code, if the value of `ifreq` is greater than 200, then the expression evaluates as true, so `ilforate` is set to 7.0. The keyword `else` is used to start the block of code that executes only if the expression is false. The entire construction ends with the keyword `endif`, on a line by itself.

If we need to allow for more than two possibilities, we can use the keyword `elseif`:

```
if (ifreq > 200) then
   ilforate = 7.0
elseif (ifreq > 150) then
   ilforate = 6.5
else
   ilforate = 6.0
endif
```

This structure is the logical equivalent of a switch statement in other programming languages. In the code above, the value of `ilforate` will depend on whether `ifreq` is above 200, between 150 and 200, or at or below 150. The key to understanding this code is that an `else` is consulted only if the `if` test returns false. If the `if` test returns true, any code in the `else` block is ignored.

If tests can be nested if desired. This type of structure is legal and sometimes useful:

```
if ifreq > 200 then
  if ival == 5 then
     iresult = 60
  else
     iresult = 30
  endif
else
   iresult = 45
endif
```

Note that the interior `if` block (beginning with the test whether `ival == 5`) terminates with its own `endif`. This is why indenting is so useful: You can easily see the structure of an interior block of statements. In extreme cases, a complex test of this sort might end with three or more `endif` statements in a row, each on its own line.

The Ternary Operator

Like many other programming languages, Csound provides a handy shorthand syntax that can be used when the if/then/else construction is simple enough. The shorthand syntax is called the *ternary* (three-part) operator. Consider this code:

```
if ival < 0.2 then
   iatk = 0.005
```

```
else
  iatk = 0.01
endif
```

This works perfectly well. But because both branches of the if/then/else tree do nothing more complex than set the value of `iatk`, we can get the same result with one line of code:

```
iatk = (ival < 0.2 ? 0.005 : 0.01)
```

This shows the ternary operator in action. The ternary operator uses two symbols—the question mark (`?`) and colon (`:`). The expression as a whole must be placed in parentheses, as shown. The compiler first evaluates the expression to the left of the question mark, in this case the test of whether `ival` is less than 0.2. This expression evaluates as either true or false. If it's true, then the output of the ternary operator is the item before the colon; if it's false, the output is the item after the colon. The output (which in this case is either 0.005 or 0.01) is given to the assignment operator (the equals sign), which assigns it to the variable on the left side, `iatk`.

Here's a nice example of a useful way to use the ternary operator. I spotted it in Steven Yi's "On the Sensations of Tone," which is distributed as an example with blue (Yi's front end for Csound).

```
ipch = p4
ipch = (ipch < 15 ? cpspch(ipch) : ipch)
```

This code lets you use either absolute frequencies or octave/pitch-class notation interchangeably in the score. If the value is less than 15.0 (which would be a very high octave but an extremely low frequency), p4 is interpreted as octave/pitch-class. If the value is 15 or higher, it will be interpreted as an absolute frequency value.

Looping Opcodes

Most computer programming languages provide looping constructs—syntax that can be used for running through one or more lines of code over and over in a loop, until some condition is met. When the condition, whatever it is, becomes true, the program exits the loop. If the condition never becomes true, then the loop keeps running forever, or at least until you shut the program down manually. (Such an infinite loop is a bug.)

Csound almost always runs in looping mode. During performance, the instrument code for each active event is processed once in each k-period. So we can take care of certain basic tasks without employing any special looping syntax. Consider this code, for instance:

```
kindex init -1
kindex = kindex + 1
if kindex < 16 then
   tablew kindex, kindex, giData
endif
```

During the first 16 k-periods, this code will write the values 0 through 15 into the table called giData. Thereafter, the value of kindex will keep increasing, but it doesn't matter, because the if test will return false, so no more table writing will take place.

Looping constructs usually use a value called an index or a counter to keep track of how often the loop has cycled through. On each pass through the loop, the counter is incremented: Its value is increased by 1. When the counter reaches a pre-defined limit, the condition being tested by the loop code returns true, and the looping ceases. That's more or less what's happening in the example above. The only detail that differs from the more usual practice in computer programming is that the loop doesn't cycle directly, on its own. Instead, Csound's rendering engine as a whole is looping, and the code simply takes advantage of that fact.

Note   To simplify the discussion in this section, I've assumed that the loop counter always increases, and that it increases by 1 on each iteration of the loop. It's sometimes more convenient to start with a large value for the counter and decrement (decrease) it instead, or to increment or decrement by a larger or smaller amount than 1. It's also possible to use some other condition to test whether it's time to exit the loop, in which case a counter may not be needed. All that's necessary is that the condition that causes the loop to exit become true at some point.

On occasion, however, we may want to write code that actually loops. This can be done using the syntax shown earlier in this chapter, in the section "Using if/goto." Here is how the loop above would be rewritten to take advantage of this possibility:

```
kindex init 0
backto:
if kindex > 15 kgoto done
tablew kindex, kindex, giData
kindex = kindex + 1
if kindex < 16 kgoto backto
done:
```

This code does exactly the same thing as before: It writes the numbers 0 through 15 into the giData table and then stops. The main difference, aside from the fact that it looks rather messy because it needs two goto statements and two labels in order to operate correctly, is that this loop executes 16 times within a single k-period. The loop in this example is simple, and 16 is not a large number, so the fact that the loop runs 16 times in quick succession is unlikely to have any audible effect on your instrument. If the code within such a loop is complex and has to be executed hundreds or thousands of times in a row, you should expect to hear a glitch in the audio output.

Csound provides four opcodes that we can use to simplify this loop just a bit: loop_ge, loop_gt, loop_le, and loop_lt. These opcodes can operate either at i-time or at k-rate, and their syntax is pretty much identical. The main difference is how the counter (index) is compared to the boundary value (the value that, when the index reaches it, will cause the loop to exit). The syntax, in pseudo-code, looks like this:

```
loop_opcode    index, increment_amount, boundary_value, label
```

- `loop_ge` tests whether the index is greater than or equal to (ge) the boundary value.
- `loop_gt` tests whether the index is greater than (gt) the boundary value.
- `loop_le` tests whether the index is less than or equal to (le) the boundary value.
- `loop_lt` tests whether the index is less than the boundary value.

To see how this works, let's rewrite the example above yet again, using `loop_lt`.

```
kindex init 0
backto:
if kindex > 15 kgoto done
tablew kindex, kindex, giData
loop_lt kindex, 1, 16, backto
done:
```

We've saved only one line of code. Instead of incrementing the index manually (with the line `kindex = kindex + 1`) and then testing whether to go back to the label, we can use `loop_lt`, which does the same thing in a single line. In some circumstances (depending on what's going on within the loop and elsewhere in the instrument), we may still need to bypass the code within the loop manually by testing the value of `kindex` and then using `kgoto done`. This instruction may appear redundant, but if we don't use it, the `tablew` line in the loop above will continue to be executed at every k-period until the instrument stops, and `kindex` will continue to increment during each k-period when the `loop_lt` opcode is reached, even if it doesn't cause a jump back to the label.

An important thing to note about `loop_lt` and its brethren is that each of them increments (or, in the case of `loop_ge` and `loop_gt`, decrements) the index variable *before* testing it against the maximum or minimum value.

As a segue to the next section, on print statements, let's use `loop_lt` to write some values to a table, this time using the i-time version of the opcode, read the values during the first k-period, and print them out to the console (or to the terminal, if you're running Csound from the command line) to make sure the table contains what we think it does.

Two things may be worth noting about this code. First, we don't have to exit the first loop (the one that writes the data to the table) explicitly, because it runs at i-time, so it won't be used during k-cycles. Second, the labels we use have to be unique, hence `backto1` and so on.

```
; in the orchestra header, create a table with 16 zeroes in it:
giData ftgen 0, 0, 16, -2, 0, 0, 0, 0, 0, 0, 0, 0, 0, 0, 0, 0, 0, 0, 0, 0
```

```
instr 1

; write integers 0-15 to the giData table:
index = 0
backto1:
tableiw index, index, giData
loop_lt index, 1, 16, backto1

; read the data from the table and print it out:
kndex init 0
kdata init -1
backto2:
if kndex > 15 kgoto done2
kdata table kndex, giData
printk2 kdata
loop_lt kndex, 1, 16, backto2

done2:

endin

</CsInstruments>
<CsScore>

i1 0 0.1
```

When you copy this code into a .csd file and run it, you should see the following output:

```
SECTION 1:
new alloc for instr 1:
i11 0.00000
i11 1.00000
i11 2.00000
i11 3.00000
i11 4.00000
i11 5.00000
i11 6.00000
i11 7.00000
i11 8.00000
i11 9.00000
i11 10.00000
i11 11.00000
i11 12.00000
i11 13.00000
```

```
i11 14.00000
i11 15.00000
```

The `printk2` opcode has run 16 times, once on each pass through the loop. Each time, it has printed out the current value of `kdata`, which was read from the `giData` table.

Incidentally, this is an unusual usage in which the value of an i-time variable can be changed by subsequent code (namely, the `loop_lt` line, which increments the value of `index`), because the loop does all its work during the initialization pass.

Print Statements

It sometimes happens, as you're developing a Csound orchestra and score, that your code doesn't behave the way you expect it to. Diagnosing the problem may take only a few seconds, or you may be tearing your hair out for an hour. (If the problem persists for longer than an hour, post a message to the email list asking for help, and then go take a long walk.)

To make the debugging process easier, Csound provides several printing opcodes. By inserting one or more of these in your code, you can inspect the values of variables as an instrument runs. This information will often reveal the source of the problem.

In CsoundQt, the print opcodes send their output to the Output Console pane, which can be displayed across the bottom of the main window. If you're running Csound from the command line, the text output will normally appear in the Command Prompt (in Windows) or Terminal (in Mac OS) window.

The trick is to know which of the print opcodes to use. I've found that this can sometimes be a bit of a challenge. In addition, some of the print opcodes have specific formatting requirements. In the next few pages we'll take a look at all of the options and requirements.

print

The `print` opcode runs at i-time, so it's useful only for printing out the values of i-time variables. Here's a not terribly useful example:

```
instr 1
idur = p3
iamp = p4
ifreq = p5
iresult = idur^iamp * ifreq
print idur, iamp, ifreq, iresult
endin

</CsInstruments>
<CsScore>

i11 0 2 0.5 440
```

The `print` opcode prints the name of each variable along with its value, so you can string together any number of arguments to `print` and easily read the output. The output of the code above should look like this:

```
instr 1: idur = 2.000 iamp = 0.500 ifreq = 440.000 iresult = 622.254
```

If you ever need to use Csound as a pocket calculator, the `print` opcode will let you view the results of your calculations.

printf

The `printf` opcode prints a formatted string. It can run either in each k-period or at i-time; the i-time version is called `printf_i`. To see this opcode in action, return to the example above in the section on `print`, and substitute this line for the `print` line:

```
printf_i "iresult is %f\n", 1, iresult
```

Now the output will be:

```
iresult is 622.253967
```

The functionality of `printf` and `printf_i` is more complex than with `print`, so let's look at the above code in detail. The first argument to these opcodes is a text string, in double-quotes. The second argument is a trigger. The trigger will cause printing whenever it's not zero. The third and any following arguments to `printf` are the values that we want to print.

When using `printf_i`, there's no harm in making the trigger 1, because an i-time opcode will run only once per score event (unless `reinit` is used to produce another initialization pass, or unless `printf_i` is being used within a loop). With `printf`, we need to create a trigger signal that is non-zero only when we want to see a new printout. This can be done in several ways. For instance, we could use a `metro` to issue triggers periodically, like this:

```
ktrig metro 5
printf "kresult is %f\n", ktrig, kresult
```

This code will cause `printf` to send a message to the console five times per second. This may not be the most efficient way to work; we can do the same thing using `printks` (see below) and skip the `metro`. But if a `metro` is already running, producing an output of 1 at periodic intervals, using its output with `printf` will cause a print operation to occur each time metro outputs a value of 1.

Conversion Specifiers and Output Formatting

The string argument above contains some mysterious characters: `%f\n`. The time has come to explain what those mean.

There are, in fact, two things going on here. %f is one thing; \n is a different thing. These symbols are borrowed from the C programming language. In C, they're used in conjunction with the printf() command. As in Csound, printf() is used to output text to the console.

When used in a text string, the percent sign followed by a single character is called a *conversion specifier*. To learn more, you can do a web search for "printf() conversion specifier". Various letters can follow the percent sign, and each of the allowed letters has a specific meaning. When a conversion specifier is used with one of the printing opcodes that accepts a text string as an argument, the string must be followed by one or more arguments containing numerical values. The conversion specifier tells the opcode to look at one of those arguments, incorporate its numerical value in the string, and format it in a specific way.

The most useful conversion specifiers in Csound coding are probably %f and %d. When printf sees %f, it prints the numerical argument as a floating-point number. When it sees a %d, it prints the argument as an integer. Conversion specifiers for exponential number display (%e) and hexadecimal (%x) are also available, among others.

The number of conversion specifiers in a string must match the number of numerical arguments that follow the string (ignoring any other arguments, such as trigger inputs, that the opcode may require). If there are too many arguments or too few, Csound will issue an error message.

 Note If you want to print an actual percent sign in a string, use a percent sign followed by another one: %%.

The backslash (\) is an *escape* character. Like the percent sign, the backslash gives a special meaning to the next character, but in this case the meanings have to do with how the text output is formatted. \n prints an invisible *newline* character, which causes the output to jump down to the next line (and also return to the left margin, which is not quite the same thing). \t prints a tab character (a fixed-width space). A backslash followed by a double-quote character prints a double-quote character, and a backslash followed by another backslash prints a backslash.

printk

If you want to observe the changing values of a k-rate variable but you don't need to print a string (presumably because you know what variable you're watching), you can do it with printk. The prototype is:

```
printk itime, kval [, ispace]
```

The first argument is the time in seconds between printings. kval is the value to be printed. The optional ispace argument is supposed to control the number of spaces between outputs, but in fact this seems not to be useful. Even without a value for ispace, printk formats its output nicely, with a column of times at which the printing occurs followed by a column of output values.

printk2

According to the manual, `printk2` is useful "for monitoring MIDI control changes when using sliders." This makes sense, as `printk2` produces a new printout each time the value you're printing changes. If you use it to monitor a signal that is changing continuously at k-rate, you'll see a whole lot of messages!

`printk2` takes two arguments—the variable to be printed and the number of spaces between printouts. Again, the output seems (in my tests, at any rate) to be formatted with one print statement per line, so specifying the number of spaces is not very useful.

printks

`printks` uses the same string-formatting conventions as `printf` (see above). The main difference between the two is that in place of a trigger argument, `printks` lets you specify the amount of time (in seconds) between printings. For example:

```
kramp line 1, p3, 2
printks "The ramp value is %f\n", 0.1, kramp
```

The value 0.1 will cause a printing every 1/10 second. Csound will not format the output for you, so a \n is highly useful for getting each printout onto a line by itself.

prints

`prints` is functionally identical to `printf_i`, except that it has no argument for a trigger. It runs at init-time and prints out a string that can include C-style conversion specifiers for numerical arguments.

sprintf

The syntax of `sprintf` is similar to that of `printf`, but `sprintf` doesn't output anything to the console. Its output is, instead, a string variable (prefix S-), which can then be used for various purposes, such as sending text strings to widgets using the `outvalue` opcode.

7 Thirty Opcodes You Must Know

Thirty? That hardly seems like enough. In this chapter we'll cover more than fifty opcodes, some of them in depth, some more quickly. In truth, you could make music with Csound using no more than four opcodes (`instr`, `endin`, `out`, and `oscil`), but you'd have to work awfully hard to produce anything like a satisfying piece of music without adding at least a few more. The more opcodes you know, the more creative options you'll have.

In some sense, this is the most important chapter in *Csound Power!* Everything that has come before it is preliminary; everything that comes after it is enhancements. Opcodes are what do the work of synthesis in Csound. Until you understand which opcodes to use and how best to use them, Csound will remain a mystery to you.

Csound boasts more than a thousand *unit generators* (more familiarly known as opcodes). Almost any of these could be useful to someone, in some piece of music. The word "almost" in that sentence is significant, however. Csound includes a number of opcodes that are *deprecated*. "Deprecated" is a fancy word for "don't use this."

Why should software include features that you're advised not to use? Primarily so that Csound will remain backward-compatible. That is, to the greatest extent possible, an orchestra and score that were written for Csound 10 or 15 years ago should still produce exactly the same sound output when they're run in the latest version of Csound. You shouldn't have to edit an older file so that it will run without errors in the current version. Anyone who has struggled with version changes and changing system resources in other software will appreciate this fact. But you'll usually find that deprecated opcodes have been replaced by newer opcodes that do the same things in better ways.

The left-side pane in the HTML version of *The Canonical Csound Reference Manual* groups opcodes into a number of main areas:

- Signal generators—primarily oscillators and envelope generators, as well as noise generators.
- Signal input and output, a category that includes routing real-time audio signals, file operations, and messages printed to the Csound console while the program is running.
- Signal modifiers—primarily filters.

- Instrument control, a complex category that includes `if`/`then`/`else` logic operators, opcodes that can start or stop instruments, and opcodes that construct on-screen sliders.

- Function table operations, which read data from stored data tables or write data to the tables.

- Mathematical operations.

- Pitch converters, which give you some useful ways to convert numerical values from one type to another.

- Real-time MIDI support.

- …and so forth. Consult the manual itself to see the other categories.

In order to keep the discussion between the covers of this book concise enough that you can pick up the book without a forklift, I'll have to pick and choose among the opcodes. We'll look at those that seem to me most generally useful and omit hundreds of others. Some of the opcodes that will be omitted from this chapter are rather obscure specialty items of limited utility. Others, while very useful, are so complex that explaining how they work would require many pages. And a few tantalizing opcodes may get skipped simply because I've never stumbled onto them! The MIDI and Python opcodes will be covered in Chapter 10, "Using Csound with MIDI, OSC, Pd, Python, and Live Audio."

We'll start by discussing the most important tone generators—primarily oscillators and noise sources. Next, we'll explore some of Csound's envelope generators, filters, and signal routing methods. But first, let's look at a few considerations that will apply across the board, no matter what opcode we're deploying.

What Is an Opcode?

An opcode is a pre-compiled chunk of computer code that does something. For a list (a *long* list) of opcodes, from a to zkwm, open the frames version of the manual in your web browser and scroll down the left column. The Reference section of this column includes a complete list. (Even the word "opcode" is an opcode.)

Every opcode has zero or more inputs, and zero or more outputs. In most (though not all) cases, an opcode is placed on a line of code by itself, with its outputs to the left and its inputs to the right, like this:

```
kr1, kr2 readk2 ifilname, iformat, iprd
```

This is the prototype of the `readk2` opcode. (For details on what `readk2` does, consult the manual. For an explanation of how to read a prototype in the manual, see below.) At the left end of the line are two output variables, separated by a comma. Next is the name of the opcode. To the right are the inputs, again separated by commas. This layout is standard: output(s), then the opcode, then input(s). (A mere handful of opcodes have an output on the right side, among the inputs.)

The arguments to an opcode are always in a fixed order. You can learn this order by consulting the manual. If you're using the CsoundQt interface, you'll see the prototype for an opcode displayed along the bottom of the main window whenever your cursor is on a line that contains an opcode. The abbreviations in this prototype, such as xamp, will often give you all the information you need about the correct order of the inputs.

At first glance, such a layout may seem backward—at least to folks who read printed languages, such as English, that are displayed from left to right. Shouldn't the outputs be on the right? But in fact it's normal in computer programming to put the result of an operation on the left side. This method is also convenient: Most opcodes have only a single output, while the list of inputs may be long and may contain optional items that can be omitted. When you want to check the name of the variable that you're using as the output, your eye will find it more easily when it's always at the left end of the line.

The technical term for an opcode's inputs and outputs is *arguments*. (Some people would say that only the inputs are arguments.) In this book I'll often use "inputs" and "outputs" rather than "arguments," because most musicians are more familiar with using the input and output jacks on hardware modules. If you think of each opcode as being like an electronic hardware module, such as you'll find on a classic analog synthesizer, you won't be far off the mark. You can plug signals (in the form of numbers, variable names such as ipan and kamp, or in some cases other types of data, such as text strings) into the inputs, which are normally written on the right side of the opcode. The opcode will chew on your inputs and produce one or more signals at its output "jacks," which are almost always found to the left of the opcode. You can then plug these signals into another opcode as if it were a hardware module, using the variable names (such as kr1 and kr2 in the readk2 example shown above) as "patch cords."

How to Read Prototypes in the Manual

To learn the precise meanings of the input(s) and the sort of data that will appear at the output(s) for a given opcode, you'll need to consult the manual. It's important to understand that the symbols used in the prototype are placeholders. That is, you can use whatever variable names you prefer for the inputs and outputs. All that matters is that you use a value of the correct type (i-, k-, a-, S-, and so on, as explained in Chapter 6).

Reading the prototype will tell you a few things. Any input or output whose name begins with i- will be sent to or received from the opcode during the *initialization pass,* before the instrument starts playing. (For more on the initialization pass, see the section "i- versus k- versus a-" in Chapter 6.) Any input or output whose name begins with k- will be sent to or received from the opcode on every control pass while the instrument is active. Any input or output whose name begins with a- will contain an audio signal. If the prototype shows an input whose name begins with x-, it can accept an a-, k-, or i-rate variable.

Many opcodes expect to receive the number of a *function table* as an input. This is the case, for instance, with the oscil opcode (see below). In the manual, the opcode prototype will generally show a function table number as ifn. Function tables are identified by integers, so this input could either be a numerical constant (such as 3) or an i-rate variable (such as iSine).

Reading the Initialization section of the manual page will tell you what type of table data the opcode expects to receive.

In general, a k-type input to an opcode will accept an i-time value or a numerical constant. For instance, given the prototype for `oscil`:

```
ares oscil xamp, xcps, ifn [, iphs]
```

you could set the amplitude and frequency to constant values like this:

```
aoutput oscil 1, 440, 1, 0.5
```

In effect, by entering a number you're using a k-rate value that never changes. This oscillator's output amplitude will be 1 continuously throughout each note, and its frequency will be 440 Hz. It will generate its output signal using the data in function table 1 as a source for the waveshape, and will begin its first cycle halfway through the table, because the start phase (`iphs`) has been set to 0.5.

Other types of conversions require special handling. If you want to send an audio signal (an a-rate variable) to an input that accepts only k-rate values, you'll need to *downsample* the audio signal to k-rate. This operation may produce audio artifacts, but there are times when it's useful. You might even want the artifacts! As you might guess, the downsampling operation is handled by the `downsamp` opcode.

Looking back at the prototype for `oscil`, you'll see an item in square brackets to the right of `ifn`. Items that appear within square brackets in opcode prototypes are *optional* arguments. That is, they're inputs for which the opcode has a preset default value. If you don't supply a value for this input, the opcode will use its default. Square brackets are also used in prototypes for opcodes that may have multiple outputs, such as `xin`:

```
xinarg1 [, xinarg2] ... [, xinargN] xin
```

In this case, the `xin` opcode will always have one output (shown as `xinarg1`). It may have additional outputs, and the exact number of outputs is unknown. Because the number is not known, the prototype includes three dots, and the final optional output has a name that ends with "N" to indicate that some unknown number belongs there. This is a prototype, however, so numbers need not be used in your code. Here are three quick examples, all of which would match the `xin` prototype:

```
asig xin
idataA, idataB xin
asig1, asig2, kenv, idelayL, idelayR xin
```

Some opcodes have several optional input arguments. Here's a good example:

```
ares dripwater kamp, idettack [, inum] [, idamp] [, imaxshake] [, ifreq] \
[, ifreq1] [, ifreq2]
```

The `dripwater` opcode requires only two inputs, `kamp` and `idettack`. The other inputs are optional. However, if you want to specify, for instance, your own value for `ifreq` with this opcode, you also have to specify `inum`, `idamp`, and `imaxshake`. Otherwise, Csound won't know how to interpret your code. If you give `dripwater` three inputs—for `kamp`, `idettack`, and one more—Csound will assume your third input is a value for `inum`, not for `ifreq`, because `inum` is the first optional input.

This is not a problem; it's just something to be aware of. The manual will almost always tell you what the defaults are for any optional inputs. Just enter the defaults for any inputs that you don't care about, enter your own value for the one you do care about, and ignore any optional inputs that fall after the one you're giving your own value to. This will give you the desired result.

Note   The backslash character at the end of the first line in the `dripwater` prototype, shown here, creates a "soft line break." This is a way of breaking up long lines of code into shorter lines that will be easier to see in your editing window; it's used throughout this book to break up long lines of code. The backslash is not required when using this (or any) opcode: You can string your code out into really long lines if you want to.

Note, however, that the backslash character cannot currently be used in CsoundQt. It can be used in your code only when you're running Csound from the command line.

A few opcodes use a different syntax. Here is the prototype for the `urd` opcode:

```
kout = urd(ktableNum)
```

This opcode uses a syntax similar to what in other programming languages would be a function call. The output value is followed by an equals sign (in fact, this is the *assignment operator*), and the input argument to the opcode is in parentheses.

Now that you know how to read prototypes, we're ready to start talking about specific opcodes.

Signal Generators

In this section we'll explore Csound's most important signal generators—oscillators, noise sources, and modulation sources such as envelopes. We'll also take a look at some of the types of synthesis you can perform using Csound. In order to give examples that you can run, listen to, and experiment with, we may in some cases use opcodes that haven't yet been discussed.

A Basic Oscillator

Probably one of the first examples of Csound code that you encountered used an opcode of the `oscil` family, which includes `oscil`, `oscili`, `oscils`, `oscilikt`, and so on. These opcodes read data out of a function table (which could be a sine wave or any other waveform) and cycle through the table repeatedly, at a rate determined by one of their input arguments. The prototype of `oscil` is given in the manual in two forms:

```
ares oscil xamp, xcps, ifn [, iphs]
kres oscil kamp, kcps, ifn [, iphs]
```

The first line is for an oscillator with an audio-rate output, the second for an oscillator with a control-rate output. You'll note that the first can accept inputs (`xamp` and `xcps`) at audio rate, while the second can't. The reason for this difference shouldn't be hard to see: Assuming that the sampling rate (`sr`) is higher than the control rate (`kr`), it would be meaningless to try to vary the amplitude or frequency of the output at the sampling rate.

The prototypes in the manual customarily use abbreviations that are easy to decipher. A symbol that includes "amp" will be used to control the amplitude of the output signal. A symbol that includes "cps" controls frequency (usually in cycles per second). The symbol `ifn` always refers to the number of a function table. And the symbol `iphs`, used above, refers to the starting phase of the output waveform. I'll have more to say about this parameter below.

Here is a simple .csd file that illustrates the use of `oscil`:

```
<CsoundSynthesizer>
<CsOptions>
</CsOptions>
<CsInstruments>
sr = 44100
ksmps = 4
nchnls = 2
0dbfs = 1

; instrument 1 - - a basic oscillator:
instr 1
iamp = 0.5
kcps = 440
ifn = p4

asig oscil iamp, kcps, ifn
outs asig, asig

endin

</CsInstruments>
<CsScore>

; table 1, a sine wave:
f1 0 16385 10 1
```

```
; table 2, a sawtooth wave:
f2 0 16385 7 -1 16384 1

; play a note with table 1, then a note with table 2:
i1 0 2 1
i1 + 2 2

</CsScore>
</CsoundSynthesizer>
```

The line we're interested in at the moment is the one that begins `asig oscil`. The input arguments to `oscil` (`iamp`, `kcps`, and `ifn`) have been set up in the preceding three lines. This is good coding practice: Your code will be easier to read and edit if you use separate lines to create named values before you use them. With such a simple instrument, though, there's little need to be this rigorous; we could get exactly the same result by omitting those three lines and writing the `oscil` line this way:

```
asig oscil 0.5, 440, p4
```

As a reminder, the name of the output (`asig`) is arbitrary. We can use whatever name we like here, as long as it begins with a- (or with k-, if we're creating a control-rate oscillator).

In this example, `oscil` first plays a tone using a sine wave (from f-table 1 in the score) and then another tone using a sawtooth wave (from f-table 2). You may notice that the sawtooth wave sounds a bit noisy, a bit grungy. This is due to a type of digital distortion called *aliasing*. The waveform we've created in f-table 2 is a pure geometrical sawtooth. As a result, it contains some overtones higher than the Nyquist frequency, which produce aliasing. (See the upcoming sidebar for more on aliasing.) Csound gives us some ways to avoid aliasing in sawtooth waves, but they can be somewhat complex. If you're curious, look up `vco2` and `vco2init` in the manual.

A simpler method, if you know the approximate pitch range of the tones your `oscil` will be creating, is to create a band-limited sawtooth using GEN 10. With GEN 10, we can add and control the relative amplitudes of a number of sine-wave partials. A sawtooth wave contains energy at diminishing amplitudes in all of the harmonically related partials. Strictly speaking, the amplitudes of the partials in a sawtooth follow the rule $1/n$, where n is the number of the harmonic. So we could create a sawtooth using amplitudes in a series such as 60, 30, 20, 15, 12, 10, and so on—or equivalently, 1, 0.5, 0.333, 0.25, 0.2, and so on. As explained later in this chapter, GEN 10 doesn't care what values we give it, because it will normalize its data to a ±1 range. If we want to avoid aliasing by using a band-limited sawtooth, we could do it like this:

```
f1 0 8192 10 60 30 20 15 12 10 8.57 7.5 6.666 6 5.45 5
```

This table will contain a waveform with the fundamental and the first 11 overtones, at successively diminishing amplitudes. The highest overtone will be three octaves and a fifth above the fundamental, which means that (assuming we're running Csound at the CD standard of 44,100 samples per second) we'll be able to use the waveform to play tones whose fundamental is as high as 1,837 Hz without risking any aliasing.

 Aliasing   Aliasing is a type of distortion that occurs in a digital audio system when the signal contains frequencies that are too high for the system to handle. There are good discussions of aliasing on the Web, so there's not much need to go into detail here. Briefly, aliasing occurs when some of the partials (overtones) in a waveform are higher than half of the sampling rate. In the examples in this book, the sampling rate is set by the line:

```
sr = 44100
```

With this line in the orchestra header, Csound will produce aliasing whenever a signal contains partials higher than 22,050 cycles per second (22.05 kHz). This value is called the *Nyquist frequency*.

Once aliasing has been introduced into a signal, it can't be removed by later filtering.

As you might surmise from the foregoing, we can use any waveform at all in an `oscil`, including a sampled wave. All we need to do is store the wave in an f-table, and then give the `oscil` the number of the table. There are constraints, however. The `oscil` opcode needs to use a waveform whose length is a power of 2, plus 1—for example, 1025 or 16385. Sampled waves are not usually of such convenient lengths, so `oscil` is not usually the right choice for sample playback. For more on this topic, see "Sample Playback," later in this chapter.

The optional `iphs` input to `oscil` controls the starting phase—that is, the point in the stored waveform at which playback will start. This parameter defaults to 0, which is the starting point of the waveform; `iphs` is expressed as a fraction of a wave cycle, so its value should be set between 0 and 1. The concept is illustrated in Figure 7.1.

It's often useful to send varying signals rather than constant ones to the `xamp` and `xcps` inputs of an `oscil`. For instance, we can patch the output of an envelope generator into the `xamp` input. The value of `iamp` (which might be coming from the score, although in the preceding example it's set as a constant) is used as the first input to `line`, which supplies an extemely simple decaying envelope.

```
kampenv line iamp, p3, 0
asig oscil kampenv, kcps, ifn
```

This is often a convenient way to work, but there are times when we would like the output level of an `oscil` to remain constant, in which case we would apply the envelope signal using a

Fraction	0.25	0.5	0.75	0 or 1
Radians	π/2	π	3π/2	0 or 2π
Degrees	90°	180°	270°	0° or 360°

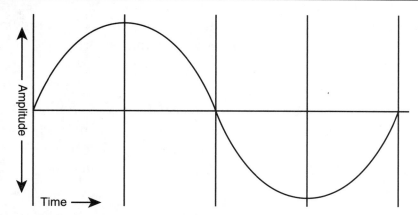

Figure 7.1 Each point in a cyclically repeating waveform has a phase. The phase is defined by the distance between the current point and the starting point of the wave. Phase is sometimes stated in radians (values between 0 and 2π) or in degrees (values between 0 and 360 degrees). In some Csound opcodes, phase is defined, more conveniently, as a number between 0 and 1. Both 0 and 1 correspond to the starting point of the waveform, since the waveform repeats. Values between 0 and 1 (or between 0 and 2π, or between 0 and 360 degrees) correspond to various point on the waveform.

separate multiplication operation. In the code below, the `oscil` has a constant output amplitude of 1, and the envelope is applied to the resulting signal using multiplication:

```
kampenv line iamp, p3, 0
asig oscil 1, kcps, ifn
aout = asig * kampenv
outs aout, aout
```

The inputs to `oscil` can also be used for amplitude or frequency modulation, which will have the effect of altering the shape of the output waveform. To hear this, try replacing the `oscil` line in the original example with these two lines:

```
amod oscil kamp, kcps * 0.5, ifn
asig oscil amod, kcps, ifn
```

The output of the first `oscil`, which is called `amod`, is being used to control the amplitude of the second `oscil`. If you try this, you may also want to delete the second line from the example score above, as modulating one sawtooth wave from another tends to sound rather nasty.

A variant of `oscil` is called `oscili`. The two are identical except that `oscili` interpolates between data points in the f-table waveform. Interpolation will produce a smoother output signal. In the early days of Csound, when computers had much less memory, interpolating oscillators were more important. An f-table might be defined with a size of only 128 or 256. Reading the data from such a small table without interpolating tended to produce audible distortion in the sound. Today, memory constraints are all but nonexistent, so an f-table size of 65,536 is just as easy to use. With such a large table, you're not likely to hear a difference in sound between oscil and oscili. If you're rendering your finished composition to the hard drive, there's no reason not to use oscili. But because it's more computationally intensive, if you're designing an instrument to be used in real time, you'll gain a small performance advantage (probably trivial on a modern computer unless you're generating a lot of signals at once) by using oscil.

Note A number of opcodes have optional interpolated forms. Usually, if the name of the opcode ends with -i, it interpolates between stored data values, producing a smoother output. The -i versions do linear interpolation. Some opcodes also have a version ending in -3, which does cubic interpolation. Cubic interpolation can produce a cleaner sound, but again, it's more computationally intensive.

We can also use oscil as an LFO (low-frequency oscillator) to generate modulation signals. For more on this topic, see "LFOs," later in this chapter. We can even use it as an envelope generator, by setting the frequency value (kcps) to $1/p3$. Since p3 always refers to the note's duration in seconds, $1/p3$ will give us exactly one cycle of the oscil waveform during the course of the note. To hear this concept in action, try this example:

```
instr 1
kampenv oscil 0.5, 1/p3, 2
asig oscil kampenv, 440, 1
outs asig, asig
endin

</CsInstruments>
<CsScore>

f1 0 16384 10 4 3 2 1
f2 0 8192 7 0 200 1 300 0 400 1 500 0 600 1 6192 0

i1 0 2
i1 + 3
i1 + 1
```

The important thing to notice here is that the control signal kampenv is being generated by an oscil, which is running at k-rate rather than at a-rate. The envelope contour (created in f-table 2 using GEN routine 07) has three quick peaks during the attack and then drops smoothly back to 0. The speed with which the peaks are articulated depends entirely on the length of the note—with slower notes, the attack peaks are spread further apart. If you want attack segments that are always the same length, no matter how long or short the note is, see the section on "Envelopes" later in this chapter.

Other Oscillators

After experimenting with `oscil`, you may want to look at `buzz`, `gbuzz`, and `vco`.

buzz and gbuzz

`buzz` and `gbuzz` are good for creating static tones containing some or many partials. You can process such tones through filters, a standard technique known as *subtractive synthesis*. Here is a simple example using `buzz`. As usual in this book, the opening and closing tags in the .csd file have been omitted.

```
sr = 44100
ksmps = 4
nchnls = 2
0dbfs = 1

; create a sine wave for buzz to use:
giSine ftgen 0, 0, 8192, 10, 1

instr 1
idur = p3
iamp = p4
ifrq = p5
icutoff = 7000
inumpartials = 35

asig buzz     1, ifrq, inumpartials, giSine

; filter the signal and modulate the cutoff with a simple descending
ramp:
kfiltenv line      icutoff, idur, ifrq
afilt lpf18        asig, kfiltenv, 0.6, 0.1

kamp linen         iamp, 0.01, idur, 0.1
afilt = afilt * kamp
outs afilt, afilt
endin

</CsInstruments>
<CsScore>

; play a three-second note at 200Hz with a filter sweep:
i1 0 3 0.8 200
```

In this example, `buzz` produces a signal with 35 partials. The tone is then lowpass-filtered by `lpf18`.

One limitation of buzz is that all of the partials will be at the same amplitude. In addition, the lowest partial will always be the fundamental. gbuzz is more flexible. Note, however, that gbuzz requires a cosine wave, not a sine wave, as its source material. We can create a cosine wave using GEN 11. The arguments of this GEN routine are slightly different from the arguments for GEN 10, but in this case it hardly matters. Using the example above, substitute the following for the ftgen line:

```
giCos ftgen 0, 0, 8192, 11, 1
```

Next, replace the buzz line with this:

```
asig gbuzz 1, ifrq, inumpartials, 1, 1, giCos
```

The sound should be exactly the same as before, because this usage of gbuzz sets the lowest partial and the multiplication factor both to 1. But now we can make a few changes. For a tone that emphasizes the upper partials, you might replace 1, 1 in the line above with 5, 1.1. This produces a tone whose lowest partial is the 5 and whose higher partials are progressively louder. (You may find this easier to hear if you get rid of the filter in the example.) Conversely, 1, 0.9 will produce a more muted tone, and 5, 0.9 will produce a tone that sounds a bit bandpass-filtered, as the lowest partials will be gone and the highest partials will be reduced in amplitude.

vco2

To generate a sawtooth or square wave for classic analog synthesis sounds, using vco2 is simple. The default output, a sawtooth, requires no inputs but the amplitude and frequency:

```
asig vco2 kamp, kfrq
```

For a square or triangle wave, add a 10 or 12 as a third argument:

```
asig vco2 kamp, kfrq, 10
```

The third argument can take other values; see the manual page for a list.

Pulse width modulation of a square wave, an effect common on analog synthesizers, requires only a bit more in the way of setup. Set the imode argument to 2 rather than 10 and then apply a signal (desired values greater than 0 and less than 1) to the kpw argument:

```
klfo lfo 0.3, 0.5
klfo = klfo + 0.5
asig vco2 kamp, kfrq, 2, klfo
```

Noise Generators

Random numbers have many uses in computer-generated music. For instance, we might want to fill a table with note pitch values at the start of a performance and let Csound choose the pitches for the table according to some quasi-random algorithm that we devise. Or we might want to add a small random value to the frequency of a vibrato LFO at the start of a note, so that the vibrato will vary slightly from note to note, thus producing a less mechanical sound.

Audio-rate signals containing random numbers are called `noise`. By mixing noise with other sound sources, we can make more realistic percussion sounds and produce other effects.

For some purposes, such as generating streams of notes, it's not desirable that the distribution of random numbers be uniform from 0 to some arbitrary value. For example, we might want mostly low numbers and only a few higher ones. Csound provides a variety of random number generators with various features, allowing us to produce weighted random series, random series that are constrained within a specific range (such as between 0 and 10), and so forth.

The precise nature of the weighted curves produced by such opcodes as `betarnd`, `cauchy`, and `poisson` is not well documented in *The Canonical Csound Reference Manual* (at least, not in the version of the manual released with Csound 5.13—future manuals may contain more information). Fortunately, specific information is readily available online: A search for "cauchy distribution" or "poisson distribution" will turn up articles full of graphs and equations.

To begin our all-too-brief survey of Csound's random signal sources, let's look at this instrument:

```
instr 1
seed 0
; generate a stream of white noise:
ahiss rand 0.5
; generate a stepped random control signal:
kstep randomh 500, 5000, 3, 3
; use the stepped signal to control filter cutoff:
aout lpf18 ahiss, kstep, 0.7, 0.5
outs aout, aout
endin
```

The `rand` opcode, which is used here to generate a stream of white noise, is one of the simpler opcodes in this group. It can produce either an a-rate or a k-rate signal. Here is its prototype:

```
ares rand xamp [, iseed] [, isel] [, ioffset]
```

In the example instrument we're ignoring the optional parameters; we're giving it only an amplitude argument, 0.5. This assumes `0dbfs=1`, as in most of the examples in this book.

The `randomh` opcode is a little more interesting. It generates random output values and then holds them for some period of time before taking a new random value. In other words, this is a classic analog sample-and-hold—at least, as that term is usually understood. A real sample-and-hold circuit can sample any input signal, not just noise. Here is its prototype of `randomh`:

```
kres randomh kmin, kmax, kcps [,imode] [,ifirstval]
```

The kmin and kmax values limit the minimum and maximum output. The kcps value tells the sample-and-hold how often (how many times per second) to take a new sample. This example uses randomh to control the cutoff frequency of a filter, so it's set to run at 3 Hz.

The two random signals, ahiss and kstep, are fed into a resonant lowpass filter, lpf18, the first as an audio signal to be filtered, the second as a control signal that controls the filter's cutoff frequency. The result is step-filtered white noise. To hear this instrument, use a single note in the score, like this:

```
i1 0 5
```

This instrument has one other important feature: It uses the seed opcode. Seeding a random number generator is an important concept in computer science. The reason is because computers can't actually generate numbers at random; their operations are entirely deterministic. Procedures that apparently generate random numbers in a computer are actually clever algorithms that use mathematical formulas to output streams of numbers—streams in which the individual numbers that appear cannot easily be predicted. That is, they're pseudo-random.

A pseudo-random number generator needs a starting point. The seed value provides this starting point. Csound gives us two ways to use seed. If we give it, as an argument, an integer between 1 and 2^32 (that is, 2 to the 32nd power), then the seeded random number generators will produce the same result every time they're run. That is, the content of the random number stream will still seem random, but it will be exactly the same each time the music is played. This can be quite useful when you're generating patterns of notes. If you think your orchestra is doing what you want, but you don't hear a pattern that pleases you, just change the seed value and play the piece again.

Conversely, if seed is given an argument of 0, the seed value will be taken from the computer's system clock. This clock will run for years without ever producing the same number, so your pattern of random numbers will be different each time the piece is run.

Some of Csound's noise sources—specifically, rand, randh, randi, rnd(x), and birnd(x)— are not affected by the seed opcode. The first three have their own private arguments for a seed value, which operate in a similar way; see the manual for details.

Next, let's use a random number generator to produce a tone with some instability. Using the same score as before (a single note of five seconds or so), try this instrument:

```
instr 1
iSine ftgentmp 0, 0, 8192, 10, 1
ahiss rand 800
afilt tonex ahiss, 10
aosc oscil 0.5, 440 + afilt, iSine
outs aosc, aosc
endin
```

The first line uses `ftgentmp` to fill a table with a sine wave. The table number, `iSine`, is passed to `oscil` to be used as a waveform. As before, we're using `rand` to produce white noise, but the amplitude (800) is higher than before. The noise is filtered using `tonex` so that only very low frequencies remain. The filtered noise is used to modulate the frequency of `oscil`. The result is a tone whose frequency wobbles up and down in a random way, but only slightly.

Experiment with different arguments to `rand` and `tonex` and listen to the result. If you increase the amount of pitch wobble (perhaps to 440 + afilt * 5), you'll discover that the output of `rand` is very non-random indeed: It loops through a cycle about once per second. Since we're creating an audio-rate signal using `rand`, it's a fair inference that it puts out on the order of 44,000 different numerical values before repeating. This is good enough in many situations, but perhaps not in this instrument. So let's try something different.

Replace the `rand` and `tonex` lines with a call to `randomi` and edit the `oscil` line, as shown below:

```
kwobble randomi -15, 15, 15, 2
aosc oscil 0.5, 440 + kwobble, iSine
```

The `randomi` opcode produces a sort of zigzag output. Periodically, it generates a new random number and then ramps smoothly up or down from the previous value to the new one. In the code above, it's selecting a new value 15 times per second, and the value will be somewhere between –15 and 15. Now there is no detectable pattern to the pitch wobble.

For our final example of randomness, we're going to let the `random` opcode choose what note an instrument will play. We'll generate a random number between 0 and 1 and then choose the oscillator frequency based on the number. Csound lacks a switch statement (a convenient bit of syntax in computer programming), so we have to use a series of `else`/`then`/`if` statements to select a pitch. This makes the instrument look a little more complex than it is. The score also takes up more lines: To make the effect of the randomness clearer, we'll play a bunch of notes.

To lead into the next section of *Csound Power!*, I've employed a `foscil` opcode in this example. Also pressed into service is the useful `cpspch` opcode, which will be discussed in the section on "Pitch Converters," later in this chapter. Here is the bulk of the .csd file (leaving off the `<...>` tags at the beginning and end):

```
sr = 44100
ksmps = 4
nchnls = 2
0dbfs = 1
seed 0

instr 1
iSine ftgentmp 0, 0, 8192, 10, 1
```

```
; generate a random number between 0 and 1:
iRand random 0, 1

; choose a definite pitch for the note, basing the choice on the random
number:
if iRand < 0.2 then
        ifreq = cpspch (7.0)
elseif iRand < 0.4 then
        ifreq = cpspch (7.04)
elseif iRand < 0.6 then
        ifreq = cpspch (7.07)
elseif iRand < 0.8 then
        ifreq = cpspch (7.09)
else
        ifreq = cpspch (8.0)
endif

kenv line 0.5, p3, 0
aosc foscil kenv, ifreq, 1, 1, 5 * kenv, iSine
outs aosc, aosc
endin

</CsInstruments>
<CsScore>

i1 0 0.2
i1 +
i1 +
i1 +
i1 +
i1 +
i1 +
i1 +
i1 +
i1 +
i1 +
i1 +
i1 +
i1 +
i1 +
```

This example will play 15 notes selected at random from a pentatonic scale in C major.

FM Synthesis

The techniques of FM (frequency modulation) synthesis were first developed in the 1970s, primarily by John Chowning at Stanford University. FM was first popularized in the Yamaha DX7 synthesizer, which debuted in 1983. Though by now the DX7 is completely obsolete, it remains one of the best-selling and most-often-heard synthesizers of all time, and FM synthesis remains a very viable way to generate complex and interesting tones. Many currently available synthesizers, especially software plug-ins, have facilities for FM synthesis, usually in conjunction with other techniques.

In FM synthesis, the frequency of one oscillator (called the *carrier*) is modulated by the signal from another oscillator (called the *modulator*). What the listener hears is normally the signal coming from the carrier. Quite often, both oscillators use sine waves as their source waveform, but in fact any waveform can be used. If the modulator is running in the sub-audio frequency range (below about 20 Hz), the result of frequency modulation is vibrato. When the modulator's frequency rises into the audio range, however, something very interesting happens: Instead of hearing the frequency changes of the carrier as pitch fluctuations, we hear them as a change in the tone color of the carrier.

Several very decent tutorials on FM are available online, so there's no need to recapitulate them here. Instead, let's dive straight in and start making some sounds.

FM Using foscil

Csound gives us several different ways to implement FM. Perhaps the easiest to use is the `foscil` opcode. This opcode models a pair of oscillators configured as a carrier and a modulator, producing a single output signal from the carrier. Here is the prototype of `foscil`:

```
ares foscil xamp, kcps, xcar, xmod, kndx, ifn [, iphs]
```

If you've read the section earlier in this chapter on `oscil`, you'll know that `ares` is the output audio signal, `xamp` is the input for the amplitude level, `kcps` the input for the frequency, and `ifn` the number of the f-table to use to generate the waveform. In FM, this should usually be a sine wave. Other waves can be used, but they tend to generate quite a lot of overtones, so aliasing distortion is likely. The optional `iphs` parameter is for setting the start phase of the signal and can almost always be ignored.

The new parameters are `xcar`, `xmod`, and `kndx`. The first two are used for setting the frequencies of the carrier and modulator relative to the value in `kcps`. In the example below, we'll set them both to 1. These settings will give `foscil` a warm, sawtooth-like tone.

The `kndx` input controls the amount of modulator signal that is applied to the carrier. As this value rises, the signal will have more and stronger partials. Because it's a k-rate input, we can easily send it a signal coming from an envelope generator. As the envelope level falls, the output of `foscil` will have fewer partials. Depending on the values of `xcar` and `xmod`, this may or may not sound similar to an envelope generator lowering the cutoff frequency of a lowpass filter. When the value of `kndx` falls to zero, there will be no frequency modulation, so only the bare tone of the carrier oscillator will be heard.

Partials, Overtones, and Harmonics   Musicians tend to use the words "overtones" and "harmonics" when describing tone color. The term "partials" is heard less often, but in some cases it's more correct.

The underlying mathematical theory is that any periodic waveform (that is, anything that's not noise) can be analyzed as a group of one or more sine waves, each having its own frequency, amplitude, and phase. When you pluck a guitar string, for instance, your ear interprets the sound as a single tone, but the tone is actually a composite: It contains sound energy at many different frequencies. That is, it comprises a number of partials.

The terms "overtones" and "harmonics" contain a hidden assumption, which is that the frequencies of the various sine-wave partials have a simple mathematical relationship to one another. Specifically, they're all whole-number multiples of some base frequency, which is called the *fundamental*. This is a fairly good (though imperfect) assumption with respect to the sound of plucked strings and vibrating columns of air. If the guitar string is tuned to 100 Hz, the tone will contain energy at 200 Hz, 300 Hz, 400 Hz, and so forth.

But in some situations, the sine-wave components of a tone don't have this simple mathematical relationship. A bell, for instance, vibrates in a more complex way than a string. The sine waves in the sound of a bell can only be termed *partials*, because they're not overtones or harmonics. Likewise, in digital synthesis, it's easy to produce tones whose sine-wave components are not related by ratios that can be described using whole numbers.

To start exploring FM synthesis, create this simple .csd file (as usual, the tags at the beginning and end of the file have been omitted in the example, to save space).

```
sr = 44100
ksmps = 4
nchnls = 2
0dbfs = 1

giSine ftgen 0, 0, 8192, 10, 1

instr 1
kampenv line 0.5, p3, 0
aosc foscil kampenv, 110, 1, 1, 5, giSine
outs aosc, aosc
endin

</CsInstruments>
<CsScore>
i1 0 2
```

Try replacing the two 1's in the `foscil` line with other values. Start with integers, and also try some decimal values, such as 1.37 for either `xcar` or `xmod`. You'll find that each combination of numbers creates a distinct tone color.

Try increasing the value for `kndx` (5 in the example). This will add partials to the tone. Another way to add partials is to edit the `ftgen` line in the header. If you look up the prototype for GEN 10, which is being used here, you'll see that the number or numbers at the end of the line add more sine wave overtones to the fundamental stored in the table. You can add several overtones and give them various strengths, like this:

```
giSine ftgen 0, 0, 8192, 10, 1, 2, 3
```

By patching an LFO or envelope generator signal into the `kndx` input of `foscil`, we can shape the tone. Change the instrument code so that it looks like this:

```
instr 1
kampenv line 0.5, p3, 0
indxmax = 10
kindex linseg indxmax, 0.2, 1, 0.1, indxmax * 0.8, p3 - 0.3, 0
aosc foscil kampenv, 110, 1, 1, kindex, giSine
outs aosc, aosc
endin
```

The FM index envelope (called `kindex` above) is generated by a `linseg` envelope generator. To make it easier to edit the envelope and thereby alter the brightness of the tone, the value `indxmax` has been pulled out as a separate i-rate variable. In a more fully developed instrument, `indxmax` would probably be controlled from the score, or perhaps from a velocity value being transmitted by a MIDI keyboard.

FM Using phasor and table

The `foscil` opcode is convenient but limited. It implements a single carrier/modulator pair; in FM parlance this is called *two-operator* FM. There are times when we may want to have two modulators modulate the frequency of a single carrier, or have a single modulator affect two carriers at once. For this, we need a more flexible instrument design. The key to developing more flexible FM synthesis lies in the use of the `phasor` and `table` opcodes.

A `phasor` is a special type of oscillator. It produces a ramp that moves upward from 0 to 1 and then repeats. Essentially, it produces a rising sawtooth wave, but you probably wouldn't want to listen to it directly, as the sound would include aliasing. A `phasor` is normally paired with an opcode that reads the data from an f-table. The most basic form of this opcode is `table`. In the code example below, I've used `tablei` instead; the `-i` on the end of the name indicates that this is an interpolating opcode, which can produce a slightly smoother output.

```
instr 1
; create a sine wave:
```

```
iSine ftgentmp 0, 0, 8192, 10, 1
; initial settings:
iamp = 0.5
ifreq = 110
index = 2
imodfactor = 1
icarfactor = 1

; envelopes:
kampenv line iamp, p3, 0
kindex line index, p3 , 0
; tone generation:
amodsig oscili kindex, ifreq * imodfactor, iSine
acarphas phasor ifreq * icarfactor
asig tablei acarphas + amodsig, iSine, 1, 0, 1

; output:
aout = asig * kampenv
outs aout, aout
endin
```

The comments in the example code above may help you see what's going on. The new function-ality is in the tone generation section. Here we create a modulator using `oscili` and a carrier using a `phasor`/`tablei` pair. The sine wave in the table (created by `ftgentmp`) is read at a fre-quency specified by the addition of `acarphas` (the output of the `phasor`) and `amodsig` (the output of the modulator).

To change the relative tuning of the carrier and modulator, enter other values for `imodfactor` and `icarfactor`.

If you play this instrument with a reasonably long note from the score—five seconds or so—you'll hear that it has a rather rich sound. Acoustic energy is moving from one partial to another during the tone. In fact, what we're doing now is not technically FM synthesis; it's phase modu-lation synthesis. Phase modulation has some advantages with more complex patches. For instance, it's more stable when we add a feedback loop, in which a portion of the carrier signal is used to modulate the carrier itself. This type of feedback, which produces a brighter sound, was implemented in the DX7.

Here is the tone generation portion of the instrument above, altered to add some feedback. Note the use of `init`. In order to include `asig` among the arguments to `tablei`, we have to initial-ize it. When we've done this, the compiler knows that it exists, so we won't get an error message when we run the instrument. I found values that I liked for the new `linseg` (the feedback amount envelope) by trial and error. This envelope sounds good to me with a tone that lasts for about five seconds. (In the DX7, if memory serves, the amount of feedback was not controllable by an envelope.)

```
; tone generation:
kfeedback linseg 0.2, 0.5, 0.1, 1.5, 0
asig init 0
asig = asig * kfeedback
amodsig oscili kindex, ifreq * imodfactor, iSine
acarphas phasor ifreq * icarfactor
asig tablei acarphas + amodsig + asig, iSine, 1, 0, 1
```

Granular Synthesis

The theory of granular synthesis is not especially complicated, but putting the theory into practice can lead to a certain amount of confusion and frustration. To see why, take a quick look at the prototype for the granule opcode:

```
ares granule xamp, ivoice, iratio, imode, ithd, ifn, ipshift, igskip, \
   igskip_os, ilength, kgap, igap_os, kgsize, igsize_os, iatt, idec \
   [, iseed] [, ipitch1] [, ipitch2] [, ipitch3] [, ipitch4] [, ifnenv]
```

That's 16 required inputs, plus half a dozen more that are optional—and no, I'm not going to pause to explain each and every one of them here. Fortunately, Csound includes several granular synthesis opcodes that are easier to use than granule. Even so, as you explore the powerful resources of granular synthesis you should plan to devote a few hours to experimentation.

In granular synthesis, a sustained sound is built up by stringing together hundreds or thousands of short "sound grains." (See, I told you the theory wasn't complex. That's really all there is to it.) The basic parameters the sound designer specifies include:

■ The source waveform used in the grains.

■ The starting points of the grains within the source.

■ The lengths of the grains.

■ The pitches of the grains.

■ The amplitude envelope used to shape the grains.

■ The amount of time that separates one grain from the next.

Specifying all of these parameters for each grain individually would be a monstrous task. Fortunately, Csound provides several granular synthesis opcodes that take care of the details. The sound designer need only provide one value for each of them, or a k-rate input to modulate them during the course of a long tone, and Csound takes care of the messy details.

It's possible to do something very similar yourself, using an event opcode in some sort of loop to start notes on your own instrument, which will then play a grain. This approach gives you a little more control over the grains; you could filter them in various ways, for instance, by employing a filter in the instrument that is playing them. An example of this technique is given at the end of this section. But the detailed, hands-on approach of using event is not always needed.

Let's look at the control parameters one at a time.

The source waveform used in granular synthesis is often a sampled (digitally recorded) sound—a file on your computer's hard drive. Sampled drum loops and spoken vocal phrases are good—anything with some variety in it. A single sampled note would probably be less interesting. Usually a monaural file will be needed; if you want to try using a stereo file as a source for granular synthesis, you'll probably want to load it into an audio editor such as Audacity and create a mono version. Alternatively, Csound lets you load each channel of a stereo file into a different table, so you could apply granular processes to the left and right channels independently. Because many granular processes involve a bit of randomization, however, it's not likely the left and right channels will stay in sync.

With a source waveform of reasonable length, the starting point for each new grain can be at a different point in the source. The starting points could proceed forward through the source, or backward, or be selected at random.

Grains are typically between 1ms and 50ms in length. As the grains become longer, the nature of the source material can be heard more easily. Using a drum loop as a source for granular synthesis and setting a larger grain size can give you a comically mangled, staggering drum track, in which the individual drum sounds are heard clearly but all rhythmic coherence is lost.

The grains can be played back at their original pitch—that is, the output rate can be the same as the rate at which the source digital recording was originally made. Or they can be played back faster or slower than the original pitch. Changing the pitch of the grains is a way of altering the pitch of a sampled sound without affecting its length.

The grain's amplitude envelope is usually defined with an attack time and a decay time. During the attack time, the envelope will rise from zero to its maximum amplitude; it will then hold that amplitude constant until the decay time starts. During the decay time, the envelope will fall back to zero (see Figure 7.2). This scheme is a bit simpler than the classic ADSR envelope found in traditional synthesizers, in that the sustain level is always 100%. In the prototype for

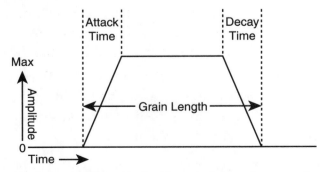

Figure 7.2 The amplitude envelope of a sound grain is usually defined by its attack and decay time. In some implementations, you may also be able to select a curve type for the attack and decay.

granule shown above, the attack and decay time of the grain envelope can be set using the `iatk` and `idec` parameters. (For details on how these inputs work, consult the `granule` page in *The Canonical Csound Reference Manual*.) Another option is to get the envelope from a function table. This approach is used in the `grain` opcode.

If there's a silent gap between the end of one `grain` and the beginning of the next, the sound will have a stuttering quality. The stuttering may be so fast, however, that it's audible only as a certain roughness in the tone or as a low frequency. On the other hand, the time between the end of one grain and the start of the next might be negative. Another way of stating this is that the grain length is greater than the difference in start times between one grain and the next. In this situation, the grains will overlap. If they overlap, the sound will be smoother and richer.

The grain Opcode

A good way to get started with granular synthesis is to copy the example code for `grain` in the manual, paste it into a CsoundQt file, and then play around with it. The source soundfile used in this example, beats.wav, is installed with Csound. You can use it as the source with this example by copying it into the directory you have set as SFDIR in the Environment tab of the CsoundQt Configuration box.

Here is the prototype for `grain`:

```
ares grain xamp, xpitch, xdens, kampoff, kpitchoff, kgdur, igfn, \
   iwfn, imgdur [, igrnd]
```

As usual, the backslash character at the end of the line is Csound's shorthand for continuing a long line of code without going off the right edge of the window.

The `xamp`, `xpitch`, and `xdens` inputs are easy to understand: They control the amplitude, pitch, and density of the grains. (The density value is in grains per second.) More interestingly, this opcode has three internal sources of controlled randomness. The value for `kampoff` determines the amount of random variation in the amplitude. When this parameter is 0, the value in `xamp` will be used directly, but when `kampoff` is not 0, the maximum amplitude will be `xamp + kampoff`, and the minimum will be `xamp – kampoff`. The same consideration applies to `xpitch` and `kpitchoff`: When `kpitchoff` is not 0, the actual output pitch of a grain will be randomly higher or lower than the value in `xpitch`. Finally, the point within the source sound file (`igfn`) where the grains will start their playback can be randomly chosen (if `igrnd` is 0) or at the beginning of the file (if `igrnd` is not 0). Because of this built-in randomness, the example in the manual produces two entirely different output audio streams from two `grain` lines of code, one being sent to the left output channel and the other to the right, even though the lines themselves are identical.

After copying the example code from the manual into your own .csd, you might try these experiments:

- Increase the end value in the line that creates `kpitch` to `ibasefreq * 4`. As the output of the `line` opcode ramps up, the pitches of the grains will rise.

- Lower the starting and ending values for kdens from 600 and 100 to 6 and 10. This will give you a much more sparse scattering of grains.

- Try different source audio files. If your file is longer than beats.wav, you may want to increase the size of f10 to some larger power of two.

Granular Synthesis by Hand

Next, let's look at an orchestra that uses event to generate grains manually. (For more on event, see "Creating Score Events during Performance," later in this chapter.) The grain-playing instrument has a sine wave as its source, but you could easily substitute any other type of tone. Adding more p-fields (perhaps for filter cutoff, varying decay time, or source waveform) and filling them with either random numbers or values that ramp up or down would be just as easy.

```
sr = 44100
ksmps = 4
nchnls = 2
0dbfs = 1
giSine ftgen 0, 0, 8192, 10, 1


instr 1 ; play a sine wave
iatk = 0.01
idec = 0.01
isus = p3 - iatk
iamp = p4
ifreq = p5
ipan = p6

ifreqrampend random 0.7, 1.3
kfreq line ifreq, p3, ifreq * ifreqrampend

kampenv linsegr 0, iatk, iamp, isus, iamp, idec, 0
asig oscil kampenv, kfreq, giSine

aoutL, aoutR pan2 asig, ipan
outs aoutL, aoutR
endin

instr 11 ; a grain generator
kamp random 0.15, 0.3
kfreq random 300, 800
kpan random 0, 1
kdur random 0.05, 0.15
```

```
ktimerand random -3, 3
ktrig metro 20 + ktimerand
if ktrig == 1 then
   event "i", 1, 0, kdur, kamp, kfreq, kpan
endif
endin


</CsInstruments>
<CsScore>
i11 0 5
e 5.2
```

As usual, I've omitted the opening and closing tags in the .csd file. The e 5.2 line at the end of the score extends the length of the score slightly, in order to allow the last grain to finish playing. Without this line, you may hear a click when the tone stops.

The grains are generated at a time determined by the metro opcode. The tempo of this is being randomized somewhat, so that the grains don't have a regular rhythm.

The grain envelope is generated by linsegr. This opcode has a release segment, so the actual grain length is idec longer than p3. It's a typical rise-sustain-decay envelope. To make the sound a little more interesting, I've given the sine-wave instrument its own random-depth pitch envelope, which can rise or fall somewhat during the grain.

Formant Synthesis

Formants are resonant regions within the frequency spectrum. The term "formant" is most often associated with the vowel sounds produced by the human voice. The human larynx (vocal cords) produces a raw tone that is somewhat like a sawtooth wave: It's rich in overtones. The overtones coming from the vocal cords pass through the resonant cavities of the mouth and sinuses, and these resonant cavities emphasize certain overtones while attenuating others. The human ear and brain are exquisitely sensitive to the differences in tone color that can be produced by changing the shape of the mouth, and for obvious reasons: Without such sensitivity, spoken language would be harder to understand. As a result, electronic tones that have a vocal quality can be surprisingly evocative.

As the description above may suggest, one way to produce this type of tone color is by starting with a broad-band tone, such as a sawtooth wave or white noise, and passing it through a set of parallel bandpass filters. A bank of such filters is sometimes referred to as a formant filter.

Csound gives us a second way to synthesize vocal tones. We can build them up additively using granular synthesis. The opcodes that are most often used for this purpose are fof, fof2, and fog.

These opcodes have enough input parameters that they can be rather intimidating. Here is the prototype for `fof`:

```
ares fof xamp, xfund, xform, koct, kband, kris, kdur, kdec, iolaps, \
   ifna, ifnb, itotdur [, iphs] [, ifmode] [, iskip]
```

For details on the meanings of the arguments, consult the manual page on `fof`. The first two arguments, `xamp` and `xfund`, aren't hard to understand: They're the amplitude of the output signal and the frequency of the fundamental tone. `xform` and `xband` are used to control the formant frequency and bandwidth.

To get you started, scroll down to the lower end of the left pane in the HTML manual. You'll see links to several Appendices. Appendix D lists the formant values for common vowels. (Note that most vowel sounds in English are actually diphthongs. That is, they're produced by gliding from one vowel sound to another. Many languages employ pure vowel sounds rather than diphthongs, and the data in Appendix D produces pure vowel sounds.)

The values for `kris`, `kdur`, and `kdec` control the rise time, duration, and decay time of individual grains within the tone. `ifna` and `ifnb` are the numbers of function tables; for vocal synthesis, the first table is normally a sine wave. The second table contains a rise shape, which is applied to the grain over the time defined by `kris` and `kdec`.

The value `koct` operates backwards from what you might expect. A value of 0 produces a "normal" vocal tone. As `koct` increases, the fundamental drops. An increase from 0 to 1 drops the fundamental by an octave (hence the name) while leaving the formants where they are.

The best way to learn to use these opcodes is probably to start with a working code example and then start varying it to see how the sound changes. The example below generates the sound of a vocal "ah" tone using four instances of `fof`, each of which generates one formant. As usual in this book, the opening and closing tags in the .csd file have been omitted.

```
sr = 44100
ksmps = 128
nchnls = 2
0dbfs = 1

instr 1 ; plays a vocal tone consisting of four formants
idur = p3
iamp = p4
ifund = p5
ioct = p6

iamp1 = ampdb(0) * iamp
iamp2 = ampdb(-4) * iamp
iamp3 = ampdb(-12) * iamp
iamp4 = ampdb(-18) * iamp
```

```
iatk1 = 0.1
iatk2 = 0.12
iatk3 = 0.14
iatk4 = 0.16

irel1 = 0.2
irel2 = 0.24
irel3 = 0.28
irel4 = 0.32

iformfrq1 = 800
iformfrq2 = 1150
iformfrq3 = 2800
iformfrq4 = 3500

ibandw1 = 80
ibandw2 = 90
ibandw3 = 120
ibandw4 = 130

; we'll leave these at their default values:
kris init 0.003
kdur init 0.02
kdec init 0.007
iolaps = 14850

ifna = 1
ifnb = 2

; now for a little fun with LFOs:
iformlforate = 4.0
iformlfoamt = 30
iamplforate = 2
iamplfoamt = 0.03
kformlfo oscil iformlfoamt, iformlforate, 1
kamplfo oscil iamplfoamt, iamplforate, 1

kformfrq1 = iformfrq1 + kformlfo
kformfrq2 = iformfrq2 + kformlfo
kformfrq3 = iformfrq3 + kformlfo
kformfrq4 = iformfrq4 + kformlfo
```

```
kenv1 expseg 0.0001, iatk1, iamp1, (idur - (iatk1 + irel1)), \
  iamp1, irel1, 0.0001
kenv2 expseg 0.0001, iatk2, iamp2, (idur - (iatk2 + irel2)), \
  iamp2, irel2, 0.0001
kenv3 expseg 0.0001, iatk3, iamp3, (idur - (iatk3 + irel3)), \
  iamp3, irel3, 0.0001
kenv4 expseg 0.0001, iatk4, iamp4, (idur - (iatk4 + irel4)), \
  iamp4, irel4, 0.0001

kamp1 = (1 + kamplfo) * kenv1
kamp2 = (1 + kamplfo) * kenv2
kamp3 = (1 + kamplfo) * kenv3
kamp4 = (1 + kamplfo) * kenv4

a1 fof kamp1, ifund, kformfrq1, ioct, ibandw1, kris, kdur, kdec, \
  iolaps, ifna, ifnb, idur
a2 fof kamp2, ifund, kformfrq2, ioct, ibandw2, kris, kdur, kdec, \
  iolaps, ifna, ifnb, idur
a3 fof kamp3, ifund, kformfrq3, ioct, ibandw3, kris, kdur, kdec, \
  iolaps, ifna, ifnb, idur
a4 fof kamp4, ifund, kformfrq3, ioct, ibandw4, kris, kdur, kdec, \
  iolaps, ifna, ifnb, idur

asig = a1 + a2 + a3 + a4
  outs asig, asig
endin
</CsInstruments>
<CsScore>

; a sine wave:
f1 0 8192 10 1
; a curve for shaping the grains:
f2 0 1024 19 0.5 0.5 270 0.5

; play three notes:
i1 0 2 0.2 250 0
i1 2.1 2 0.1 350 0
i1 4.2 3 0.2 350 2
e
```

This example produces three stationary tones with a bit of vibrato and tremolo. Because each formant has its own overall attack and release time (not to be confused with the `kris` and `kdec` values for the individual grains), the tone has a bit of shape. But much more can be done with this example. The code example for `fof` in the manual, for instance, uses `line` opcodes to glide the formant frequencies, amplitudes, and bandwidths during the course of a single note, so that the vocal tone shifts from one vowel to another. For more realistic vocal synthesis, you may want to vary the speed and depth of the LFOs or glide smoothly from one pitch to another. And of course, many combinations of formants produce vowel-like tones that are not possible with the human vocal tract, so singing aliens are a distinct possibility.

Sample Playback

Csound has a number of opcodes with which you can play back audio samples stored on your hard drive. Normally these samples will be in the form of .WAV or AIFF files. In addition, a whole family of opcodes (the so-called Fluid opcodes) is available for playing files in the popular SoundFont format. We'll have more to say about the Fluid opcodes below.

Before playing a .WAV or AIFF file, you'll need to load it into an f-table. This is done using GEN 01. One potentially tricky point about GEN 01 is that it expects you to tell it the size of the file in samples. You may not know this. You can enter a 0 as this parameter and let Csound figure it out, but if you do so, you may have trouble further on down the line, as the `table` opcode doesn't like deferred-size tables.

To find the size of a file, you can start with a deferred-size table (setting size to 0 in the GEN routine), use the `tableng` opcode to determine the size, and then use `print` to print the value out to the Console:

```
giSample ftgen 0, 0, 0, 1, "gtrA4.aiff", 0, 0, 0
instr 1
ilen tableng giSample
print ilen
endin
```

When I played a short score that triggered `instr 1`, I learned that my file was 168,020 samples long. Normally, a GEN routine needs to see a power of 2 or a power-of-2-plus-1 as its size, but you can override this by setting a negative value for size, so I replaced my `ftgen` line with this:

```
giSample ftgen 0, 0, -168020, 1, "gtrA4.aiff", 0, 0, 0
```

Once you've gone through these steps, you'll be ready to try sample playback.

Sample Playback Using table

The simplest way to play a sample uses the `table` opcode. Starting with the monaural waveform loaded into the `giSample` table as shown above, the instrument below will play the sample exactly once, at its original pitch. It will play the sample from start to end, no matter how long or short it is, and no matter how long or short the score event triggering the instrument may be:

```
instr 1
iamp = p4
ilen tableng giSample
p3 = ilen/sr
aphas phasor 1/p3
aphas = aphas * ilen
asig table aphas, giSample
asig = asig * iamp
outs asig, asig
endin
```

This instrument gets the length of the sample using `tableng` and then resets p3 (the length of the score event) to the length divided by the sample rate at which the orchestra is playing. A `phasor` then creates a ramp that moves from 0 to 1 exactly once during the (revised) length of the note. This phase value is multiplied by the sample length, so that the `table` opcode can sweep through the entire table exactly once during the note.

Starting from this template, you should find it fairly easy to play the sample faster or slower, to repeat it in a loop, or to start at a later point than the beginning of the sample. For instance, if you want to play the sample an octave lower (in which case it will last twice as long), substitute this line:

```
p3 = (ilen/sr) * 2
```

However, Csound provides some tools to make such modifications easier.

Using loscil

When using `loscil`, we can skip the messy calculations in the example above. The following instrument is much simpler. If all we want to do is play a sample at its original pitch, we'll get the same result:

```
instr 1
iamp = p4
ilen tableng giSample
p3 = ilen/sr
asig loscil iamp, 1, giSample, 1, 0
outs asig, asig
endin
```

Here, I've taken advantage of the ability of `loscil` to figure out the sample's pitch. I've set the arguments for `kcps` and `ibas` both to 1. I also set `imod` to 0 to tell `loscil` that I didn't want a loop. But much more can be done with `loscil`. For reference, here is its prototype:

```
ar1 [,ar2] loscil xamp, kcps, ifn [, ibas] [, imod1] [, ibeg1] [, iend1] \
    [, imod2] [, ibeg2] [, iend2]
```

You'll find several examples illustrating the use of `loscil` in Chapter 3. Reading the manual will provide details on the meanings of the arguments shown in the prototype. Two or three points may be worth mentioning. First, `loscil` will work with either mono or stereo soundfiles. Second, it always starts playback from the beginning of the file—it doesn't provide a way to skip the beginning of the file. If you want to start playback at some point after the beginning of the file, you'll want to adapt the code shown earlier that uses `phasor` and `table`.

Third, with `loscil` you can specify both sustain and release loops. The release loop makes use of the same mechanism as envelope generators with the -r suffix, such as `linsegr`. If one of these is included in the instrument, then `loscil` will finish the sustain loop and move on to the release loop when the normal duration of the note (set by p3) is finished and the release segment (the final time value of the -r envelope) begins. Here's an example. It mangles a sampled stereo drum pattern by interrupting the loop with a short back-and-forth loop and also introducing a pitch envelope. The length of the entire sample (298,141 sample words) was determined using the technique discussed earlier in this section, using `tableng` and `print`.

```
giSample ftgen 0, 0, -298141, 1, "Drumloop 01.wav", 0, 0, 0
instr 1
idur = p3
iamp = p4
iatk = 0.005
isus = idur - iatk
irel = 5
kamp linsegr 0, iatk, iamp, isus, iamp, irel, 0
kfrq linseg 1, iatk, 1.2, isus, 0.8, irel, 2
aL, aR loscil kamp, kfrq, giSample, 1, 2, 10000, 18000, 2, 39000, 46000
outs aL, aR
endin
```

Using flooper

If you don't need both sustain and release loops, `flooper` may be the tool for the job. Its prototype is:

```
asig flooper kamp, kpitch, istart, idur, ifad, ifn
```

The value of kpitch is interpreted as a multiplier of the base frequency of the loop; it can be negative for reverse playback. The other parameters specify the start point of the playback loop, the loop's duration, the crossfade time, and the f-table number.

Crossfading between the end of a loop and the start of the next play-through of the loop has been a standard technique of sampling since the 1980s. It isn't always needed with drum loops, where a clearly articulated rhythm is preferred, but can work very well to smooth out loops of sustaining sounds.

Smooth Loop Strategies   When an audio recording (a sample) is played back over and over in a looped fashion, the playback mechanism (such as a Csound opcode) jumps from the end of the loop back to the beginning. If the value of the last data word at the end of the loop is not the same as the value of the first data word at the beginning of the loop, you'll hear a click.

If both the end of the loop and the beginning are on zero-crossings—points where the waveform crosses from a positive value to a negative value or vice versa—there won't be a click. In fact, the loop start and end points can be at any value, as long as the two values are the same, but for technical reasons, some early samplers required that the loop points be at a zero-crossing, so setting loop points at zero-crossings has become standard practice.

Another technique that avoids clicks is back-and-forth looping. The loop is played forward until the end point is reached, then played backward until the start point is reached, then played forward again, and so on. In this situation the start point is never directly joined to the end point, so there's no click.

A third method is to crossfade between the data at the end of the loop and the data at the start.

flooper operates in mono, so if we want to use it to play a stereo sample, we have to create two separate f-tables using GEN 01. One table will contain the left-channel data and the other table the right-channel data. This is done by setting the channel argument (the final argument) to GEN 01 to either 1 (for the left channel) or 2 (for the right channel). During playback, the two channels don't have to stay in sync; the left and right channel loops can split apart if desired.

The start, duration, and crossfade time of flooper are set in seconds. The crossfade must be shorter than the duration of the loop.

Using diskin2
All of the sample playback methods discussed so far in this section require that the audio data be loaded into RAM before (or during) playback. Given the amount of RAM available in today's computers, this may not seem to be a problem, but due to the way Csound uses floating-point arithmetic, the upper limit of RAM-based audio is about a minute per sound. (You can load

many sound samples into RAM, of course.) In order to play single sounds that are longer than a minute, you'll need to stream audio directly from a hard disk file using the `diskin2` opcode.

`diskin2` provides several options, including transposing the audio up or down in pitch and playing it backwards, but the basic version could hardly be easier to use:

```
instr 1
aL, aR diskin2 "finalMix.wav", 1
outs aL, aR
endin
```

The Fluid Opcodes

SoundFonts are a data format for music synthesis that was developed by E-MU Systems and Creative Labs in the early 1990s. SoundFonts are instrument definitions in which samples are mapped to a MIDI keyboard, often with other features such as envelopes and sample loop points built into the SoundFont. Given that this format was developed for consumer-grade devices, primarily PC soundcards, it may seem odd to want to use SoundFonts in a high-quality system optimized for experimental sound programming—but if you want to use SoundFonts in Csound you can do it, using the Fluid opcodes. You might want to do this if you have a SoundFont that you're fond of and want to use in a piece of music, or for satirical purposes.

SoundFonts of various kinds are available for download from the Internet, some of them free and some as commercial products. If you're using a recent installation of Csound for Windows, you'll find the file sf_GMbank.sf2 in the Samples directory of your Csound directory; if you're running Mac OS or Linux and want to use this file, post a message to the Csound mailing list, and probably somebody will be willing to send it to you. This 4-MB file includes a full set of General MIDI sounds.

To use a SoundFont in Csound, you need to take five steps. The first three would normally be done in the orchestra header, the final two in one or more instruments.

1. Activate the FluidSynth engine using `fluidEngine`.

2. Load a SoundFont file using `fluidLoad`.

3. Tell the engine what sound within the file you want to play by passing a specific bank and preset number to `fluidProgramSelect`.

4. Play one or more notes on the sound using `fluidNote`.

5. Capture the output sound stream using `fluidOut` and send it to Csound's output.

Some of these opcodes have features we won't discuss here; they're explained in the manual. Instead, we'll jump straight to a code example that uses them to play a little music. Before we do that, though, we need to clear up one question.

A single SoundFont file can contain numerous sounds. The sf_GMbank.sf2 file, in fact, contains a couple of hundred. In Step 3, you'll be choosing a particular sound by bank and preset number.

So how do you know what's available in the file? The solution is to pass a non-zero number to `fluidLoad` as the optional `ilistpresets` argument. This will cause the entire contents of the file to be listed to the Output Console, complete with sound names and their associated bank and preset numbers. Scroll up in the Console pane in CsoundQt (or in the terminal, if you're running Csound from the command line) to view the list.

The example below instantiates a FluidSynth engine and selects presets for it on channels 1 and 2, in order to play two different GM sounds. The SoundFont file can be specified using a complete directory structure from the root of your hard drive, or the file can be stored in the SSDIR you have chosen.

```
sr = 44100
ksmps = 4
nchnls = 2
0dbfs = 1

; start an engine:
giEngine fluidEngine

; load the GM SoundFont bank into the engine:
giSFnum fluidLoad "sf_GMbank.sf2", giEngine, 1

; select active sounds for two channels (bank 0, preset 0 and bank 0,
; preset 83):
fluidProgramSelect giEngine, 1, giSFnum, 0, 0
fluidProgramSelect giEngine, 2, giSFnum, 0, 83

instr 1, 2          ; play a note, using p1 to choose a channel:
ichan = p1
inote = p4
ivel = p5
fluidNote giEngine, ichan, inote, ivel
endin

instr 99            ; capture the stereo output signal
                    ; and send it to Csound's output:

iamp = p4
asigL, asigR fluidOut giEngine
asigL = asigL * iamp
asigR = asigR * iamp
outs asigL, asigR

</CsInstruments>
<CsScore>
```

```
t0 100

; play some notes on channel 1:
i1  0   7    48   60
i1  0   7    52
i1  0   7    55
i1  0   0.8  60   100
i1  1   .    64   70
i1  2   .    67   100
i1  3   .    64   70
i1  4   3    60   100

; play some notes on channel 2:
i2  0   0.333 72  60
i2  +   .     71
i2  +   .     72
i2  +   .     67
i2  +   .     69
i2  +   .     71
i2  +   4     72

; capture the output and play it:
i99 0 8 7
```

To play a SoundFont from a MIDI keyboard would require a few minor alterations to this code; see Chapter 10 for more on real-time MIDI with Csound.

It's also quite practical to send MIDI control change messages to a SoundFont preset while it plays using `fluidCCk`. Of course, you may not know how the preset will respond (if at all) until you try it. To add a mod wheel (CC1) move to the code above, create this instrument:

```
instr 11  ; send mod wheel to channel 2:
kmod line 0, p3, 127
kmod = int(kmod)
fluidCCk giEngine, 2, 1, kmod
endin
```

Then add this line to the score:

```
i11 2 2
```

Assuming you're using the sf_GMbank.sf2 file, you should hear vibrato being added to the lead synth sound on the final note.

Physical Models

Physical modeling is a general term for the concept of building a mathematical model of a physical process and then using the model to synthesize sound. The physical process might involve striking an object (such as a piece of wood or metal) or blowing into a tube. Inevitably, the model will be a less than exact description of every aspect of the physical process, but some physical models reproduce the most audible characteristics of acoustic sounds with remarkable fidelity.

Csound includes a number of opcodes that implement physical models of various kinds. You'll find a link to the "Models and Emulations" page in the Signal Generators section in the left pane of the HTML manual. More models are found on the "Waveguide Physical Modeling" page. We don't have space in *Csound Power!* to discuss all of these opcodes in detail. Some are better designed than others, and some are easier to use than others.

Experimentation may help you find some good settings, but there are no guarantees. Physical models tend to be very sensitive to the settings you give them, and extremely loud outputs are not unheard of. I failed to find anything that I liked using `gogobel` or `marimba`. With proper settings for `bar-model` I got a lovely metallic tone, but it had a null in the middle—it faded out and then back in.

The `bamboo` opcode models a shaken set of bamboo sticks. It's easy to use and sounds good. You can specify three resonant frequencies; if you don't use the defaults, your "bamboo" may sound nothing like the real thing, but it might have a hauntingly harsh or hollow quality. These settings, chosen almost at random, give a gargling effect:

```
asig bamboo 0.2, p3, 3, 0, 0.3, 500, 1078, 2249
```

You'll find that the output amplitude of `bamboo` is higher than the `xamp` argument would indicate. It depends partly on the value for the `imaxshake` argument (0.3 in the code above).

Another winner is `vibes`. Like some other models, `vibes` requires a sampled impulse to model the striking of the mallet against the metal bar. The file marmstk1.aif is suitable, and it may be distributed with your copy of Csound. If not, it's available online. A sine wave table is also needed, to model the vibraphone's characteristic tremolo (referred to in the manual, incorrectly, as vibrato). Here is an example:

```
giSine ftgen 0, 0, 8192, 10, 1
giSample ftgen 0, 0, -1023, 1, \
  "C:/Users/Jim Aikin/My Documents/csound scores/audio/marmstk1.aif",
0, 0, 0

instr 1
asig vibes 0.2, p4, 0.5, 0.5, giSample, 0.8, 0.6, giSine, 0.1
```

```
outs asig, asig
endin

</CsInstruments>
<CsScore>

i1 0 3 300
i1 0.5 . 400
i1 1 . 500
```

I derived the values for the tremolo (0.8, 0.6) experimentally; they seem realistic. The amplitude value shown (0.2) produces an output signal with a value of more than 0.6. As usual with physical models, be prepared to lower the output amplitude as needed.

Waveguide Models

Among the waveguide models, `wgbowedbar` produces a pleasant tone, though I found it desirable to use an amplitude envelope, as this opcode seems to start with a pop that overloads the audio output briefly.

`wgpluck` makes pleasant plucked-string tones. You'll want the damping argument to this opcode to track the pitch argument in some manner; a single damping value across a wide pitch range will produce unrealistically long sustains at low pitches or very short tones at high pitches.

As a string player, I don't feel `wgbow` is terribly realistic, but it produces tones that are bound to be useful in some musical situations. You can easily experiment with the example in the manual by substituting moving envelopes for the fixed k-rate values given.

Envelope Generators

Shaping each sound in your music so that it changes, subtly or drastically, from moment to moment is a basic necessity of sound synthesis. Csound provides several ways to generate moving control signals (envelopes). We can read the data in a table directly and modulate some aspect of the signal with it; see the section "Table Operations" later in this chapter for more on this idea. An instrument can receive and make use of external signals, which could come from MIDI, from another software program running concurrently, or from another Csound instrument. The `follow` and `follow2` opcodes (not discussed in this book) perform as envelope followers.

The most basic way of creating envelopes, however, is using Csound's rich supply of envelope generators—and these are the subject of this section of *Csound Power!* You'll find these opcodes listed on two pages in the Opcodes Overview list in the left pane of *The Canonical Csound Reference Manual*: They're listed in the "Envelope Generators" and "Linear and Exponential Generators" pages.

The linseg Opcode

A good basic envelope generator to know about is `linseg`. As the name might suggest, `linseg` constructs an envelope out of line segments—an arbitrary number of them. Here is the prototype for `linseg`:

```
kres linseg ia, idur1, ib [, idur2] [, ic] [...]
```

The inputs to `linseg` are, alternately, levels and durations (the latter in seconds). The `ia` parameter is the starting level, `idur1` is the amount of time required to reach level `ib`, and so forth. There must always be an odd number of inputs, because the last value has to be a level, not a duration.

Tip   The `linseg` page in the 5.13 version of the manual is in error on one important point. It alleges that if the note hasn't ended, the output level of this opcode will continue to rise or fall after the final level is reached. This is not correct. When `linseg` reaches its last level, it stays there. Other modulation sources, including `line` and `expseg`, will, however, continue to rise or fall after their final defined point is reached if the note event is still active.

Because `linseg` can be given as many segments as you like, it's useful for producing complex attack transients. Here is an example of an amplitude envelope with a triple attack:

```
iamp = 0.5
ifall = p3 - 0.25
kamp linseg 0, 0.01, iamp, 0.03, 0, 0.05, iamp, 0.07, 0, 0.09,\
   iamp, ifall, 0
asig oscil kamp, 400, giSine
```

The level values in this example are, in order, 0, `iamp`, 0, `iamp`, 0, and `iamp`. The durations are 0.01, 0.03, and so forth. The value of `ifall` is calculated by subtracting the total of the other durations from p3, which as usual is the length of the note as set by the score.

The levels of a `linseg` envelope don't have to be positive, nor does the first or last level have to be 0. If it's being used as an amplitude envelope for an audio signal, however, both of these would be standard practice. From my experiments, it appears that the first duration value for `linseg` can't be 0, though subsequent times can be. This is sensible: If you want zero time to elapse between the first and second level values, just start the envelope with the second level. Setting two initial levels to 0, however, is useful: This will delay the onset of the envelope:

```
kamp linseg 0, 1, 0, 0.1, iamp, p3 - 1.25, iamp, 0.15, 0
```

You'll note that the arguments to `linseg`, as with other Csound envelope generators, are i-time arguments. That is, they're set up at the beginning of the note and don't change after that (unless the instrument code uses `reinit`, which can restart the envelope with different values—for more on `reinit`, see the "Instrument Control" section later in this chapter). The main exception to this rule is `loopseg`, which is discussed below.

The line Opcode

`line` is very simple: It takes starting and ending values, and a time duration. During the specified time, `line` produces a ramp from the starting value to the ending value. If the note hasn't ended at that point, the value produced by `line` will continue to rise or fall at the same rate. If you need to stop the rise or fall before the end of the note, use `linseg` instead.

The expseg Opcode

`expseg` operates much like `linseg`, but with one important difference: The segments of the output envelope contour are exponential curves rather than straight lines. This has an important consequence: The level values of `expseg` cannot be 0, and they all have to have the same sign. That is, they can all be negative or all positive, but the values in the output can't cross zero. If you want an `expseg` envelope to have a level that is functionally 0, give it a very small positive level, such as 0.0001.

The difference in shape between linear and exponential envelope segments is partially a matter of musical taste, but it can have some significant consequences. Perhaps the easiest way to hear the difference is to use the envelope to modulate the pitch of an oscillator. Here's an instrument and a score:

```
instr 1
iamp = 0.5
kpitch expseg 0.001, 1, 400, 2, 0.001
kpitch = kpitch + 400
asig oscil iamp, kpitch, 1
aout linen asig, 0.01, p3, 0.1
outs aout, aout
endin
</CsInstruments>
<CsScore>
f1 0 8192 10 1
i1 0 3
```

The `expseg` pitch envelope here is the same duration as the note (three seconds). Because the start and end levels are well below 1, the concave curvature of the segments is very audible: The envelope spends most of its time below 1, then rises quickly to 400 and almost as quickly falls back. If you replace `expseg` with `linseg` in this instrument, the difference will be clear.

If you need an envelope whose curvature varies from segment to segment, use `transeg`.

-r, release, and xtratim

Normally, a Csound event starts and stops at precisely the time specified in the score. If you're starting an event from an instrument using the `event`, `scoreline`, or `schedkwhen` opcode, the start time will depend on when the opcode is invoked, but the duration of the event, as determined by p3, is not in doubt. After p3 seconds (or p3 beats—if the event is listed in the score, the actual value of p3 will depend on the tempo setting as defined in the t statement), the event will stop.

This makes calculating the lengths of envelopes a bit tedious. If the waveform being generated by the instrument doesn't happen to be at a zero-crossing when the event ends, you'll hear a click, so you need to reason backwards in order to calculate the desired values for the amplitude envelope.

Fortunately, there's an easier way. Several of Csound's envelope generators, including linseg, expseg, and transeg, have alternate versions whose names end with -r: linsegr, expsegr, and transegr. These envelope generators will automatically sustain at their next-to-last level setting until the note reaches its nominal endpoint. They will then add a release segment to the envelope. The release segment adds actual time to the length of the note, during which the opcode will proceed through its last time value to its last level value.

Here's a simple example. The note in the score lasts for only one second, but the audio output is a four-second note, because linsegr has a three-second release segment:

```
instr 1
iamp = 0.5
kamp linsegr 0, 0.1, iamp, 0.1, iamp, 3, 0
asig foscil kamp, 300, 1, 1, 1, 1
outs asig, asig
endin
</CsInstruments>
<CsScore>
f1 0 8192 10 1
i1 0 1
```

The main limitation of these opcodes is that the envelope can have only a single release segment. If you need more complex behavior from a note as it is dying away, the opcodes to use are release and xtratim.

As you might guess from its name, xtratim adds length to the end of a note. It takes one input—the number of seconds to add. release is a sensing opcode: It outputs 0 until the extra time segment added by xtratim begins, and thereafter it outputs 1. release also senses when the note event has gone into its release segment due to the use of an -r envelope opcode.

Using a little logic and Csound's kgoto opcode, we can create a second envelope that only kicks in when the release starts. This can then be used to create a composite envelope shape that has several release segments. Here's an example that illustrates this technique:

```
instr 1
iamp = 0.5
xtratim 2
```

```
krel init 0 ; a trigger for the release envelope --
krel release ; krel goes to 1 when the release segment begins
if krel == 1 kgoto rel

kmp1 linseg 0, .3, 1, 0.7, 0.3
kamp = kmp1*iamp
kgoto done

rel:
kmp2 linseg 1, .08, 0, .08, 1, .08, 0, .08, 1, .08, 0, .08, 1, 1.5, 0
kamp = kmp1*kmp2*iamp

done:
asig foscil kamp, 300, 1, 1, 1, 1
outs asig, asig
endin

</CsInstruments>
<CsScore>

f1 0 8192 10 1
i1 0 1
```

This instrument uses Csound's ability to jump to a user-named label while the instrument is running. For more on this technique, see "Logic and Flow Control" in Chapter 6. In this instrument, when the release segment begins, release gives krel a value of 1. As long as krel is 0, the first linseg operates. It puts a value in kmp1. This is multiplied by iamp (the overall amplitude value). Then the instrument jumps straight over the second linseg and goes to the label done:.

When krel becomes 1, the flow of operations through the instrument changes. The first linseg envelope is now bypassed. Instead, the flow jumps ahead to the rel: label. The first linseg is no longer active, so its final output value (whatever that happens to be) stays in the variable kmp1. The second linseg now begins to run. Its output (kmp2) is multiplied appropriately, producing a new value for kamp.

The linen Opcode

Most Csound envelope generators simply produce control signals. linen is unusual in that it can also *process* a signal, eliminating the need for a separate output variable. If you're familiar with analog synthesis, you can think of linen as including both a simple contour generator and a VCA.

Here is the prototype of linen. It has both a-rate and k-rate forms.

```
ares linen xamp, irise, idur, idec
kres linen kamp, irise, idur, idec
```

The three parameters irise, idur, and idec are all time values, stated in seconds. irise is the amount of time linen takes to rise from 0 to the value in xamp or kamp, and idec is the amount of time it takes to fall back to 0.

Because of the way the input parameters are laid out, it would be easy to assume that idur represents the sustain portion of the envelope—that is, that after rising to its peak during the time of irise, linen will remain at the peak for idur seconds and then begin to fall. This is not correct. In fact, idur represents the total length of the envelope, from the beginning of the rise segment to the end of the decay segment.

As the manual points out, another common error is to assume that after falling back to 0 at the end of the decay segment, the output of linen will stay at 0. In reality, it will continue to fall. If the note hasn't yet ended, linen will "go negative." The result will depend on how you've designed your instrument. If you're using linen for an amplitude envelope, you need to understand that a negative amplitude is the same as a positive amplitude with the polarity of the signal reversed. Incorrectly calculating the length of idur can cause the instrument's output level to increase drastically during the final portion of a note, so be careful.

If you use a constant value for the kamp argument, linen will produce a rise/sustain/fall envelope signal, which can be used as an input for some other module, or in an equation. But you can instead feed a signal into linen, like this:

```
iatk = 0.1
idec = 0.1
idur = p3
asig oscil iamp, 400, giSine
aout linen asig, iatk, idur, idec
outs aout, aout
```

Here, the signal coming from oscil is an input to linen, and the output of linen is sent directly to outs so we can listen to it. This works perfectly well. Still another alternative is to feed an LFO signal through linen and use it to shape the amount of LFO modulation. What linen doesn't do in the latter situation is, it doesn't operate as a lag processor. That is, if you use an LFO signal with a rapid rise and fall, while linen itself has a slow rise and fall, you'll still hear the full LFO waveform during the sustain portion of the linen contour; the peaks and dips of the LFO wave won't be smoothed out. (And that's a good thing, because if they were, linen wouldn't be usable as an audio-rate VCA.)

transeg

If you've ever programmed sounds in a feature-rich software synthesizer plug-in, you may know that the line segments that make up an envelope don't have to be straight lines; nor does the sound designer have to make an either-or choice between a straight line and an exponential curve. Instead, you can grab a "curvature handle" in the middle of any envelope segment and drag the handle up or down. The curve of the segment can be very convex, very concave, or anywhere in between.

In Csound, the same results are achieved (without graphic editing) using transeg. Using transeg is slightly more complicated than using linseg or expseg, because each segment of the envelope needs three input values, not two. After the initial level parameter (the point at which the envelope starts), transeg expects to see a duration, a curve type, and a destination level for each segment.

The type parameter operates in a sensible way. A value of 0 produces a linear segment. When the value is above 0, the segment moves toward the destination level more slowly and then speeds up. When the value is below 0, the segment moves more rapidly toward the destination level and then slows down as it nears the destination. With envelope segments that rise, in other words, a curve value greater than 0 produces a concave shape, while a value less than 0 produces a convex shape. With segments that fall, it's the other way around: Values greater than 0 produce a convex curve.

This explanation may be clearer if you experiment a bit with transeg. Start with this instrument and score:

```
instr 1
iamp = 0.5
icurve1 = 0
icurve2 = 0
kpitch transeg 300, 1, icurve1, 450, 1, icurve2, 300
kamp linseg 0, 0.1, iamp, p3 - 0.25, iamp, 0.15, 0
asig foscil kamp, kpitch, 1, 1, 1, 1
outs asig, asig
endin


</CsInstruments>
<CsScore>


f1 0 8192 10 1
i1 0 4
```

Here, transeg is creating a pitch envelope, because that makes it easier to hear what it's doing. The two curve type parameters are 0 in the code above. Replace them with values between –100 and 100, and listen to the results.

loopseg

The Csound envelope generators we've looked at so far are one-directional: They start and then move forward until either they reach their end or the note event ends. With `loopseg`, we can construct a looping envelope. This opcode has a couple of features that differ from the features of other envelope generators. Here is the prototype:

```
ksig loopseg kfreq, ktrig, ktime0, kvalue0 [, ktime1] [, kvalue1] \
   [, ktime2] [, kvalue2] [...]
```

Whenever `ktrig` is non-zero, the envelope will start over. This feature has to be used with care, as `loopseg` will simply jump back to its starting value, which may cause a click.

Unlike other Csound envelope generators, `loopseg` interprets the time values starting with `ktime1` not as absolute measurements in seconds, but as proportions of the whole envelope length. The length of the envelope is inversely proportional to `kfreq`: That is, a larger value of `kfreq` will produce a faster loop. The value for the `kfreq` input should be in Hz (cycles per second). If `loopseg` sees three time parameters of 2, 1, and 1, for instance, it interprets these as proportions. The first segment will take up half of the total length, whatever that is, while the latter two segments will each take a quarter of the length. The envelope will sound exactly the same if the three time parameters are set to 200, 100, and 100, because the proportions will be the same.

However, the value of the `ktime0` parameter is different. This parameter is interpreted as a starting phase value. It tells `loopseg` how far into the loop you want the cycle to start. For instance:

```
kpitch loopseg 1, ktrig, 0.6, 0, 0.01, 1, 0.99, 0, 0.01, 1, 0.49, 0, \
   0.01, 1, 0.49, 0, 0.01, 1, 0.49, 0
```

This looping envelope has a five-beat pattern. (If you add the values for `ktime1` and so on, you'll find that they total 2.5.) The first peak lasts for two beats, the following three peaks for one beat each. If we consider that it's a pattern in 5/8 time, the loop would be QEEE, QEEE, and so on (where Q=quarter note and E=eighth note). Because `ktime0` is set to 0.6, the pattern will start playing 3/5 of the way into the loop: The first iteration will be EE, followed by QEEE and so on. Note, also, that this parameter is misnamed in the manual: It's an i-time parameter and won't accept a k-rate input. It really ought to be called `iphs`, not `ktime0`.

The frequency of `loopseg` can be either positive or negative. If it's negative, `loopseg` will run backward. You can even run `loopseg` forward and backward alternately, using a `phasor`, like this:

```
kphas phasor 0.8
kphas = (kphas - 0.5) * 2
kpitch loopseg kphas, 0, 0, 0, 0.01, 1, 0.99, 0, 0.01, 1, 0.49, 0, \
   0.01, 1, 0.49, 0, 0.01, 1, 0.49, 0
```

If you do this, you'll discover that the value of ktime0 will affect not only the starting point of the loop, but the shape of the loop on each iteration. I'm not sure exactly what's going on in this situation, but it may not matter: Adjust the values until you like what you hear, and you'll be fine.

The next example, which produces a sort of odd satirical take on the four-on-the-floor kick drum, uses three instances of loopseg to control amplitude, pitch, and FM index. The first is set to a frequency of 1 Hz, the second to 0.8 Hz, and the third to 1.2 Hz. As a result, the loop pattern repeats once every five seconds. However, if you uncomment the line with metro (by removing the semicolon), the composite loop will re-trigger every 2.5 seconds.

```
instr 1
iamp = 0.5
ktrig init 0
; ktrig metro 0.4

kamp loopseg 1, ktrig, 0, 0, 0.01, 1, 0.99, 0, 0.01, 1, 0.49, 0, \
    0.01, 1, 0.49, 0
kdeclick linseg 1, p3 - 0.2, 1, 0.15, 0
kamp = iamp * kdeclick * kamp

kpitch loopseg 0.8, ktrig, 0, 0, 0.01, 1, 0.99, 0, 0.01, 1, 0.49, 0, \
    0.01, 1, 0.49, 0, 0.01, 1, 0.49, 0
kpitch = 60 + (40 * kpitch)

kindex loopseg 1.2, ktrig, 0, 0.75, 0.6, 2, 0.4, 0, 0.5, 0.75

asig foscil kamp, kpitch, 1, 1, kindex, 1
outs asig, asig
endin

</CsInstruments>
<CsScore>

f1 0 8192 10 1
i1 0 15
```

There's a lot more to explore in loopseg territory; I'll leave you to dig into it on your own. Each of the arguments to loopseg (except for ktime0, as noted above) can be k-rate if desired, so the shape of a loop can be changed drastically while it's playing. The loopsegp opcode is even more interesting, because it takes a moving phase input instead of a frequency. As a result, it can slow down and speed up during a given cycle, or even reverse direction. Finally, looptseg is a hybrid of loopseg and transeg: Each segment has a type parameter, which controls its curvature.

LFOs

As discussed in the previous section, the `loopseg` opcodes are a powerful source of repeating low-frequency modulation signals. In other words, they can operate as LFOs. But in many musical situations, simpler solutions will work. Even `oscil`, which can produce a wide variety of waveforms and provides control over the starting phase, may provide more features than we need. The simplest way to set up an LFO is by using the `lfo` opcode.

This opcode can run at a-rate. Most often the k-rate version will do the job. Here is the prototype:

```
kres lfo kamp, kcps [, itype]
```

The amplitude (`kamp`) and frequency (`kcps`) inputs should be familiar to you if you've been patiently plodding through *Csound Power!* page by page. The `itype` parameter can be set to an integer between 0 and 5. As the manual explains, these settings will produce, respectively, sine, triangle, bipolar square, unipolar square, rising sawtooth, and falling sawtooth waves. Both of the sawtooth outputs are unipolar. The default is the sine wave.

The vibrato of singers and performers on acoustic instruments is not absolutely steady, but alters in speed and depth in response to moment-to-moment expressive concerns. Some sound designers feel that this type of "human" vibrato can be effectively mimicked using subtle random changes. To provide an LFO that produces such changes, Csound provides the `vibrato` opcode. This has eight k-rate inputs; I'll leave you to discover them by reading the manual. Here is a basic example that uses `vibrato`:

```
instr 1
iamp = 0.4
kvib vibrato 7, 5, 0.1, 0.1, 3, 5, 4, 7, 1
kamp linseg 0, 0.1, iamp, p3 - 0.25, iamp, 0.15, 0
asig foscil kamp, 200 + kvib, 5, 1, 1.5, 1
outs asig, asig
endin

</CsInstruments>
<CsScore>

f1 0 8192 10 1
i1 0 6
```

The random amount of pitch and amplitude variation can be controlled with `vibrato`, as can the rapidity with which new random values are generated for each. And because the inputs for `kAverageAmp` and `kAverageFreq` are k-rate, the possibility of shaping the vibrato in non-random ways is preserved.

A significant limitation of `lfo` is that its square wave always has a 50% duty cycle. That is, you can't vary its pulse width: It always spends 50% of its time in the "up" portion of the waveform and 50%

in the "down" portion. What if you want a trill (a common situation where a square wave is called for) but you want the lower pitch within the trill to last longer than the upper pitch or vice versa?

 A *pulse wave* spends some portion of its total wave cycle at a higher value and the rest at a lower value. In Csound, these values might be +1 and −1, so the pulse wave signal would be at +1 for a while, then at −1 for a while. The transition between −1 and +1 is called the **rising edge**, and the number of rising edges per second determines the frequency of the wave. The portion of the waveform that is +1 is called the **duty cycle**, and the percentage of time that the wave spends in its +1 state is called its **pulse width**. When the pulse width is 50%, the pulse wave is better known as a square wave.

The trick, in this case, is to apply the `pdhalfy` opcode to the output of a `phasor`, and then use `tablei` to read a table containing a square wave. (In fact, you can read any waveshape you like at this point. The signal coming from `phasor` will be skewed so that the first half of the table is read more quickly or more slowly than the second half.) For details, consult the page in the manual on `pdhalfy`. Here is a working example, which omits, like many of the examples in this book, the standard orchestra header:

```
giWave ftgen 0, 0, 8192, 10, 1, 0.7, 0.4
giSquare ftgen 0, 0, 8192, 7, 0, 2, -1, 4092, -1, 4, 1, 4094, 1, 2, 0

instr 1
; the pulse width is specified from -1 to +1:
kpw line -0.99, p3, 0.99
aphas phasor 3
ashift pdhalfy aphas, kpw
atrill tablei ashift, giSquare, 1 ; trill output is +/-1
ktrill downsamp atrill
ktrill = ktrill * 0.5 + 0.5

ibasefreq = 300
itopfreq = 450
kpitch = ibasefreq + (ktrill * (itopfreq - ibasefreq))

asig oscili 0.8, kpitch, giWave
outs asig, asig
endin

</CsInstruments>
<CsScore>

i1 0 10
```

When you run this, you should hear that when the trill starts, the lower pitch lasts longer than the upper pitch. As the note continues, the percentage of time spent in each state will tilt toward the upper pitch. This is because of the `line` opcode, which is ramping the value of `kpw` upward. This variable instructs `pdhalfy` how to tilt the value in `aphas`. The result, `atrill`, is then downsampled to k-rate using `downsamp`. (This is not necessary in the example, but if you want to use `foscili` rather than `oscili` to generate an FM tone, it becomes necessary, because `foscili` won't accept an a-rate input for its pitch.)

The rather odd-looking formula used to compute `kpitch` relies on the fact that the data stored in `giSquare` has a value that runs from –1 to +1. We multiply this by 0.5 and then add 0.5, so that the value of `ktrill` is now in the 0–1 range. When it's 0, we hear the pitch value stored in `ibasefreq` unaltered. When it's 1, we add the difference between `itopfreq` and `ibasefreq` to `ibasefreq`, thus producing the value of `itopfreq`. In practice, you might define both of these frequencies using p-fields in the score, so as to be able to produce trills of any pitch depth.

Just for fun, you might want the modulating pulse wave to pan the output alternately to the left and right speakers as well as changing the pitch. If you apply the `ktrill` signal to the `pan2` opcode, you'll hear clicks as the signal jumps around. We need to smooth it out a bit. In other words, we need to lowpass-filter it. A good opcode for lowpass-filtering is `tone`. However, `tone` won't filter k-rate signals, so we can't process `ktrill` through `tone`. Instead, we'll use `tonek`. Try replacing the `outs` line in the example with these three lines:

```
kpan tonek ktrill, 10
aoutL, aoutR pan2 asig, kpan
outs aoutL, aoutR
```

Now you should hear the pulse wave modulating the panning position of the signal, so that the lower pitch is heard in the left speaker and the upper pitch in the right speaker.

Filters

In the early days of electronic music synthesis, prior to about 1980, the raw tones that synthesizers could produce were quite limited. Analog synths were capable of generating only a few basic waveforms, sawtooth, pulse, triangle, and sine waves being the most common. Consequently, the filter was the most potent sound-shaping tool in the sound designer's toolbox. The mythology of filters—the legendary "fat" Moog filter, for instance—dates from this period.

Today, digital synthesizers can create tones of far greater complexity and interest. Consequently, the role of filters is somewhat reduced in importance. Nonetheless, filters remain an essential component in many types of sound design. Csound provides an almost bewildering variety of filters, which may be suitable for different purposes or different tastes.

A filter is a frequency-dependent amplifier. That is, it processes an audio signal by attenuating (reducing the amplitude of) the sound energy within some range of frequencies, while allowing the sound energy in other frequency ranges to pass through without attenuation. It may also boost the level of the sound energy in some range of frequencies.

Most sounds consist of or can be analyzed as a number of discrete sine waves, each with its own frequency and amplitude. These sine waves are called *partials*. A filter will typically alter the amplitudes of some of the partials in a signal, but not others. Noise signals are a special case, in that they contain (in theory) an infinite number of partials, each of which is randomly changing in amplitude. Nonetheless, noise contains sound energy at many different frequencies, so a filter can attenuate portions of the frequency spectrum of a noise signal.

The filter family also includes a specialized device called an *allpass filter* (implemented in Csound by the `alpass` opcode), which neither reduces nor boosts the sound level in any frequency range. Instead, it changes the phase relationships of various partials within the signal. Allpass filters are used in constructing reverb modules; by themselves, they have little or no effect on a tone passing through them, because the human ear is not sensitive to phase changes.

 Filter Terminology

- **Bandpass filter.** A filter that attenuates both low and high frequencies, allowing frequencies that lie between the stop-bands to pass through. A bandpass filter has two stop-bands, one below the pass-band and one above it.

- **Bandwidth.** The width of the pass-band in a bandpass filter.

- **Cutoff frequency.** The frequency that defines the transition point between a filter's pass-band and its stop-band. At the cutoff frequency, the filter should attenuate the signal by 3 dB.

- **Highpass filter.** A filter that attenuates low frequencies while allowing high frequencies to pass through.

- **Lowpass filter.** A filter that attenuates high frequencies while allowing low frequencies to pass through.

- **Multimode filter.** A filter with several outputs (either simultaneous or switchable). One output provides a lowpass response, another a highpass response, and so on. Typically, all of the outputs share a common cutoff frequency and resonance amount.

- **Notch (band-reject) filter.** A filter that attenuates a selected band of frequencies while allowing frequencies both below and above the stop-band to pass through.

- **Pass-band.** The range of frequencies that a filter allows to pass without attenuation.

- **Pole.** A term from circuit design that designates the sharpness of the rolloff slope of a filter. Each pole increases the rolloff slope by 6 dB per octave, so a two-pole filter has a rolloff slope of 12 dB per octave and a four-pole filter a rolloff slope of 24 dB per octave.

- **Q.** *See resonance.*

- **Resonance.** The amount by which a narrow band of frequencies lying near the cutoff frequency of a resonant filter is boosted. Resonance imparts a characteristic nasal or "peaky" quality to the tone of a filter. With high resonance settings, a filter may self-oscillate, producing something like a sine wave near the cutoff frequency.

- **Rolloff slope.** A measurement of the amount by which frequencies in the stop-band of a filter are attenuated. Frequencies farther into the stop-band with respect to the cutoff frequency will be attenuated further, and the amount by which a given frequency will be attenuated depends on both its distance from the cutoff frequency and the sharpness of the rolloff slope. When the rolloff slope is shallow (6 dB per octave), partials that lie further into the stop-band will still be audible, though at a lower amplitude. When the rolloff slope is steeper (24 dB per octave), partials within the stop-band will be more attenuated and may no longer be audible.

- **State-variable filter.** A filter whose output can vary continuously from one mode (such as lowpass) to another mode (such as highpass).

- **Stop-band.** The range of frequencies that is attenuated by a filter.

More about Q   There are two ways of specifying the pass-band of a bandpass filter or the emphasized frequency region of a resonant filter: We can talk about bandwidth, or we can talk about Q. (Q is an abbreviation for "quality," but nobody talks about "filter quality." The abbreviation is always used.) Some Csound filters have an input for bandwidth, and some have an input for Q.

Mathematically, the two are roughly reciprocal: A higher Q setting is equivalent to a narrower bandwidth, and a lower Q is equivalent to a wider bandwidth. A Q setting of 1.5 gives the pass-band or emphasized region of the filter a width of about one octave, while a Q of 2.5 narrows this to about a perfect fifth.

Because bandwidth is usually specified in Hz rather than in a musical intervals, a filter with a fixed bandwidth will be effectively narrower (in a musical interval sense) when the center frequency is higher. If the bandwidth of a filter is 200 Hz, for instance, when the center frequency is also 200 Hz the pass-band will be an octave and a fifth wide (from 100 Hz to 300 Hz). When the center frequency of this filter is raised to 2 kHz (2,000 Hz), a bandwidth of 200 Hz will pass only a small fraction of an octave (from 1.9 kHz to 2.1 kHz). A filter with a Q parameter should behave differently. A given Q setting should produce a bandwidth of the same musical interval, irrespective of the center frequency. However, there's no guarantee that all Csound filters will be implemented in this way. As always when using filters, you should be guided by your ears, not by the theory.

Resonant Lowpass Filters

The first filter you may want to try, if you're familiar with analog synthesis, is `moogvcf`. This is a resonant lowpass filter, and it has a rather fat sound. The sound of `moogladder` is very similar. These filters have inputs for an audio signal and control signals governing cutoff frequency and resonance. Here is a basic instrument that uses moogvcf:

```
instr 1
iCos ftgen 0, 0, 8192, 11, 1
iamp = 0.6
ifreq = 50
asig gbuzz 1, ifreq, 95, 1, 1, iCos
ifiltrise = p3 * 0.01
ifiltdecay = p3 * 0.99
kfiltenv linseg 300, ifiltrise, 4500, ifiltdecay, 300
afilt moogvcf asig, kfiltenv, 0.7
aout linen afilt * iamp, 0.01, p3, 0.1
outs aout, aout
endin
```

The Wrong Trousers   Diagnosing problems with Csound can be tricky, because a problem may show up in an unexpected or misleading place. When I started writing the section on filters, I decided to use gbuzz as an oscillator. When I sent the signal from gbuzz into moogvcf, I found that moogvcf was blowing up when the cutoff frequency and resonance were set even moderately high. But the problem wasn't with moogvcf. I posted a "help" message to the Csound mailing list, complete with the source code for my instrument, and Iain McCurdy quickly spotted the problem: I was using a sine wave as the source waveform for gbuzz, but gbuzz expects to use a cosine wave. The fact that gbuzz appeared to work fine when its output was processed by other filter opcodes was an illusion. When I replaced the source waveform with a cosine, which was as simple as using GEN 11 rather than GEN 10, the apparent problem with moogvcf vanished.

The moral of the story—well, it has two morals: First, read the manual carefully. (The page for gbuzz does indeed say a cosine wave should be used.) Second, be careful about making assumptions. What appears to be a bug in a Csound opcode will sometimes turn out to be user error.

The cutoff frequency of moogvcf can be modulated at a-rate, but in my experiments the sound produced by modulating it with an audio-range sine wave oscillator was rather thin. It didn't produce the rich, swirling sidebands that I remember when doing the equivalent patch on a Minimoog. I got better results with moogladder. However, the cutoff frequency of moogladder can only be modulated at k-rate. If you want this type of sound, you'll get the smoothest results by setting ksmps = 1 in the orchestra header. Here is an example instrument that gets fairly close to the classic Minimoog sound. Play it with a note about 10 seconds long.

```
sr = 44100
ksmps = 1
nchnls = 2
0dbfs = 1

instr 1
iSine ftgen 0, 0, 8192, 10, 1
iCos ftgen 0, 0, 8192, 11, 1
iamp = 0.4
ifreq = 300

asig gbuzz 1, ifreq, 75, 1, 0.9, iCos
ifiltrise = p3 * 0.1
ifiltdecay = p3 * 0.9
kfiltmod oscil 800, ifreq * 2, iSine
kfiltenv linseg 300, ifiltrise, 2500, ifiltdecay, 500
afilt moogladder asig, kfiltenv + kfiltmod, 1

asine oscil 0.3, 500, iSine
abal balance afilt, asine
aout linen abal * iamp, 0.01, p3, 0.1
outs aout, aout
endin
```

If you replace `moogladder` in the code above with `moogvcf`, without making any other changes, you'll find that the difference in tone color is very noticeable.

 Caution Note the use of the `balance` opcode in the code for producing audio sidebands with `moogladder`. The `balance` opcode is designed to tame an overly loud signal and bring it back into the normal amplitude range. An extra sine wave has been pressed into service for `balance` to use as a reference signal. If you neglect to use `balance`, this instrument will be painfully loud and might even damage your speakers. For more on `balance`, see the section on "Dynamics Control and Panning," later in this chapter.

Csound's other lowpass resonant filters include `rezzy`, `lowpass2`, `lowres`, and `lpf18`. Each has a slightly different sound, so experimenting with them is worthwhile. (For safety, continue to use the `balance` opcode while doing so.) `lpf18` has an input for distortion amount, which can warm up the tone. The resonant peak in `lowpass2` is a thin whistle, which sounds rather artificial but might be perfect for some musical situations.

These filters do not necessarily expect to see the same range of values for the resonance amount. Several of them expect a resonance amount between 0 and 1, with 1 producing self-oscillation.

`lowpass2`, on the other hand, looks for a resonance amount between 1 and 500, while the resonance of `rezzy` should be between 1 and 100. For details on these filters, consult the manual.

State-Variable Filters

Csound's `statevar` and `svfilter` opcodes are not, strictly speaking, state-variable filters. A state-variable filter in an analog synth has a single output, which can be modulated under voltage control to sweep from lowpass response to bandpass and thence to highpass. These two Csound filters are, in fact, more flexible in design: They're multimode filters with several simultaneous outputs. `svfilter` has simultaneous lowpass, bandpass, and highpass outputs, while `statevar` has a fourth output with a notch (band-reject) response. To produce the sound of a state-variable filter, you'll need to crossfade between two or more of the outputs. Here is an example that does such a crossfade. To hear the result, play this instrument with a note about 10 seconds long.

```
instr 1
iSine ftgen 0, 0, 8192, 10, 1
iCos ftgen 0, 0, 8192, 11, 1
iamp = 0.4
ifreq = 100

asig gbuzz 0.7, ifreq, 35, 1, 0.95, iCos
ifiltrise = p3 * 0.01
ifiltdecay = p3 * 0.99
kross line 1, p3, 0
alow, ahigh, aband svfilter asig, 100 + (3000 * kross), 60
alow = alow * (1 - kross)
ahigh = ahigh * kross
afilt = alow + ahigh + (aband * 0.5)

asine oscil 0.7, 500, iSine
abal balance afilt, asine
aout linen abal * iamp, 0.01, p3, 0.1
outs aout, aout
endin
```

The amplitude of the crossfading tone pulses due to phase cancellation, at a speed and intensity that varies depending on how the filter's cutoff frequency is modulated and how the outputs are mixed.

Basic Tone-Shaping

Basic tone-shaping can be handled in Csound using the `tone`, `atone`, `butterlp`, and `butterhp` filters. These are not resonant filters. The rolloff slope of the Butterworth filters is steeper than the rolloff slope of `tone` and `atone`; the latter provide a fairly gentle sound. While `butterbp` and `butterbr` (bandpass and band-reject filters, respectively) are not, technically, resonant filters, they have a bandwidth input. A narrower bandwidth for `butterbp` will produce a more precise peak in the tone. Here is an example that uses `butterbp`:

```
giCos   ftgen 0, 0, 8192, 11, 1

instr 1
idur = p3
iamp = p4
icps = cpspch(p5)
kline1   line 0.1, p3, 4.5
kfco = p6 * kline1
asig   gbuzz iamp, icps, 75, 1, 0.9, giCos
afilt   butterbp asig, kfco, p7
outs afilt, afilt
endin


</CsInstruments>
<CsScore>

i 1 0.0 3.0 0.5 6.00 500 300
i 1 3.0 4.0 0.5 6.03 1000 50
```

The second event uses a much narrower bandwidth (p7 in the score is only 50), so you'll hear individual overtones in the upward sweep of the filter. Notice that the amplitude of both of these events is set to greater than 1.0. This doesn't cause clipping, because `butterbp` reduces the amplitude of the signal passing through it.

Global Signal Routing

Generating an audio signal within an instrument and sending it directly to Csound's output is often all that's needed—but sometimes we need to bus signals from one instrument to another. In particular, effects processors such as reverb and delay are usually implemented in Csound as separate instruments.

 Tip It's usually better to make an effect a separate Csound instrument for a couple of reasons. First, effects like reverb and delay typically linger for a few seconds after the last note that they're processing has stopped. If the effect is written as part of the instrument playing the note, the effect will end when the note ends. It's possible to work around this limitation by extending the note event, but it's tricky and not necessary. Second, because reverb can be a fairly CPU-intensive process, it's usually better to run only one instance of a reverb, by having the reverb instrument run throughout the piece, than to give each note its own reverb processor.

Csound provides four different methods of routing signals from one instrument to another. Each is the best choice in certain situations. The use of global variables was already covered in Chapter 6. A global variable is the easiest choice if you only need one or two signal paths between instruments. Simply declare values in the orchestra header, like this:

```
gaReverbInL init 0
gaReverbInR init 0
```

and you're ready to go. Here's an example that plays a pitch-swept tone and sends it to a reverb using global variables:

```
sr = 44100
ksmps = 4
nchnls = 2
0dbfs = 1

gaReverbInL init 0
gaReverbInR init 0

instr 1
iCos ftgen 0, 0, 8192, 11, 1
iamp = 0.7
kfreq line 300, p3, 600
asig gbuzz 1, kfreq, 75, 1, 0.9, iCos

ifiltrise = p3 * 0.1
ifiltdecay = p3 * 0.9
kfiltenv linseg 300, ifiltrise, 2500, ifiltdecay, 500
afilt moogladder asig, kfiltenv, 0.2

ashaped linen afilt, 0.01, p3, 0.1
gaReverbInL = gaReverbInL + ashaped
gaReverbInR = gaReverbInR + ashaped
aout = ashaped * iamp
outs aout, aout
endin

instr 101
ioutlevel = p4
ainL = gaReverbInL
ainR = gaReverbInR
gaReverbInL = 0
gaReverbInR = 0
```

```
aoutL, aoutR reverbsc ainL, ainR, 0.8, 6000
outs aoutL * ioutlevel, aoutR * ioutlevel
endin

</CsInstruments>
<CsScore>

i1 0 10
i101 0 12 1.2
```

A few things about this example are worth pointing out. First, the reverb instrument starts running at the beginning of the score, and runs for a couple of seconds after the last note in the score ends. (In this case, there's only one note.) Its output level is controlled from p4 in the score. Second, because reverbsc is a stereo reverb opcode, we're sending left and right signals to it, though in this case the two signals happen to be the same. Finally, the bus signals have been zeroed out in the reverb after being copied into local variables. If you're mixing the signals from several instruments (or, for that matter, several instances of a single instrument that is being used polyphonically) into the reverb bus, this step is essential. If you fail to zero out the bus, the signal in it will quickly build to an astronomical level.

We're going to edit this example to illustrate the other possibilities. When your busing needs are more complex, you can turn to the chnset and chnget opcodes, or to the zak family of opcodes. chnset and chnget are convenient when you want to use named channels. The zak family of opcodes is a better choice when you have quite a few buses and want to refer to them (perhaps by selecting the bus from a p-field in the score) by number. They're also convenient if you want to let an instrument choose which effect send bus to use, either at random or in response to some external control message. You could do the switching to a different bus using either global variables or chnset/chnget, but doing so would be messy. It's easier with zak.

One advantage of the chnset/chnget mechanism is that the channels don't need to be declared in the orchestra header. Starting from the code in the example above, delete the declaration of the global audio variables. Then, in instrument 1, replace these two lines:

```
gaReverbInL = gaReverbInL + ashaped
gaReverbInR = gaReverbInR + ashaped
```

with these two:

```
chnmix ashaped, "RevInL"
chnmix ashaped, "RevInR"
```

Next, replace these four lines in instrument 101, the reverb:

```
ainL = gaReverbInL
ainR = gaReverbInR
```

```
gaReverbInL = 0
gaReverbInR = 0
```

with these four lines:

```
ainL chnget "RevInL"
ainR chnget "RevInR"
chnclear "RevInL"
chnclear "RevInR"
```

The result should sound exactly the same as before. The `chnmix` opcode mixes an audio signal with whatever is already in the named channel (in this case, "RevInL" and "RevInR"), so the signals from multiple notes can be sent to the bus at the same time. The `chnclear` opcode resets the data buffer of the channel to zero on every k-period.

The zak Opcodes

Using the `zak` opcodes is almost as easy, but it does require that you remember which of the numbered buses are being used for what. Begin by initializing a couple of buffers in the orchestra header:

```
zakinit 2, 2
```

The `zakinit` opcode initializes an arbitrary number of a-rate and k-rate buffers. In this case, we're not using the k-rate buffers, but `zakinit` requires a non-zero value for its second argument, so we'll set it to 2 so as to be symmetrical. Next, use the `zawm` opcode to send the signal from instrument 1, like this:

```
zawm ashaped, 0
zawm ashaped, 1
```

The name of this opcode is terse but readable: The "a" means "audio," the "w" means "write," and the "m" means "mix." Finally, in the reverb, replace the four lines using `chnget` and `chnclear` with these three lines:

```
ainL zar 0
ainR zar 1
zacl 0, 1
```

The "r" in `zar` means "read," and `zacl` clears all of the audio buffers between the two numbers given as arguments. The last line of code above uses `zacl` to clear (set to 0) the buffers between 0 and 1, inclusive. Again, the sound should be exactly the same as before.

The Mixer Opcodes

The mixer opcodes provide yet another way to mix audio signals before sending them to the output. The manual explains these opcodes pretty clearly, but a few points are worth reiterating here:

- `MixerSetLevel` (or `MixerSetLevel_i`) must be used in a lower-numbered instrument than the instrument using the corresponding send bus.

- `MixerSend` must be used in a lower-numbered instrument than the one using the corresponding `MixerReceive`.

- After using `MixerReceive`, you must use `MixerClear` to zero out the signals in all of the busses.

- Using `MixerSetLevel` or `MixerSetLevel_i` is mandatory, as this creates the bus.

You may find it useful to let the number of the send bus be the same as the number of the instrument, but this is not mandatory. `MixerSetLevel_i` can conveniently be placed in the orchestra header; `MixerSetLevel` can accept k-rate signals as inputs, which makes it ideal for fade-outs, fade-ins, and crossfades.

Here is a not-too-convoluted example. It includes two instruments, basically identical, whose outputs are sent to the mixer. Instrument 1 uses a p-field to send the signal either to the 0 (left) or 1 (right) channel of the bus. Instrument 2 sends to both channels and is set to a lower level by the second `MixerSetLevel_i` line.

```
giSine ftgen 0, 0, 8192, 10, 1


; set the send and receive channels for two busses, and their levels:
MixerSetLevel_i 1, 101, 1
MixerSetLevel_i 2, 101, 0.4

instr 1
kenv line 0.25, p3, 0
asig foscil kenv, p4, 1, 1, kenv * 3, giSine
MixerSend asig, p1, 101, p5
endin

instr 2
kenv line 0.35, p3, 0
asig foscil kenv, p4, 1, 1, kenv * 3, giSine
MixerSend asig, p1, 101, 0
MixerSend asig, p1, 101, 1
endin
```

```
instr 101 ; mixer
aL MixerReceive p1, 0
aR MixerReceive p1, 1
outs aL, aR
MixerClear
endin

</CsInstruments>
<CsScore>

; start the mixer instrument:
i101 0 5

; play some notes and send them to the left channel:
i1 0 3 300 0
i1 0.5 . 400 0
i1 1 . 500 0

; play some notes and send them to the right channel:
i1 0 3 700 1
i1 0.5 . 800 1
i1 1 . 900 1

; play some notes that will be sent to both channels:
i2 0 0.25 150
i2 +
i2 +
i2 +
i2 +
i2 +
i2 +
i2 + . 175
i2 +
i2 +
i2 +
i2 +
i2 + 0.75
```

MixerSend has four input arguments—the audio signal, the send channel, the receive bus, and a channel number. The term "channel number" may be slightly misleading. If nchnls=2, the final argument to MixerSend should be 0 for the left channel and 1 for the right channel.

Pitch Converters

Many of the examples you've seen so far in *Csound Power!* use a preset value for the oscillator frequency, or input a raw value for frequency from the score, as in "The Mixer Opcodes," above. This is fine for tutorials, but it's not always useful in musical situations. More often, we want to control the frequencies of notes—that is, their musical pitches—from the score, so as to play melodies, chords, or bass lines, and to do so with some sort of shorthand rather than having to calculate all of the desired frequencies by hand. Csound lets us do this in a variety of ways. Here is an example that illustrates the concept in a deliberately clumsy way:

```
instr 1
; setup:
iCos ftgen 0, 0, 8192, 11, 1
iamp = p4
ifreq = p5

; tone generation:
asig gbuzz 1, ifreq, 75, 1, 0.9, iCos
ifiltrise = 0.005
ifiltdec1 = 0.05
ifiltdec2 = p3 - (ifiltrise + ifiltdec1)
kfiltenv linseg 300, ifiltrise, 2500, ifiltdec1, 1000, ifiltdec2, 300
afilt moogladder asig, kfiltenv, 0.2

; output:
aout linen afilt * iamp, 0.01, p3, 0.1
outs aout, aout
endin

</CsInstruments>
<CsScore>

t 0 100

i1 0 0.5 0.5 250
i1 + . . 225
i1 + . . 200
i1 + . . 225
i1 + . . 250
i1 +
i1 + 1
```

(For details on the odd-looking data in the score, see Chapter 8, "Writing a Csound Score.") If you enter this as shown, instrument 1 will play the opening phrase of "Mary Had a Little Lamb." The frequency values sent to the oscillator (gbuzz) come directly from p5 in the score. In this score, we're playing "Mary Had a Little Lamb" in just intonation, but that's little more than a detail. Or is it? If we wanted to play the same tune, in C major, using the standard 12-note-per-octave equal temperament used on a piano, the score would look like this:

```
i1 0 0.5 0.5 329.627
i1 + . . 293.665
i1 + . . 261.625
i1 + . . 293.665
i1 + . . 329.627
i1 +
i1 + 1
```

There just has to be a better way! And of course, there is. The tool to use is the cpspch opcode. Derive ifreq in instrument 1 using this line:

```
ifreq = cpspch(p5)
```

and edit the score so that it looks like this:

```
i1 0 0.5 0.5 8.04
i1 + . . 8.02
i1 + . . 8.00
i1 + . . 8.02
i1 + . . 8.04
i1 +
i1 + 1
```

With these two changes, the score should sound exactly as it did before. The input to cpspch (in this case, the value being sent by p5 in the score) is in Csound's *octave/pitch-class* format. This format uses numbers with two decimal places. The integer part (8, in the example above) is the octave designation. The two decimal places give the number of the chromatic half-step within that octave.

Caution   When using pitch-class data, be careful not to omit the leading zero in the decimal part of numbers like 8.02. Csound will interpret a value of 8.2 as if it were 8.20.

cpspch assumes that your music is based on conventional Western tuning, with 12 equally spaced pitches per octave and octaves that are defined by doubling the frequency. This may or may not be a tuning system that you want to use. To produce some other equal-tempered scale, use cpsxpch. With this opcode, you can choose the number of equally spaced steps per octave, the frequency width of the "octave," and the base frequency that corresponds to a pitch-class value of 0.0. Try replacing the line with `cpspch` in the previous example with this line:

```
ifreq cpsxpch p5, 11, 2, 1
```

The phrase will sound much as it did before, but if you add harmonies the difference will quickly become clear: This scale has only 11 equally spaced notes per octave, not 12, so all of the intervals are a bit too wide. Creating music with 17, 19, or 31 notes per octave is just as easy. And if you replace the 2 in the code line above with some other value, such as 3 or 1.75, you'll get an even more exotic tuning.

cpsmidi

If you're playing a Csound instrument live from a MIDI keyboard, the opcode to use for deriving a frequency from the MIDI note number is `cpsmidi`. This can only be used in an instrument that has actually been triggered by a MIDI note. If you need to translate an integer coming from elsewhere into a frequency value, use `cpsmidinn`.

`cpsmidi` has a sibling, `cpsmidib`, which incorporates pitch-bends into its output. The bend depth in semitones is given as an argument to `cpsmidib`. For instance:

```
kpitch cpsmidib 2
```

This will give you the pitch value including a possible pitch-bend with a maximum depth up or down of two semitones.

String Manipulation Opcodes

Some Csound opcodes allow double-quoted text strings to be used as input arguments—for instance, as filenames. Because you may want your instrument to respond differently depending on other factors, you may find it convenient to assemble a string on the fly, in the instrument code, before passing the result to an opcode as an argument. String variables begin with a capital S- (or gS-, for global variables).

The string manipulation opcodes are well explained in *The Canonical Csound Reference Manual*, on the pages called out in the left pane of the HTML manual, so there's little need to discuss them here.

The Important GEN Routines

The purpose of Csound's GEN routines is to generate or load data that will be stored in function tables. The term "functions" may be a bit misleading to knowledgeable programmers, as the tables don't store functions; they store data. Once created, a table can be read or edited by the `table` family of opcodes, which are discussed in the next section of this chapter. Currently, Csound provides about 40 GEN routines, some of which you'll be likely to use only if you know a fair amount about mathematics. Others are more broadly useful in everyday synthesis operations.

The f-Statement

GEN routines can be invoked in two ways. The original mechanism provided by Csound for this purpose utilized an f-statement in the score. For example:

```
f 1 0 8192 10 1
```

If you look up the syntax of the f-statement in the manual, the meaning of this code should be fairly clear. It has five parameters (p1 through p5). p1 is the number by which the table will be used in the orchestra, and should usually be unique. You can create several tables with the same number if you like, but only the most recently created of them will exist in memory. p2 is the time in the score at which the table will be created. Often this is 0—that is, the table is created before the score plays—but you can easily replace one table with another at a later point in the score by using the same value for p1.

p3 is the size of the table to be created, in data words. At present, Csound is available in 32-bit and 64-bit versions, so the actual size of a given table in bytes will be twice as large in the latter case, even though the number of points in the table is the same. You don't need to worry about this when creating the table; just give it a size. You do need to be aware, however, that some Csound operations require a table of a size that is a power of 2 or a power of 2 plus 1. This is true with simple waveforms like the sine wave created in the example above. 8192 is 2 to the 13th power. The extra point that may be added at the end (the table above could have been created with a size of 8193) is a *guard point*. In fact, a table created with a size of 8192 also has a guard point: Its actual size is 8193 data words. But the data in the guard point may be different, depending on which size you specify in your code. (The manual page on the f-statement explains how the two ways of specifying table size differ with respect to the guard point.) The guard point is needed with opcodes such as oscili and tablei, which derive their output using a process of interpolation between points in the table.

Note The reason why waveform tables have guard points is efficiency. It's faster to calculate the interpolation when an opcode reaches the last point of the table if there's a guard point, because the code doesn't have to accommodate the special case where it's interpolating between the last point in the table and the first one.

If you want to create a table with a size that's *not* a power of 2 or a power of 2 plus 1, you must specify its size as a negative number. If you forget to do this, your .csd file will compile, but you'll get an error message at run time if any instruments try to use the table, because it won't actually exist.

Tables containing samples loaded from the hard drive can be given a size of 0, which tells Csound to determine the size of the table at run time based on the size of the file. Such tables will work with some opcodes, but not with others.

Returning to the syntax of the f-statement, p4 is the number of the GEN routine. This, too, can be negative, and the minus sign has a very specific meaning. When you use a positive integer to specify the GEN routine, the table will be rescaled after it is created, so that its data falls within the range −1 to +1. (See the "Post-Normalization" sidebar.) When the number of the GEN routine is negative, however, rescaling is omitted. This is useful for things like tables of frequencies that are used to construct microtonal scales.

The meanings of the other parameters in an f-statement (p5 and following) depend on the specific GEN routine. For details, you'll need to consult the manual page for the specific GEN routine you're using.

 Post-Normalization   When we construct tables that will be used as audio waveforms, or for certain other purposes such as envelope contours, we normally want the wave data to have a range of ±1. Csound's GEN routines take care of this chore for us: After the data in the table is generated, it is *normalized* (increased or reduced in amplitude as needed) so that it fits neatly within this range.

Some types of data should not be normalized, however. If we're writing a sequence of note pitches in octave/pitch-class format (perhaps a series that begins 8.00 8.02 8.04 7.11), the very last thing we want is to have Csound reduce these values to fit within a smaller range. We can defeat the normalization feature if we need to by making the number of the GEN routine negative.

The ftgen Opcode Family

Instead of using f-statements in the score, you can invoke GEN routines using the opcodes `ftgen`, `ftgenonce`, and `ftgentmp`. The difference between the latter two is rather technical; for details, consult the manual page for `ftgenonce`. Basically, `ftgenonce` economizes on computer memory by checking to see whether an identical function table already exists. If so, the data in that table is used; no new table is created by the opcode. If some instrument is writing new data to the table during performance, and if some other instrument (or another event that uses the same instrument) is accessing the table, you'll need to think carefully about whether to use `ftgentmp` or `ftgenonce`.

The arguments to `ftgen` and its siblings are very similar to those used with f-statements in the score, but with three differences, two of them rather trivial. First, the arguments to `ftgen` must be separated by commas. Second, the value for time of creation (p2) is ignored, as the table is created whenever `ftgen` runs. If it's in the orchestra header, for instance, it will run when the performance starts. Third, you don't need to specify a table number if you don't want to. If you provide a p1 value of 0, Csound will automatically generate a unique table number. The automatically generated number is returned—that is, it's an output value—when `ftgen` runs. For example, in place of the f statement in the previous section, we could do this:

```
giSine ftgen 0, 0, 8192, 10, 1
```

At this point, the return value (`giSine`) is the number of the table. Because it's a global variable, it can be used in any instrument in the orchestra in order to access the table. This is convenient because it makes the code easier to read, and because it eliminates the need to think about your table numbers.

Most often, you'll invoke `ftgen` within the orchestra header, so its output will be a global value, as indicated by a name beginning with g-: `giSine`, for instance. `ftgentmp` is more often used within an instrument, and the table it creates exists only as long as the instrument is running. Because it's local, a name beginning with i- would normally be used:

```
iSine ftgentmp 0, 0, 8192, 10, 1
```

With this preamble out of the way, we're ready to look at some GEN routines.

Sinusoids with GEN 09, 10, and 11

The sine wave is one of the basic building blocks of sound synthesis. Using GEN 10, we can create a waveform containing harmonically related sine waves of various amplitudes. For example:

```
instr 1
iamp = 0.5
iWave ftgentmp 0, 0, 8192, 10, 1, 0.8, 0.6, 0.4, 0.2
asig oscil iamp, 200, iWave
outs asig, asig
endin
```

Here, we have invoked GEN 10 using `ftgentmp`. The five values after the 10 (which is the GEN number) specify the relative strengths of the first five harmonics. The fundamental has a strength of 1, and the higher harmonics get progressively weaker. This will produce the tone of a very muted sawtooth wave. For a brighter sound that is still sawtooth-like, substitute this line:

```
iWave ftgentmp 0, 0, 8192, 10, 1, 1, 1, 1, 1, 1, 1, 1, 1, 1, 1, 1
```

Now the wave has 10 sine harmonics of equal amplitude.

Sine Waves   The sine wave (refer to Figure 7.1) is a mathematically defined entity and one of the most basic building blocks of sound synthesis. If you want to understand the technical definition, your best bet may be to go to the library and take out a good introductory book on trigonometry. Sine waves are explained in a number of articles online, but some of the articles use advanced math and others are rather eccentric.

In music synthesis, a sine wave produces a smooth, pure sound. It has no overtones. This makes it useful as a starting point for generating more complex sounds, for example in FM synthesis.

The easiest way to understand sine waves may be to imagine a freely rotating circle, with a dot at some point on the rim of the circle. As the circle rotates at a constant speed, the dot on the rim will move first upward and then downward, alternately. If we draw a diagram that shows the distance of the dot above or below the horizontal axis at the center of the circle as that distance changes over time, we have a diagram of a sine wave.

Because the tables created by GEN routines are rescaled unless we use a negative GEN number, the waveform created here can be weighted toward the higher harmonics without risk of overloading the audio output. Try replacing a few of the parameter values, along these lines:

```
iWave ftgentmp 0, 0, 8192, 10, 0.5, 0, 3, 0.7, 0.6, 4.5, 0, 2.3, 0.2, 3.1
```

This is not necessarily the most interesting way to create tone colors, but even with something as simple as GEN 10 we have some useful options.

With GEN 09, we have to give three values—the partial number, the strength, and the phase—for each partial. We have to call them partials at this point, not harmonics, because with GEN 09 the value for the partial number need not be an integer. In other words, GEN 09 lets us stack sine waves with arbitrary frequency relationships to one another. We could specify three partials with partial numbers 1, 1.37, and 1.944. This is less interesting than you might imagine, however, because the waveform will start over when the end of the table is reached. If you create such a wave and then use it in an oscil, you won't hear three non-harmonically related partials— you'll hear a buzzy tone with no apparent inharmonicity. The bright, buzzy quality of the sound will be caused by the abrupt discontinuity in the waveform when the end of the table is reached and the oscillator jumps back to the beginning. If you want to generate a tone containing non-harmonically-related partials, there are other ways to do it (using the adsynt2 opcode, for instance). GEN 09 is not the right choice for this type of tone.

 Inharmonicity is out-of-tuneness. The word is generally used to refer to the sound of partials within a composite tone that are not harmonically related. If the partials are close to pure harmonic (whole-number) ratios, the composite tone has only a slight inharmonicity. The amount of inharmonicity, while not rigorously defined in a mathematical sense, is the aggregate distance of the partials from harmonically pure overtones—the amount of out-of-tuneness.

GEN 09 is useful, however, for creating a smooth curve that rises from –1 to +1, perhaps with some bumps along the way. Such a table can be useful in building a waveshaper. Here's a simple example:

```
instr 1
iMap ftgentmp 0, 0, 8192, 9, 3.5, 1, 270
iWave ftgentmp 0, 0, 8192, 10, 1
kamp line 0.01, p3, 0.49
```

```
asig oscil 1, 200, iWave
atab tablei asig * kamp, iMap, 1, 0.5
aout linen atab, 0.1, p3, 0.1
outs atab, atab
endin
```

GEN 09 is used, in the first line of the instrument, to create a table called iMap. The partial used is 3.5; to hear more overtones, try a higher value such as 7.5. This waveform starts with a phase value of 270 degrees, which is the bottom of the trough of a sine wave (refer to Figure 7.1). After generating a sine wave with oscil, we use the sine wave to read the iMap table using tablei, and the width of the sine wave's swing through the table is controlled by a line value that increases from 0.01 to 0.49. The result is a tone that acquires more harmonics as the line rises. Not supremely interesting with a sine wave as the source, but with a sampled sound as the input from the oscil, the distortion will get more pungent.

GEN 11 creates a table containing one or more cosine waves rather than sine waves. The difference between a sine wave and a cosine wave is not audible, but it's mathematically significant. Both are smooth curves that alternately rise above 0 and fall below 0. Assuming an amplitude of ±1, a sine wave starts with a value of 0, rises to 1, then slides down to –1, rises back to 0, and so on. A cosine wave starts at 1, slides down to –1, then rises to 1 again, and so on.

This difference—that a sine wave starts at 0, while a cosine wave starts at its maximum amplitude—is significant in Csound in at least two ways. First, a few opcodes, such as gbuzz, require cosine waves rather than sine waves as source data. Second, if you want to define a curve for some purpose, such as for an envelope segment or a waveshaper, you might want to use GEN 09 or GEN 11, and you'll need to know where the curve starts.

The syntax of GEN 11 is:

```
f # time size 11 nh [lh] [r]
```

In this prototype, nh is the number of harmonics requested, lh is the lowest harmonic, and r is a multiplier that is applied to the amplitudes of successively higher harmonics. The syntax of GEN 11 is efficient if you want to produce a tone that has a number of harmonically related partials. For instance:

```
giCos ftgen 0, 0, 8192, 11, 7, 5, 1.2
```

This line of code produces a wavetable constructed additively using seven cosine waves, the lowest being the fifth harmonic, and the higher harmonics being somewhat louder than the lower ones.

Building Tables out of Segments

Sometimes we want to store the shape of a contour in a table, and we want to specify the shape of the contour ourselves rather than have it constructed automatically using sine waves. The basic tools for this are GEN 07 and GEN 27, both of which build tables using segments of straight lines. Such tables are very useful for creating modulation contours, such as amplitude envelopes. As far as I can determine, these two GEN routines give exactly the same result, but the syntax is different.

When GEN 07 is used, the first data p-field (p5) is a value—the value of the first location in the table. The remaining fields alternately specify the lengths of the segments and the data values at the ends of those segments. The sum of the lengths of the segments will normally equal the size of the requested table.

When GEN 27 is used, again, alternating p-fields are used to define the values stored in the table—but in this case the values alternate with the points in the table at which that value is reached, rather than the lengths of the segments. An example may make this clearer. The following two f-statements construct the same table data:

```
f1 0 256 7  0 63 1 1 -1 127 1 1 -1 64 0
f2 0 256 27 0 0 63 1 64 -1 191 1 192 -1 256 0
```

In the first statement, using GEN 07, three segments are defined with lengths 63, 127, and 64. Two abrupt discontinuities—segments of 1 length—are also defined, where the table data jumps down from 1 to –1. The result is a rising ramp wave. In the second statement, using GEN 27, each segment is defined by its start and end points (0–63, 64–191, and 192–256 respectively).

Here is a simple instrument and score with which you can listen to and compare these tables:

```
instr 1
iWave ftgentmp 0, 0, 8192, 10, 1, 0.7, 0.4, 0.1
kphase phasor 1
; replace with: kphase, 2, 1
kramp tablei kphase, 1, 1
asig oscil 0.7, 300 + (50 * kramp), iWave
outs asig, asig
endin
</CsInstruments>
<CsScore>

f1 0 256 7  0 63 1 1 -1 127 1 1 -1 64 0
f2 0 256 27 0 0 63 1 64 -1 191 1 192 -1 256 0


i1 0 5
```

Try replacing 1 with 2 as the second argument to `tablei`. Sounds like a car alarm either way. I can't hear the difference—can you?

GEN 16 and GEN 25 produce tables using variable curves. GEN 25 operates much like `expseg`: The curvature of the segments is exponential, and the breakpoints of the curve must all have the same sign (either positive or negative). GEN 16 produces only one curve between its start and end points, but the start and end points don't have to be alike in sign, and the curve can be adjusted to have a slightly or radically convex or concave shape. The curvature produced by GEN 16 is handled exactly like the curvature produced by `transeg`.

Reading Audio Files

GEN 01 reads a mono or stereo .WAV or .AIFF file from your hard drive and stores the data in a table. GEN 49 does the same thing with .mp3 files. These files should be stored in the directory you define as the SSDIR or SFDIR in the Environment tab of the Configuration box in CsoundQt. Note, however, that in version 0.6 these settings are broken. If Csound can't find the audio files, you may need to specify the full path from the root of your hard drive as part of the f-statement, like this:

```
f1 0 1048576 1 \
   "C:/Users/Jim Aikin/Documents/csound scores/samples/olive.aiff" \
   0 0 0
```

(The backslash is used for a line of code that is too long to fit conveniently on one line in the screen.) As you can see, spaces are allowed in directory and file names, and forward-slashes are used as separators in the file name string, not backslashes.

GEN 49 is a relatively recent addition to Csound—at this writing, it's less than three years old. It didn't work for me using Csound 5.13 in Windows 7, but it worked fine on my MacBook Pro. Here's a test file I created, which played egyptian.mp3:

```
instr 1
aphas phasor 0.023
asigL tablei aphas, 1, 1
asigR tablei aphas, 2, 1
aoutL linen asigL, 0.1, p3, 0.1
aoutR linen asigR, 0.1, p3, 0.1
outs aoutL, aoutR
endin
</CsInstruments>
<CsScore>
f1 0 2097152 49 "egyptian.mp3" 4 3
f2 0 2097152 49 "egyptian.mp3" 4 4
i1 0 60
```

The number after the file name in the f-statements is a skip time. Since my audio started several seconds into the file, I entered a 4 here. The last number specified the left channel of the stereo source file for `f1` and the right channel for `f2`. I then read the data in these two tables using a pair of `tablei` opcodes, one for the left channel and one for the right channel, in the instrument. The value for the frequency of the phasor was derived empirically. In this instrument the phasor frequency determines the speed and therefore the pitch of the audio playback.

Your Own Data

Two GEN routines are especially useful when you know exactly what data you want to store in a table: GEN 02 and GEN 23. These routines are the tool of choice, for instance, when you want to create a complex tuning table and fill it with your own frequency values, or when you want to build a step sequencer.

With GEN 02, you enter the data by hand into the .csd file, either in the f-statement or in the call to the ftgen opcode. In either case, the data is transferred directly from the p-fields into the table. Don't forget that the data will later be rescaled to a ±1 range unless you make the GEN number negative.

According to the manual, numeric values in a text file used by GEN 23 can be separated by spaces, tabs, newline characters, or commas. Words can be added to the file as comments and will be ignored when GEN 23 loads the file into a table.

Here is an example that loads values from a table created with GEN 02 in order to play an arpeggio within a single note event. In this example we're using the table opcode rather than tablei, because there's no need to interpolate between the data values in the table.

```
instr 1
iWave ftgentmp 0, 0, 8192, 10, 1, 0.7, 0.4, 0.1
iPitchTable ftgentmp 0, 0, 8, -2, 300, 375, 450, 525, 600, 525, 450, 375
kfreq init 300
kstep init 0

ktrig metro 8
if ktrig == 1 then
   kfreq table kstep, iPitchTable
   kstep = kstep + 1
   if kstep > 7 then
     kstep = 0
   endif
endif

asig oscil 0.7, kfreq, iWave
outs asig, asig
endin

</CsInstruments>
<CsScore>
i1 0 5
```

This instrument plays an arpeggio. The successive steps in the arpeggio are triggered by a `metro`, which outputs a value of 1 at a frequency of 8 Hz. Except when these pulses occur, the value of `ktrig` is 0. The first if-test encloses a block that runs only when `ktrig` is 1. In this situation, `table` reads from the table whose ID is `iPitchTable`, which was created by `ftgentmp`. The rest of that code block increments the value of the counter `kstep`. If we've reached the end of the table, `kstep` is set back to 0.

This arpeggio is implemented in a basic way, using actual frequency values. Also, the frequencies are in just intonation, which may not be what you want. Let's edit this instrument slightly so it will use 12-note-per-octave equal temperament. We'll use `cpspch`, which was introduced earlier in this chapter.

```
instr 1
iWave ftgentmp 0, 0, 8192, 10, 1, 0.7, 0.4, 0.1
iPitchTable ftgentmp 0, 0, 8, -2, 8.00, 8.04, 8.07, 8.10, 9.00,\
    8.10, 8.07, 8.04
kfreq init 100
kfreqval init 8.00
kstep init 0

ktrig metro 8
if ktrig == 1 then
   kfreqval table kstep, iPitchTable
   kfreq = cpspch(kfreqval)
   kstep = kstep + 1
   if kstep > 7 then
     kstep = 0
   endif
endif

asig oscil 0.7, kfreq, iWave
outs asig, asig
endin
```

The table now contains data in octave/pitch-class format. We've introduced a new k-rate variable, `kfreqval`, which receives the data from the table in its original form. `cpspch` then converts this data into a frequency value that `oscil` can use.

To try out GEN 23, copy the eight data values from the `iPitchTable` `ftgentmp` above and paste them into a new text file in a text editor (not a word processor). Save this file to some suitable location and then replace the GEN 02 line with GEN 23. On my machine, the new code looks like this:

```
iPitchTable ftgentmp 0, 0, 8, -23, \
  "C:/Users/Jim Aikin/My Documents/csound scores/arpeggio.txt"
```

The sound should be exactly the same as before. GEN 02 is more convenient if you only need to enter a few values, or if you want to keep all of your code in a single file. GEN 23 is more useful if you're using an external program to write a large amount of data to a text file.

Table Operations

In the discussion of GEN routines in the preceding section, we've been using a couple of table-reading opcodes, but without saying much about what they do or how to use them. The time has come to rectify that situation.

Csound has more than three dozen opcodes that can be used with tables. You can read the data from tables in order to use the data in an instrument; edit the data in a table one data item at a time while the score is playing; write new data automatically to a table while the score is playing, and read it out; copy one table to another; mix the contents of two tables; morph between tables; write table data to a file on disk; or load data from a file on disk into a table.

The first point to understand is that these opcodes all make use of previously allocated tables, which are created using GEN routines (either via f-statements in the score or using the `ftgen` family of opcodes). The integer that refers to the table is specified using the `ifn` argument in the manner shown in the prototype for the opcode. If Csound can't find the table you're requesting, you'll get an error message in the Console, and nothing will happen.

Note Some table opcodes can switch from one table to another while operating. In the prototype for an opcode of this type (such as `tableikt`), the table number is specified as `kfn`.

Reading from Tables

The basic tools for reading data from tables are the `table` and `tablei` opcodes. We have already seen these at work in the section on GEN routines, a few pages back. They're identical except that the latter interpolates between two adjacent values in the `table` when it needs to, thus producing a smoother output.

For a quick illustration of interpolation, let's suppose that step 2 in a small table contains a value of 10, while step 3 contains a value of 15. If the index (the point in the table that is to be read by the opcode) happens to be 2.5, halfway between 2 and 3, then `tablei` will output a value of 12.5—halfway between 10 and 15. Given an index of 2.5, however, `table` will output a value of 10, because it only reads the integer part of the index.

These opcodes can run at i-time, k-rate, or a-rate. Here is the k-rate prototype for `tablei`:

```
kres tablei kndx, ifn [, ixmode] [, ixoff] [, iwrap]
```

In this prototype, the output is `kres`. The `kndx` argument is the index—the point in the table that is to be read. `kndx` will quite often be a moving value. It may ramp up or down, for instance, or be varied randomly. `ifn` is the table number. The remaining three arguments are optional but useful. `ixmode` is a switch that tells `tablei` the type of value to look for in the `kndx` input. If `ixmode` is 0, `kndx` is interpreted as a raw number. For instance, if the table is 512 elements long and you want to read the entire table, you'll need to sweep the `kndx` input from 0 to 511. However, if `ixmode` is set to 1, the `kndx` input is assumed to be normalized to a 0–1 range, so you can read the whole table by sweeping through that range. Since a `phasor` outputs a sweep from 0 to 1 during its cycle, an `ixmode` setting of 1 is convenient to use with `phasor`. If you need to use `ixmode` 0 for some reason, you'll need to multiply the output of the `phasor` by the length of the table before sending it to `kndx` in order to read the entire contents of the table.

If you aren't sure of the length of the table, you can get it with the `tableng` opcode. This could be useful if you're selecting different tables on the fly, and they're not all of the same length.

The easiest way to explain the other two optional parameters may be by example. Let's return to the example given in the section "Your Own Data" a page or two back, but with a couple of minor changes:

```
giPitchTable  ftgen  0,  0,  8,  -2,  7.00,  7.04,  7.07,  7.10,  8.00,\
    8.04, 8.07, 8.10

instr 1
iWave ftgentmp 0, 0, 8192, 10, 4, 3, 2, 1
kfreq init 100
kfreqval init 8.00
kstep init 0
ktrig metro 8

if ktrig == 1 then
    kfreqval table kstep, giPitchTable
    kfreq = cpspch(kfreqval)
    kstep = kstep + 1
    if kstep > 7 then
        kstep = 0
    endif
endif

asig oscil 0.7, kfreq, iWave
outs asig, asig
endin
```

If you play this instrument for a few seconds, you'll hear it stepping rapidly through an ascending arpeggio. (I've moved the table up into the orchestra header, because in the next section we'll be writing data to it.)

The `ixoff` argument is an offset. It tells the opcode where in the `table` you want to start reading. If you replace the call to `table` with the following line, you'll hear the difference:

```
kfreqval table kstep, giPitchTable, 0, 4
```

The argument to `ixmode` is the default (0), so that won't change anything. We have to specify it, because we're going to pass a non-default value of 4 to `ixoff`. At this point, the table will be read starting at index 4, so we'll hear the upper half of the arpeggio. And when we hit the end of the table, the output will "pin." You'll hear the B-flat sustain for a bit before the cycle starts over, again starting from index 4 in the table. Essentially, `ixoff` adds its value to the `kndx` input. We're sending `kndx` integers from 0 to 7, but `table` is translating these into a series of integers from 4 to 11. There's nothing past `table` position 7, so `table` keeps outputting that value in response to an index of 8, 9, 10, or 11. This may not be what you want musically.

To remedy the situation, we'll use the other optional argument, `iwrap`:

```
kfreqval table kstep, giPitchTable, 0, 4, 1
```

Now the table will start being read at index 4, as before, but when the index (as adjusted by `ixoff`) goes up to and past 8, `table` will wrap around, starting over at index 0. Now we'll hear steps 4, 5, 6, and 7 followed by steps 0, 1, 2, and 3. The cycle will then repeat.

Other opcodes also read from tables. We've been using `oscil`, which reads from a table, for many of the examples of this book. `oscil` doesn't have to play a sine wave; it will happily read data of almost any kind from a table. Its more specialized cousins include `oscil1` and `oscil1n`.

`oscil1` reads through a table exactly once, at k-rate. Its start can be delayed and its duration (the amount of time it takes to read the table) specified. When it reaches the end of the table, it "pins" at the last value in the table and stays there. It's useful for attack transients; you could use it instead of using a `linseg` or other envelope generator, and get similar results. `oscil1n` is somewhat like `oscil1`, but it operates at a-rate, making it a good choice for playing back sampled (digitally recorded) attack transients. It can also loop a sample several times and then stop.

Writing to Tables

For writing new data to small tables by specifying one value at a time, the `tablew` opcode should be used. After copying the example from the previous section into your .csd file, add this new instrument:

```
instr 2
ktrig metro 2
krand init 0
kval1 init 0
kval2 init 0

if ktrig == 0 kgoto done
```

```
krand random 0, 10
if krand < 5 kgoto done

; select the data in two randomly chosen steps:
krand1 random 0, 7
krand1 = int(krand1)
kval1 table krand1, giPitchTable
krand2 random 0, 7
krand2 = int(krand2)
kval2 table krand2, giPitchTable

; swap the data:
tablew kval1, krand2, giPitchTable
tablew kval2, krand1, giPitchTable

done:
endin
```

To hear the result, play both instruments 1 and 2 at the same time from the score:

```
i1 0 10
i2 0 10
```

The new instrument chooses two steps in the `giPitchTable` at random and copies the values from those steps into the internal variables `kval1` and `kval2`. It then swaps them, writing each into the table, using `tablew`, at the index of the other. When you play the score, you should hear the arpeggio as before, but it will mutate gradually as values in the table are swapped. For more variety, you may want to seed the random number generator in the orchestra header:

```
seed 0
```

This instrument uses a random number to decide whether to do a swap operation; you can make swaps more likely by adjusting `if krand < 5` to test for some other number. It uses the `kgoto` syntax to skip the swapping if the test fails. For more on `kgoto`, see "Logic and Flow Control" in Chapter 6.

Dynamics Control and Panning

Because Csound uses floating-point audio internally, the signal level can rise to astronomical levels—far beyond anything that your output hardware (or your ears) can hope to deal with. In order to prevent clipping and have a pleasant listening experience, you'll often want to employ one or more techniques for controlling the audio signal level. Appropriate tools for the job are the `balance` and `compress` opcodes, which are useful for designing individual instruments. In addition, I find it useful to set up i-time or k-rate level controls in the orchestra header, so that I have quick access to what is essentially a mixing console. For instance, the header might include code like this:

```
giMasterVolume = 1.0
giBassVolume = 1.0
giSnareVolume = 1.0
```

Then, in the bass instrument, I would do something like this:

```
iamp = p4 * giMasterVolume * giBassVolume
```

If, while developing a piece of music, I find that the mix as a whole is clipping, I can adjust everything downward by setting `giMasterVolume = 0.95` or whatever. Likewise, I can adjust all instances of the bass instrument downward from one easy-to-find parameter, without having to edit the score or hunt through the orchestra for the bass instrument. (The same results can be achieved using the Mixer opcodes, as explained earlier in this chapter.)

balance

The most basic opcode for controlling the signal level within an instrument is `balance`. `balance` compares a signal to a reference signal. The output of `balance` is the same as the main input signal, but adjusted up or down in level so that it doesn't exceed the level of the reference signal. `balance` doesn't always do a perfect job of this; it does some averaging, so shorter peaks may slip through without being entirely squashed. So you'll still need to use your ears and check the messages in the output console for indications of clipping.

I usually use `balance` by creating a dummy sine wave (a wave I'm not using for anything else) as its comparison input. Here's an example that illustrates the technique:

```
0dbfs = 1

instr 1
iCos ftgen 0, 0, 8192, 11, 1
iSine ftgen 0, 0, 8192, 10, 1
ifreq = p4

; generate a tone, and process it through a resonant filter:
asig gbuzz 100, ifreq, 75, 1, 0.9, iCos
ifiltrise = p3 * 0.01
ifiltdecay = p3 * 0.99
kfiltenv linseg 2500, ifiltrise, 3700, ifiltdecay, 800
afilt rezzy asig, kfiltenv, 85

; generate a reference tone, and adjust the filter output to match the
```

```
; level of the reference:
icomplevel = 0.2
asine oscil icomplevel, 500, iSine
abal balance afilt, asine
aout linen abal, 0.01, p3, 0.1
outs aout, aout
endin

</CsInstruments>
<CsScore>

i1 0 1 100
i1 + . 125
i1 + . 150
```

As usual, this orchestra has 0dbfs = 1, but the careless programmer has given the signal from gbuzz (the oscillator we're listening to) an amplitude of 100. The filter (rezzy) is happy to process this signal, but the result—the signal in afilt—will be much too loud. A comparison signal is created by an oscil playing a 500-Hz sine wave, and afilt is passed through balance, giving us a new output signal called abal. This is then enveloped using linen and sent to the output. You'll note that the level of asine is set to 0.2, yet the output level of the signal is about 0.9. There's no clipping, which is good, but balance doesn't always reduce a signal to the expected level, so creating an i-time argument (named icomplevel in the code above) to control the level of the comparison signal makes the code easy to read.

You can control the output more crudely and drastically with the limit opcode. In the example above, replace the balance line with this code:

```
abal limit afilt, -0.9, 0.9
```

The output signal will be reported by the console as having a perfectly even level of 0.9, but you'll still hear lots of clipping, because clipping the signal is what limit does. Once in a while this may be the effect you want, but it's important to understand that limit is not a high-end soft-knee compressor/limiter: It just performs a simple mathematical operation. Rather than processing audio through limit, you're more likely to want to use it to limit the range of control signals. That's what it's mainly designed for. For good-sounding limiting, use compress.

compress

The compress opcode implements a soft-knee sidechain compressor with standard envelope attack and release settings and an adjustable threshold. The first thing to note about this opcode is that as of Csound 5.13, the opcode assumes 0dbfs = 32768, which was the maximum signal level in early, 16-bit versions of Csound. I'm told this requirement will disappear in the next release of Csound, so if you're using 5.14 or later, you shouldn't need to worry about it.

For details on this opcode, you'll need to consult the manual. But here's an example to get you started. I set up my orchestra so that neither the synthesizer instrument nor the reverb uses `outs` to send the final signal to Csound's audio output. Instead, they use global variables to send to an output processor "instrument" whose sole purpose is to apply `compress`. Because this .csd file has `0dbfs=1.0` in its orchestra header, the output processor has to do a little extra math on the input and output of `compress`. And because the signal is stereo, I needed a `compress` on each channel.

Note that the synth output needs to be zeroed in the output processor instrument, because the synth instrument will be played polyphonically. There's only one reverb, however, so its output, which is also arriving at the output instrument, simply overwrites whatever is in the bus rather than adding to it. Thus the reverb bus doesn't need to be zeroed.

```
instr 201 ; output compressor
ainL = gaRevOutL + gaSynthOutL
ainR = gaRevOutR + gaSynthOutR
gaSynthOutL = 0
gaSynthOutR = 0

; get rid of DC:
ainL atone ainL, 10
ainR atone ainR, 10

; boost (and later reduce) the level for Csound 5.13:
ainL = ainL * 32768
ainR = ainR * 32768
aoutL compress ainL, ainL, 0, 60, 76, 2, 0.001, 0.05, 0.005
aoutR compress ainR, ainR, 0, 60, 76, 2, 0.001, 0.05, 0.005
aoutL = aoutL / 32768
aoutR = aoutR / 32768

outs aoutL, aoutR
endin
```

The inputs are being used in both the first and second arguments to `compress`. The second input is the signal that is to be analyzed for purposes of deciding what to do with the signal at the first input. In other words, `compress` has a built-in sidechain input. Since we're not using a second signal for sidechaining, this is how we tell `compress` to analyze our main signal.

The output processor above is designed for live use, so the final argument to `compress` is only 5 milliseconds (0.005 second). A larger value here might give a slightly smoother response, but it would also add latency to a MIDI keyboard performance, because the output of `compress` will always be delayed by this amount of time. 5ms seems a good compromise.

Because of the sidechain input, `compress` can also be used for ducking. Below is an instrument that illustrates this idea. You can substitute your own voice wave (or a drum loop sample, or whatever). The tone produced by `gbuzz` will duck during the amplitude peaks in the voice signal.

```
instr 1
iCos ftgen 0, 0, 8192, 11, 1
iVoiceTable ftgen 0, 0, 524288, 1, "olive.aiff", 0, 0, 0
ibasefreq = 44100 / ftlen(iVoiceTable)

; play the voice signal:
aphas phasor ibasefreq
avoice tablei aphas, iVoiceTable, 1, 0, 1
avoice = avoice * 0dbfs

; create a tone:
abuzz gbuzz 0dbfs, 200, 75, 1, 0.9, iCos

; duck the tone in response to peaks in the voice signal:
acomp compress abuzz, avoice, 0, 48, 60, 10, 0.005, 0.01, 0.05
outs avoice, acomp
endin

</CsInstruments>
<CsScore>

i1 0 35
```

Note the use of the global variable `0dbfs` to set the amplitudes of the two signals. Because this file does not have `0dbfs=1` in its orchestra header, this variable has the default value 32768.

Try changing the values for the attack and release parameters, and notice how the output changes.

pan and pan2

If you use Csound to generate stereo audio—probably the most common situation, in which the orchestra header specifies `nchnls=2`—you'll often need a way to control the point in the stereo field at which a signal will be heard. The tool for this is `pan2`. Here is its prototype:

```
a1, a2 pan2 asig, xp [, imode]
```

`pan2` takes one audio input (called `asig` above) and produces left and right outputs. The latter are called `a1` and `a2` in the prototype, but I feel it's less confusing in actual instrument code to name them something like `aL` and `aR`. The value sent to `xp` is the pan position and should be somewhere between 0 (hard left) and 1 (hard right).

By default, `pan2` runs in equal-power mode, but there are two other options, as explained in the manual: linear and square-root-of-two.

 In *equal-power* panning, a signal that is panned smoothly from the left speaker to the right or vice versa will sound equally loud at each point in the stereo field. With linear panning, the amplitude level will drop by 6 dB in the middle of the stereo field.

There are two or three basic ways to use the `xp` input. If you know that the pan position of the instrument will remain fixed throughout the score, you can set this argument to a constant. If various notes will be panned to various positions, you can set it from a p-field in the score; in this situation it will presumably be an i-time value, which will be a constant in any given note, but may change from one note to the next. Because this parameter can also be sent a changing k-rate value, you can easily modulate pan position from an envelope or LFO, like this:

```
kpan lfo 0.5, 2
kpan = kpan + 0.5
aL, aR pan2 aout, kpan
outs aL, aR
```

The raw signal from `lfo` is bipolar; that is, it will run from –0.5 to 0.5. We need to add 0.5 to it so it will vary from 0 to 1. This code will cause the LFO to pan whatever signal is in `aout` between the stereo outputs.

The `pan` opcode is more powerful. It's designed for quadrophonic audio systems, in which four speakers are positioned at the corners of a square. In addition to specifying the X and Y coordinates of the apparent sound source within the square, the user has to create a table that defines the curve with which the amplitude will grow as the X or Y value increases.

Audio Output

Because Csound is all about generating audio signals, perhaps it's not surprising that several methods are available for getting audio out of (and into) Csound while it's running.

If you're using CsoundQt, you will normally produce real-time output to your system's audio driver by clicking the Run button. If you're running Csound from the command line, you'll need to specify an output using the `-odac` command-line argument. (See the section on command-line arguments in Chapter 2 for more details.) Likewise, output can be directed to a disk file using CsoundQt's Render button or by specifying an output filename from the command line.

Normally, these outputs will tap directly into the `out` (or, if `nchnls=2`, into the `outs`) opcode, which is used throughout this book. These are not the only options, however.

Audio input from a previously recorded file was covered earlier in this chapter, in the "Sample Playback" section. Real-time audio input is discussed in Chapter 10, "Using Csound with MIDI, OSC, Pd, Python, and Live Audio."

out and outs

Let's suppose your score has five instrument instances (which could be the same instrument or different ones) running at the same time. Each instrument generates an ongoing audio signal and then sends it to the output via the `outs` opcode. Without any hand-holding on the user's part, Csound transparently mixes all of these signals to produce a single output audio stream.

If your orchestra header specifies `nchnls=1`, your orchestra will be monaural, so use `out` with a single argument:

```
out asig
```

If `nchnls=2`, use `outs`:

```
outs asigL, asigR
```

Needless to say, the left and right signals to `outs` need not be different; if they're the same, you'll get a monaural output.

In the event that you have an audio system with more than two channels, you'll need to use `outc`, which accepts an arbitrary number of audio signals. With two audio variables as input arguments, `outc` is exactly the same as `outs`.

fout

In some circumstances, such as producing submixes as separate audio files, standard rendering won't do the job. Instead of, or in addition to, `outs`, you can use `fout`. The only thing that's at all tricky about `fout` is specifying the format in which you want the file saved. You can refer to the manual for details, but briefly, an argument of 14 will give you a standard 16-bit .WAV file, while 24 will give you a standard 16-bit .AIFF file.

If you're using `fout` in a mixer/output instrument, in order to collect the signals from several instruments before writing the result to disk, you need to be aware that, unlike the `outs` family opcodes, `fout` does not zero the audio variables after using them. This can be done manually or using the `clear` opcode.

Effects

Effects processes such as reverb, chorus, and delay are not special: They're implemented in Csound using the same kind of code used for synthesis. It's possible to create an effect within the instrument whose signal will be processed by the effect, but this is not usually the best approach. For more on this topic, see "Global Signal Routing," earlier in this chapter.

Reverb

With Csound, you can build your own reverb using comb and allpass filters, which can be configured however you like. This is an exercise for DSP experts, and we won't get into it in this book. (See the upcoming sidebar for a cautionary note, however.) Fortunately, you don't have to go there if you don't want to, as several good reverbs are available among Csound's opcode complement.

The `reverbsc` opcode is a good choice for making a stereo reverb. The basic way to use this has already been covered in the QuickStart tutorial in Chapter 3 and earlier in this chapter in the section on global signal routing.

`freeverb` is easy to use and sounds good. The room size and high-frequency damping are set in arbitrary values between 0 and 1, and can be modulated in real time. High values for room size (around 0.99) coupled with low values of damping produce a repetitious looping quality, but below are some values that produce a pleasant wash of reverb:

```
aoutL, aoutR freeverb ain, ain, 0.89, 0.47
```

Also worth exploring is `babo`. (The name is short for "ball in a box.") `babo` takes a mono input and produces a stereo output by modeling the echoes bouncing off the walls of a room. The dimensions of the room and the amount of diffusion from the walls are controllable, as are the position of the listener, the position of the sound source, and the distance between the listener's ears. A set of eight default parameters can be user-programmed using a small data table created with GEN 02. Here is a simple reverb instrument that uses `babo`:

```
instr 101 ; a modeled room reverberator
ain = gaRevIn
gaRevIn = 0
giData ftgen 0, 0, 8, -2, 0.99, 0.9, 0, 0, 0, 0.3, 1, 0.8
aoutL, aoutR babo ain, 6, 4, 3, 14.39, 11.86, 10, 0.9, giData
outs aoutL, aoutR
endin
```

If you're curious how this works, you should definitely study the `babo` page in the manual. We won't cover the details here. Basically, the `ftgen` line uses GEN 02 to create eight optional parameter values that are then passed to `babo`, overriding the defaults. Most of the values shown above are defaults, but I've increased the high-frequency damping from 0.1 to 0.9, increased the attenuation of the direct signal to 1 from the default of 0.5, and reduced the diffusion from 1 to 0.9 because the default of 1 produces a long-lasting roar. The values for the room dimensions are taken from the `babo` page in the manual.

 Filters Aren't Just for Tone-Shaping   One of the things that can happen, when you start writing DSP code, is that the values produced by your code or by the opcodes you're employing can gradually spiral higher and higher. This is especially likely with any process, such as reverberation, that involves delay lines and feedback. When the values of an audio signal gradually drift higher (or lower), you may not be able to hear the difference immediately, but the dynamic range of your system will be compromised. When this happens, clipping distortion is likely to occur sooner than it would otherwise, and your speakers will work less efficiently.

This type of mathematical error is often referred to as DC, because it's analogous to the direct current in an analog audio system. Another way of looking at it is that it's a signal with some non-zero amplitude and a frequency of 0 Hz. A standard method of getting rid of DC is to run the output of a reverb-type instrument through an `atone` opcode with a half-power point of 15 or 20 Hz. Recent versions of Csound include the `dcblock2` opcode, which does the same thing.

Delay

Delaying an audio signal before sending it to the output is a surprisingly powerful sound modification technique. In addition to simple echoes, delay can be used for pitch changes, chorusing, and comb filtering. Csound is well equipped to create effects of this type. The primary opcodes you need to know are `delayr`, `delayw`, and `deltapi`. The `vcomb` opcode is described in the manual as "reverberating" a signal, but in my tests it seems to behave like a delay line with a built-in feedback loop. While not covered in this book, it's also worth looking at if you're seeking ways to build complex delay effects.

The `delayr` opcode reads the output of the delay and also sets the length of the delay. `delayw` writes a signal to the input of the delay. `deltapi` is a "tap" into the data being held by the delay; it can be used to create multi-tap delay effects.

You'll often hear the term "delay line" used to refer to a delay effect. You might imagine the signal traveling down the line from the input (the write operation) to the output (the read operation). In fact, this is more or less what happens. A delay line is implemented in software as a "first-in, first-out" memory buffer. As a signal is received at the input of the delay, during each k-rate cycle the data in the buffer is passed from one memory location down the line to the next location. When the data reaches the end of the buffer (after some number of k-rate cycles), it is sent to the output.

delayr and delayw

The first example below creates a very simple delay line with feedback. The delay line is implemented as instrument 101. It receives a plucked sound from instrument 1. Take a look at this code and then read the explanation that follows. (The tags at the beginning and end of the .csd file have, as usual in this book, been omitted.)

```
sr = 44100
ksmps = 4
nchnls = 2
0dbfs = 1
gaDelayBus init 0
```

```
instr 1 ; a plucked sound
; setup
iCos ftgen 0, 0, 8192, 11, 1
idur = p3
iamp = p4
ifreq = cpspch(p5)

; synthesis
kampenv line iamp, idur, 0
asig gbuzz kampenv, ifreq, 25, 1, 0.8, iCos
kfiltenv line 3500, idur, 500
afilt lpf18 asig, kfiltenv, 0.3, 0

; output
gaDelayBus = gaDelayBus + afilt
outs afilt, afilt
endin

instr 101 ; a simple delay
; setup
ain = gaDelayBus
gaDelayBus = 0
iamp = p4

; delay line with feedback:
ifdbk = 0.5
aout delayr 0.25
  delayw ain + (aout * ifdbk)

; output
aout = aout * iamp
outs aout, aout
endin

</CsInstruments>
<CsScore>

i101 0 4 0.5
i1 0 0.5 0.8 7.00
i1 + . . 7.04
i1 + . . 7.07
```

The first thing to note is that the delay line (instrument 101) has to be started in the score. Thanks to a p3 value of 4, it runs for a couple of seconds after the end of the last note coming from instrument 1. This gives the echoes coming from the delay time to die away.

The second thing to note is that delayr, which reads the output of the delay, is used *before* the input is created using delayw. At first glance this may seem backward, but it's actually very sensible. The argument to delayr tells Csound how long (in seconds) the delay will be. This argument causes Csound to set up a memory buffer of the proper length. The output variable (aout) can then be passed back to the input to create feedback—hopefully at a reduced level. The value ifdbk in this instrument controls the feedback amount. In a more complex orchestra, both the delay time and the feedback amount might be controlled using p-fields in the score.

The third thing to note is that this delay line is a wet-only effect; the delay instrument has no dry (un-delayed) output. The dry output is handled by the instrument generating the tones. As an exercise, you might try rewriting this example so that the delay instrument produces all of the output and has control over the wet/dry mix.

To create a stereo delay effect, you can use two separate delay lines, like this:

```
instr 101 ; a stereo delay
ain = gaDelayBus
gaDelayBus = 0
iamp = p4

; delay lines with feedback:
ifdbkL = 0.75
ifdbkR = 0.4
aoutL delayr 0.125
delayw ain + (aoutL * ifdbkL)
aoutR delayr 0.25
delayw ain + (aoutR * ifdbkR)

; output:
aoutL = aoutL * iamp
aoutR = aoutR * iamp
outs aoutL, aoutR
endin
```

This example could be spiced up by adding a cross-delay amount. With cross-delay, the output of the left delay line is used as an input to the right delay line, and vice versa. (One of the audio variables has to be created ahead of time using init.) If you try this, be careful that the total amount of delay feedback doesn't exceed 1.0. If it does, runaway feedback will occur.

deltapi

The simplest way to use `deltapi` is with a fixed delay time. This opcode should be positioned between the `delayr/delayw` pair. The next example shows a multitap delay with four taps, two of which are panned left and two right. When using this in the .csd file given at the beginning of this section, you may want to increase the length of the `i101` event in the score.

```
instr 101 ; a multitap delay
ain = gaDelayBus
gaDelayBus = 0
iamp = p4

; multitap delay with feedback:
aout delayr 1.5
aout1 deltapi 0.25
aout2 deltapi 0.75
aout3 deltapi 1.00
aout4 deltapi 1.25
delayw ain + (aout * 0.2)

; output:
aoutL = (aout1 + aout3) * iamp
aoutR = (aout2 + aout4) * iamp
outs aoutL, aoutR
endin
```

A more interesting use of `deltapi` is to sweep the delay time in some manner. This is most often done with an LFO. You'll notice that `deltapi` is an interpolating opcode. This is important, because the interpolation smooths the audio signal when the delay time is changing. Below is a basic stereo chorus constructed with `deltapi`. Instrument 1 uses the same code given earlier in this section, but the notes in the score have been lengthened to make it easier to hear the chorus effect.

```
instr 101 ; a stereo chorus
ain = gaDelayBus
gaDelayBus = 0
iamp = p4

; swept delay with feedback:
klfo1 lfo 0.003, 1.0
klfo2 lfo 0.003, 0.8
aout  delayr 0.1
atap1 deltapi 0.03 + klfo1
atap2 deltapi 0.05 + klfo2
```

```
    delayw ain + (atap1 * 0.3) + (atap2 * 0.3)

; output:
aoutL = atap1 * iamp
aoutR = atap2 * iamp
outs aoutL, aoutR
endin

</CsInstruments>
<CsScore>
i101 0 7 0.8
i1 0 2 0.8 7.00
i1 + . . 7.04
i1 + . . 7.07
```

When using `deltapi`, it's important that you keep the minimum delay time greater than zero and the maximum less than the total delay time created by `delayr`. In the code above, `delayr` creates a memory buffer containing 0.1 second of audio. This is actually more than is needed. The delay time for the first `deltapi` output varies from 0.027 to 0.033 as it is swept by the LFO, while the second varies from 0.047 to 0.053. You can experiment with a wider LFO sweep, as long as you're careful that the maximum and minimum values stay in range. The values I used for the LFOs in this instrument were arrived at empirically: I like the sound. When I increase the LFO amplitude, the chorusing starts to sound wobbly to me.

vdelay

Using `vdelay` is a bit easier than using a `delayr/deltapi/delayw` set, because the Csound code is more concise. The main limitation of `vdelay` is that it only produces one tap into the delay line. Within a `delayr/delayw` pair, you can run a number of taps. Another difference is that `delayr` expects to see a delay time in seconds, while `vdelay` expects the delay time to be given in milliseconds. Even though its name doesn't end with -i, `vdelay` is an interpolating opcode, so it will produce smooth audio.

Here's a simple example in which a stereo chorus, constructed using two `vdelay` units, is build into an instrument. The same principle could be used to build a six-voice chorus modulated by several LFOs. Play a note on this instrument for five or six seconds to hear the chorusing:

```
giSine ftgen 0, 0, 8192, 10, 1
giWave ftgen 0, 0, 8192, 10, 1, 1, 1, 1, 1, 1, 1, 1, 1, 1
instr 1
kpitchramp expseg 800, 2, 200, 1, 200
asig oscil 0.3, kpitchramp, giWave
```

```
imoddepth = 2.5
imodrate = 0.7
aLFO oscil imoddepth, imodrate, giSine
imaxdel = 15
adelL vdelay asig, 8 + aLFO, imaxdel
adelR vdelay asig, 8 - aLFO, imaxdel
kampenv linseg 0, 0.1, 1, p3 - 0.11, 1, 0.1, 0
aL = (adelL + asig) * kampenv
aR = (adelR + asig) * kampenv
outs aL, aR
endin
```

vdelay is one of a family of closely related opcodes. The details will be found in the manual.

Distortion

Rumor has it that the deliberate use of distortion began in the 1960s, when guitarists found that they could make a nastier, more aggressive sound by slicing through their speaker cones with a razor blade. Not long afterward, the fuzz tone effect pedal, which produced a similar sound but without physical damage to the equipment, was introduced. In any event, the introduction of deliberate distortion has become an important technique in electronic music-making.

There are various ways to add distortion to a signal. Modulating the frequency of an audio oscillator with a noise source, for instance, is a form of distortion. In this section we'll take a quick look at *waveshaping* distortion. Waveshaping introduces new partials (frequency components) into the sound. Generally this is an amplitude-dependent process. That is, the louder an input signal is, the more distorted it will be, and the more new partials will be added.

Waveshaping with mirror

The mirror opcode provides a quick, easy way to do waveshaping. It has lower and upper thresholds. Signals that exceed these thresholds are "reflected" back into the range between the thresholds in a way that sounds pleasant and natural. Play this instrument with a 12-second score event to hear the effect. When the waveform of the audio signal has an amplitude greater than ± 0.4, waveshaping takes place.

```
giSine ftgen 0, 0, 8192, 10, 1

instr 1
kamp linseg 0, 1, 0.4, 5, 1.3, 1, 1.3, 2, 0.4, 3, 0
asig oscil kamp, 200, giSine
amir mirror asig, -0.4, 0.4
outs amir, amir
endin
```

Waveshaping with table

The example below doesn't make use of any opcodes not already covered in this chapter. It shows a way of using `table` at audio rate so as to add distortion. Instrument 1 in this example generates a sine wave with a gradually increasing amplitude, but it doesn't send the resulting signal to the output; instead, the signal is routed to the distortion instrument. The latter contains an f-table generated using GEN 08. GEN 08 produces a smooth curve with arbitrary peaks and valleys.

The input signal (coming from `gaDistBus`) is expected to have a maximum amplitude of 1.0. It's multiplied by 8,192 because that is the length of the `iShape` table that has been created using `ftgen`. The signal is then used as an index into the `iShape` table. The output is no longer a sine wave; instead, it has whatever peaks and valleys were defined in the table.

```
giSine ftgen 0, 0, 8192, 10, 1
gaDistBus init 0


instr 1
idur = p3
iamp = p4
ifrq = p5
iatk = 0.01
idec = 0.1
isustime = idur - 0.11

kamp linseg 0, iatk, 0.01, isustime, iamp, idec, 0
asig oscil kamp, ifrq, giSine
gaDistBus = gaDistBus + asig
endin


instr 11 ; distortion
iamp = p4
iShape ftgen 0, 0, 8192, 8, 0, 1024, 1, 512, -1, 512, 1, 2048, -1, 4096, 0
ain = gaDistBus
gaDistBus = 0

asig table ain * 8192, iShape
asig = asig * iamp
outs asig, asig
endin


</CsInstruments>
<CsScore>


i1 0 10 0.6 200
; uncomment the next line to hear intermodulation distortion:
```

```
; i1 3 7 0.4 350
i11 0 10 0.5
```

This effect could easily be modified by adding a lowpass filter to produce a fatter sound.

Instrument Control

Once in a while, you may need to reinitialize an instrument while it's running. This is done using the `reinit` opcode. The reinitialization can be done for all of the instrument code or only for a selected portion of the code. During the reinitialization, all of the i-time values that are set forth within the designated code lines will be recalculated. Envelope generators will start over from their starting points. The phase of oscillators will be reset.

The syntax of `reinit` is simple:

```
reinit label
```

As the manual explains, during a reinitialization pass, performance is temporarily suspended (without any effect on the audio output, unless the reinitialization itself causes an effect or takes so long that the output buffer is emptied) while an initialization pass is run. This pass begins at the label specified as the argument to `reinit` and continues either to the end of the instrument or to an earlier point in the code designated by a `rireturn` statement. Performance is then resumed at the point where it left off.

`reinit` will often be used in conjunction with `timout`, but it doesn't have to be. The syntax of the `timout` opcode looks like this:

```
timout istrt, idur, label
```

This opcode creates a conditional branch during k-period cycles. Beginning at time `istrt` (which should usually be zero), `timout` causes processing to jump to the point specified by `label`. After `idur` seconds, the jump ceases, and whatever code lies between the `timout` statement and the label will be executed. This code may include a `reinit`.

Here is an example of `timout` that delays the start of a second oscillator:

```
instr 1

asig2 init 0

timout 0, 0.5, contin
asig2 oscil 0.4, 500, giSine
```

```
kamp2 linseg 0, 0.1, 1
asig2 = asig2 * kamp2

contin:

asig oscil 1, 200, giSine
asig = asig + asig2
kamp linen 0.7, 0, p3, 0.2
asig = asig * kamp
outs asig, asig

endin
```

In this example, the second oscillator (whose output is `asig2`) and its associated amplitude envelope are ignored for the first 0.5 second, because during that time `timout` causes a branch to the `contin` label. When 0.5 second has passed, `timout` ceases to cause a jump, so the second oscillator will be heard.

With that preamble, the usage of `reinit` and `timout` may be easier to understand. The example given in the manual for `reinit` is rather artificial, but I was unable to come up with anything much more musical. In the following example, the frequency of the oscillator (set by `ifreq`) is changed during a `reinit` pass. The frequency is coming from a global k-rate variable, `gkPitch`, which might be doing anything.

```
instr 1
reset:
  ifreq = i(gkPitch)
  timout 0, p3/40, contin
  reinit reset
contin:
  asig oscil 1, ifreq, giSine, -1
rireturn
kamp linen 0.7, 0, p3, 0.2
asig = asig * kamp
outs asig, asig
endin
```

The point of this example is that the `reinit` line is executed only when `timout` has timed out. While `timout` is active, the k-period execution of the instrument code never sees `reinit`; it jumps past `reinit` to the `contin` label. And the value of `ifreq` doesn't change, because it's an i-time variable. Periodically, however (in this example, it happens 40 times during the note event, because the duration value for `timout` is p3/40), `reinit` causes a jump back to the `reset` label. Each time this happens, `ifreq` is given a new value based on the current value of `gkPitch`. The reinitialization pass then continues downward through the code, first restarting `timout` (so that its start time and duration will be reset in terms of the current moment) and then sending the new value of `ifreq` to the oscillator. The reinitialization pass then hits the `rireturn` opcode and terminates.

You'll notice that the value of the optional phase parameter for `oscil` has been set to –1. This causes reinitialization of the waveform phase to be skipped. In the absence of a negative value for this argument, the oscillator will click whenever a reinitialization pass occurs, because its phase will be reset to the starting point.

Analysis and Resynthesis

Csound provides a number of tools for advanced types of synthesis. We don't have space in this book to discuss all of them in detail, but we'll take a quick look at one of them.

If you look at the manual pages for opcodes like `pvoc` and `adsynt`, you'll discover that they need file analysis data in order to function. This analysis data is generated by Csound's built-in utilities. If you click on the Utilities icon in the CsoundQt toolbar, you'll find a dialog box (see Figure 7.3) with which you can run the `cvanal`, `hetro`, `lpanal`, `pvanal`, and `atsa` utilities. Each of these creates an analysis file that can be used with a different group of opcodes.

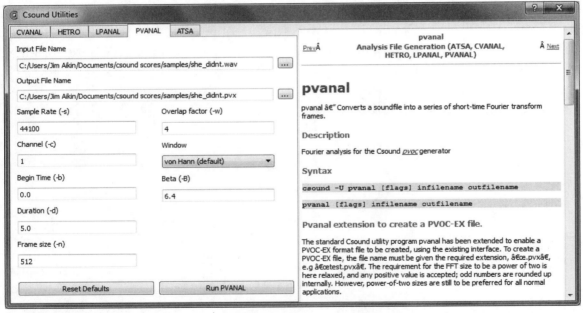

Figure 7.3 From the Utilities box in CsoundQt, you can run five different audio analysis routines. The right side of the window displays the manual page for the current routine, which you'll want to consult while setting the parameters. These utilities can also be run from the command line, if desired.

The settings used with these utilities require some experimentation. The `atsa` utility has an especially daunting number of settings. In Csound 5.13, I was unable to get `lpanal` to work, no matter what settings I tried. (I'm told that `lpanal` is very old code and is something of a vestige.) However, `pvanal` works very well, and the results are musically versatile.

The pvanal utility generates a file for use with the pvoc opcode. This opcode gives you independent control over the speed and pitch of the sampled sound. A good source sound to experiment with might be a short sample—a few seconds—of a voice speaking a phrase. You can select the source file in the top field in the dialog box; CsoundQt will then fill the second field with the same filename, but with a .pvx extension.

Feel free to experiment with the values in this box. The manual notes, for example, that the frame size (-n, if you're working from the command line) should be "larger than the longest pitch period of the sample." However, a smaller value, such as 128, can produce some interesting gargling effects. With a value of 1024, which is the default in CsoundQt, pvoc can reproduce the original sound with only a slight smearing quality. Using pvoc can be simple or complex; here's a simple example:

```
isamplelength = 5.0
kphas phasor 1/p3
kphas = kphas * isamplelength
ktransp init 1
asig pvoc kphas, ktransp, "she_didnt.pvx"
```

This plays the source file once, at original pitch, during the duration of the note in the score. You could easily add a pitch envelope by generating the value of ktransp as the output of a linseg.

For producing abstract sounds, you may find that a more interesting approach is to ramp through the analysis file (via the first argument to pvoc) very slowly. With a vocal sample as the source audio, this technique can produce rich sheets of slowly evolving metallic tone. For instance, you might replace the code shown above with this:

```
ioffset = p4
kphas phasor 0.1
kphas = kphas * 0.025 + ioffset
ktransp init p5
```

User-Defined Opcodes

The opcodes included with Csound are written in the C programming language. While they'll do lots and lots of things, you may not always be able to find one that does precisely what you need. If you're fluent in C, you can write a new opcode using the guidelines in the manual, compile it, and place it in the plugins64 directory of your Csound program directory. Some users do precisely this.

If you're not conversant with C, you may be delighted to find that there's an easier way. You can create new opcodes using the Csound language itself and include them in your .csd file. This is done using a special syntax for creating *user-defined opcodes* (UDOs). In the next couple of pages, you'll learn how to do this.

Technically, you can't do anything by writing your own opcode that you couldn't do just by writing the code for the new opcode as part of an instrument. (This is not 100% true, as we'll see, but it's a good approximation.) So why write a UDO? There are two main reasons: encapsulation and reusability.

Encapsulation makes your code easier to read and maintain. Instead of writing 30 lines of code in the instrument, you write a one-line call to a UDO. The UDO is in a different part of your source code file. Once you've debugged it, you don't need to look at or worry about it. In addition, if five different instruments in your orchestra need to make use of the same complex procedure, you only need to write the code once. All five instruments can use the same UDO, exactly the way they would use any other opcode. On that basis, a UDO is a bit like a GOSUB statement in BASIC.

Once you've created a useful opcode, such as your own custom reverb or filter bank, you can save it to your hard drive as a separate file. Having done that, you don't even need to open the file and copy the code into your next project. To reuse it, just use an #include directive, and the file will be included in your orchestra when the orchestra is compiled. After creating a file called my_opcodes.txt, you would put this line in the orchestra header:

```
#include "my_opcodes.txt"
```

Csound will look for the included file first in the same directory as the .csd file and then in the directory you've specified using the INCDIR environment variable. (In CsoundQt, this directory can be set in the Environment tab of the Configuration window.)

User-defined opcodes will generally be less efficient at the code level than opcodes written in C. That is, they'll use up more CPU time when running. Generally, the convenience factor outweighs the performance hit.

User-defined opcodes are created with the opcode opcode. The prototype of this opcode is a little different from other prototypes. It looks like this:

```
opcode name, outtypes, intypes
```

What this says is that we need to give the opcode a name (in order to be able to call it from our instrument code). We also need to tell Csound what type(s) of input(s) and output(s) the opcode will receive and send. The name can consist of any combination of letters, digits, and underscore characters, but should not begin with a digit. It may be a good idea to start the name of your opcode with a capital letter, as this will make the fact that it's a UDO more obvious when you're reading your code. Names such as myfilter and my_filter are legal, but MyFilter works better visually.

The outtypes and intypes of the UDO are defined using the familiar letters i, k, a, and S, but with a couple of extra possibilities. Here, for instance, is an opcode that accepts three k-rate inputs and outputs two a-rate outputs:

```
opcode MyOp, aa, kkk
kdata1, kdata2, kdata3 xin
```

```
; processing code would go here, including lines that create two audio
; variables
xout audio1, audio2
endop
```

The first thing to note about this is that there is a comma after the name of the UDO. There won't be a comma after the name when you use it in your instrument code, so omitting the comma here is an easy mistake to make. The inputs are assigned to local variables using the `xin` opcode, and the outputs are transmitted back to the calling instrument using the `xout` opcode. The number of arguments to `xin` and `xout` must always match the opcode header. The opcode ends with `endop`.

The line containing `xin` should be the first line of the code in the UDO, and the line containing `xout` should be the last line. It's legal to put code before `xin` or after `xout`, but if you do this, your code may not run the way you expect it to. This is because `xin` and `xout` are actually init-time opcodes. They initialize the data connections between the UDO and the instrument that invokes it, but they're ignored during k-rate operations. As a simple illustration, consider this rather silly opcode:

```
opcode Mult, k, kk
kval1, kval2 xin
kresult = kval1* kval2
kstorage = kresult
kresult = 0
xout kresult
kresult = kstorage
endop
```

Logically, you might expect it to output 0, since `kresult` is set to a value of 0 just before `xout` is called. But the UDO will output the product of the two inputs, which probably won't be 0, because the last line restores `kresult` to its previous value before the output is sent to the calling instrument.

An opcode with neither inputs nor outputs is legal, though it's not likely to be very useful. If you don't need ins or outs, put 0's in those arguments. For example:

```
giSine ftgen 0, 0, 8192, 10, 1

opcode MyTone, 0, 0
asig oscil 0.5, 220, giSine
outs asig, asig
endop
```

```
instr 11
MyTone
endin
```

This produces the same signal as if the calls to `oscil` and `outs` had been in instrument 11 itself. Even if your opcode needs no inputs, it would be better practice to pass the audio output(s) back to the calling instrument and use `outs` in the instrument.

As with many of Csound's built-in opcodes, UDOs can be given default values for optional i-time input arguments. If an i-time argument is included among the inputs, it can be symbolized by `j` (in which case the default will be –1), `o` (which defaults to zero), or `p` (which defaults to 1). These are the only default values that can be used, but they cover a lot of territory.

For example, suppose the opcode is defined this way:

```
opcode MyOp, aa, kjp
```

The k-rate input will always be required. The instrument calling the opcode can give a non-default value to the two i-time arguments, but it's not required to do so. If it doesn't, then following this:

```
opcode MyOp, aa, kjp
kdata1, idata2, idata3 xin
```

the variable `idata2` will have a value of –1 and the variable `idata3` will have a value of 1.

If you use a capital `K` in defining the opcode's inputs, the value will be read from the calling instrument during the initialization pass and then in each k-period. If you use a lowercase `k`, the input will *not* be read during the initialization pass, which may result in unexpected behavior.

The one thing that makes a UDO different from ordinary code, which was alluded to earlier, is this: An opcode can be given a lower value of `ksmps`. This can sometimes provide better audio quality when the opcode is engaged in complex DSP—if you're writing your own reverb, for example. The orchestra as a whole might have `ksmps=10`, yet the UDO could run with `ksmps=1`.

This is done using the `setksmps` opcode:

```
setksmps 1
```

The new, temporary value of `ksmps` must always be a factor of the orchestra's setting for this value. If the orchestra has `ksmps=10`, for example, then a value of 5, 2, or 1 could be used in the UDO.

As the manual notes, when `ksmps` is set to a lower value, global a-rate operations must not be used in the opcode. You can't access ga- variables or use the a-rate zak opcodes, for instance.

Creating Score Events during Performance

The list of events in a Csound score is pretty much set in stone at the time the score is compiled. During the compilation process, the events are sorted, looping sections are spelled out as linear lists of events, and so forth, and then the score is played. For some types of musical compositions, this is perfectly appropriate. But there are other situations in which we might want to insert new events during performance. One way of doing this is with real-time MIDI input, as discussed in Chapter 10. Another method is to use the Live Events feature in CsoundQt, as explained in Chapter 5. Yet a third method is to create new score events from within the orchestra.

Three families of opcodes are available with which to accomplish this: schedule, scoreline, and event. To some extent, which one you use is a matter of taste; they'll all do the job. However, scoreline is a bit different in that it accepts a new score event in the form of text. This can make it a good choice when used in conjunction with embedded Python code, as you can assemble strings in a Python routine and return them to Csound so as to generate notes with them. The use of Python within Csound is discussed in Chapter 10.

Ordinarily, the event-generating opcodes will be used by a master sequencing or loop-generating instrument. They will be used to generate new events by a different instrument, which will produce the actual sounds. With the usual amount of care, however, they can be used recursively, as the next example illustrates.

Note   In some versions of *The Canonical Csound Reference Manual*, due to block-copying of text, reference is made on a few manual pages to trigger arguments that will cause a score-scheduling event to fire, even though no such argument can be used with that particular opcode.

schedule and schedwhen

schedule is an i-time opcode. Its arguments exactly parallel the p-fields of a score statement: instrument number (or name as a double-quoted string), starting time (in relation to the moment when schedule is invoked), duration, p4, p5, and so on.

In the example below, schedule is being used recursively to call another instance of the same instrument:

```
giSine ftgen 0, 0, 8192, 10, 1

instr 1
idur = p3
iamp = p4
ifrq = p5
icount = p6

if icount > 0 then
```

```
        schedule 1, 0, idur, iamp * 0.65, ifrq * 1.35, icount - 1
    endif

    kamp linseg 0, 0.01, iamp, idur - 0.11, iamp, 0.1, 0
    asig oscil kamp, ifrq, giSine
    outs asig, asig
    endin


</CsInstruments>
<CsScore>


i1 0 2 0.3 200 4
```

This example produces a four-note chord. Each note is higher and quieter than the note before it. The value of `icount` is decremented before being passed to `schedule`, and when `icount` reaches zero, no more notes are generated.

Though the presence of a k-rate trigger argument would seem to imply otherwise, `schedwhen` behaves somewhat like an i-time opcode. In fact, it runs during k-rate passes, but a given instance of it runs only once—the first time its trigger is non-zero. You can use it several times within a single score event by setting up an `if/elseif` switching block, like this:

```
instr 1
kcount init 0
ktrig metro 3
if ktrig == 1 then
    kcount = kcount + 1
endif

kdur line 0.1, p3, 0.5

if kcount == 1 then
    schedwhen 1, 2, 0, kdur, 0.3, 200
elseif kcount == 2 then
    schedwhen 1, 2, 0, kdur, 0.3, 300
elseif kcount == 3 then
    schedwhen 1, 2, 0, kdur, 0.3, 400
elseif kcount == 4 then
    schedwhen 1, 2, 0, kdur, 0.3, 500
elseif kcount == 5 then
    schedwhen 1, 2, 0, kdur, 0.3, 600
elseif kcount == 6 then
```

```
      schedwhen 1, 2, 0, kdur, 0.3, 700
endif


endin
```

This code will fire six notes in succession, and the duration of each successive note will be longer because kdur is ramping upward. But the values sent to the new event's p-fields by the schedule family of opcodes must always be i-time. To use varying k-rate values in p-fields, you'll need to use the event opcode. schedkwhen can generate a cloud of notes, but again, they will all have the same p-field values, because the p-field arguments are i-time values.

schedkwhen adds a few features: It can be triggered more than once, and it will limit the maximum number of simultaneous events that it will produce, as well as the minimum time between events.

scoreline

Instead of firing new score events with numerical values for the p-fields, scoreline accepts a text string as its first argument (and a trigger as its second). This has two advantages. First, the text can contain multiple lines. Second, you can assemble the text on the fly. Here's an example of the first technique:

```
instr 1
Strudel = {{i2 0 0.5 0.5 200
i2 1 . . 300
i2 2 . . 400 }}

ktrig init 1
scoreline Strudel, ktrig
ktrig = 0


endin
```

This instrument plays three notes, one second apart. The double curly braces are used around the text because it has multiple lines. Note that the carry symbol (.) can be used in the string sent to scoreline, but some other shortcuts, such as +, can't be. ktrig is set to 0 after being used, so the three score lines will play only once. As the manual notes, if the actual score comes to an end while some of the events queued up by scoreline are still waiting, playback will stop. An e-statement with a p-field to control the score's ending time may come in handy as a way of preventing this. Note, also, that scoreline takes no notice of the current tempo in the score. It always interprets p2 and p3 in seconds.

To put varying values into a string, we can use sprintfk. The resulting string can then be passed to scoreline. Here is an example in which a stream of notes (played by instrument 2, not shown) gets shorter in duration, closer together, and higher in pitch:

```
instr 1
ktempo line 3, p3, 7
ktrig metro ktempo
kpitch line 100, p3, 600
kdur line 0.5, p3, 0.15
Strudel sprintfk "i2 0 %f 0.3 %f", kdur, kpitch
scoreline Strudel, ktrig
endin
```

The call to `sprintf` uses formatting strings to put the current (floating-point) values of `kdur` and `kpitch` into the string, which happens to be called `Strudel`. The string is then passed to `scoreline`, which fires a new event each time the value of `ktrig` is 1. `ktrig` comes from the `metro` opcode, which is increasing in tempo during the course of the instrument 1 event.

event

In some ways `event` is the most flexible opcode for generating score events from within the orchestra. This is because the p-fields for the newly generated event can be filled with k-rate values. The syntax of `event_i` is identical, but because it runs at i-time, only i-time variables can be used as arguments. Here is a simple example that uses `event` in conjunction with `metro`; `metro` produces a regular series of pulses, each of which causes a new call to `event`.

```
instr 1
ktrig metro 4
kdur line 0.3, p3, 0.03
kamp expseg 0.5, p3, 0.05
kfreq expseg 200, p3, 600
if ktrig != 0 then
    event "i", 2, 0, kdur, kamp, kfreq
endif
endin
```

The first argument to event is normally `"i"`, the score character that defines the event. However, `"f"` is also legal here; you can create a new f-table on the fly using `event` or change the data in an f-table that already exists. The second argument is the instrument number. The third argument is the start time with reference to the moment when `event` is called; this is generally zero, but needn't be. The fourth argument has the same meaning as the third p-field in a score event: It sets the duration of the note. The meanings of the remaining arguments are p-fields and depend on the nature of the instrument being triggered.

8 Writing a Csound Score

The score portion of a Csound .csd file is found between the `<CsScore>` and `</CsScore>` tags. Alternatively, the score can be contained in a separate .sco file if you're working the old-fashioned way, with separate .orc and .sco text files. The score contains a list of events. When you click the Run button in CsoundQt (or invoke Csound from the command line and pass it some command-line flags, one of which will be the name of your .csd file), Csound first compiles the code in your orchestra into a form that can produce sound. It then sorts the events in the score and puts them in a form that can play the instruments defined in the orchestra. In this chapter we'll take a close look at exactly how to create Csound scores, and what happens when the score is sorted by the preprocessor.

In the absence of at least one score event, Csound would have nothing to do. Or so we might expect. If you're using real-time MIDI input to play the instruments in the orchestra, however, you can in fact create a score that contains no events, but simply runs silently for some period of time, waiting for MIDI input. For details, see Chapter 10, "Using Csound with MIDI, OSC, Pd, Python, and Live Audio."

The Canonical Csound Reference Manual explains the score syntax in detail. In the left pane of the HTML manual, click on The Standard Numeric Score. The syntax of Csound scores is not difficult to master, but there are a few tricky bits. If you've been reading straight through this book, you've already seen dozens of Csound scores, most of them short and simple. In this chapter we'll explore scoring in greater detail. We'll look at the meanings of the various types of score statements and look at the shortcuts that can make producing complex scores somewhat easier.

Score Statements

Csound score code is like orchestra code in one important way: Each score statement is on a line by itself. Csound has no special "line terminator" character. The carriage-return/line-feed character (normally invisible) that you create by hitting the Enter or Return key on your keyboard terminates one score statement and begins a new one. Blank lines are ignored. Anything that appears on a line after a semicolon is a comment and is also ignored. Comments can also be entered using C-style syntax, in which a comment begins with the character pair `/*` and ends with `*/`:

```
/* This is a comment. */
```

Each score statement begins with a letter or with a curly bracket; curly brackets have a special meaning, as explained in the section "Looping Score Sections," later in this chapter. The characters that can begin a score statement are: a, b, e, f, i, m, n, q, r, s, t, v, x, {, and }.

Following each of these characters, you'll enter zero or more numbers or other symbols, separated by spaces or tab characters. It's a matter of coding style whether you place a space after the initial letter and before the first number; it makes no difference to Csound. These two lines are equivalent:

```
i1   0 2 0.6
i 1  0 2 0.6
```

The numbers in a score statement are referred to as *p-fields*. They're numbered consecutively beginning with 1. Thus it makes sense to talk about p1, p2, and so on. The meanings of the values in the p-fields depend on the type of statement and, in the case of i- and f-statements, on the values in other p-fields. That may sound a bit intimidating if you're new to Csound, but the process of putting numbers into p-fields is actually very straightforward.

With a couple of exceptions, any other symbols used in a score statement will be translated into numbers by the preprocessor, so the score as actually performed consists primarily of lines of numbers.

 Tip   Csound score lines that contain more than a few numbers can get very hard to read. For this reason, you may want to separate the numbers and other symbols with tab characters, so that they will align in neat vertical columns and therefore be easier to read and edit. On the line before a score statement or a series of similar statements, you can insert a comment, also divided up by tabs, to label the columns. The result might look something like this:

```
;        start  dur   amp   pitch  atk   rel   pan
i 101    3      2.25  0.7   6.09   0.03  0.17  0.2
i 101    3.25   2.0   0.7   7.00   0.03  0.17  0.8
```

Unlike a score in conventional music notation, where the left-to-right and top-to-bottom order of notes on staves is significant, Csound score statements can be typed out in any order that's convenient for you. If you're writing a polyphonic passage, for instance, in which notes will sound as chords, it makes no difference whether you enter all of the note events for the first chord, then all of the events for the second chord, and so on; or, alternatively, enter all of the notes for the top chord voice, then proceed to enter all of the notes for the second chord voice, and so on.

This freedom has to be wrapped in a few caveats, however. First, Csound scores can be divided into sections by the s-statement. It's only within a given section that you can place statements in whatever order you like. Second, if you're using shortcut symbols to carry values from one statement to the next, as explained in the "Carry Symbols" section later in this chapter, the statements obviously need to be listed in a certain order. Third, the placement of a b-statement or v-statement at a specific point in an event list does make a difference in how the p-fields in subsequent events are interpreted (see below). Fourth, the `np` and `pp` symbols, discussed below, refer to the previous and following lines, so changing the order of the lines may change the values that will be substituted for these symbols as the score is being processed.

The i-statement

By far the most common statement in a Csound score is the i-statement. In composing a given piece you may need only a few i-statements, or you may need hundreds of them. Each i-statement invokes an instance of an instrument that is defined in the orchestra. The number in p-field 1 is the number of the instrument. For example, this line:

```
i 21  3  1.2
```

has the number 21 in `p1`, so it causes instrument 21 to play a note (or to do whatever it does, which may or may not include producing an audio output).

An i-statement must have values in at least the first three p-fields. `p1` designates the instrument, `p2` is the start time of the event, and `p3` is the length of the event. The meanings of these p-fields are fixed. An i-statement can include other p-fields, if desired. The meanings of `p4`, `p5`, and so on are defined by the instrument itself, so they will quite likely be different for `i21` than for `i19`. (And of course `i21` in one orchestra may be entirely different from `i21` in a different orchestra. What matters is how the current instrument uses the data in the p-fields.)

Some Csound users prefer to grab the values in the p-fields and assign them local variable names at the start of the `instr` code, like this:

```
instr 1
idur = p3
iamp = p4
ifreq = cpspch(p5)
ipan = p6
; ... and so on
```

Other composers just use the symbols p3, p4, and so on wherever they're needed in the instrument code. This is purely a matter of coding style; it makes no difference, but naming the values in your orchestra code will make the code easier to read, edit, and debug.

You may be wondering: Start time? Duration? How are these numbers defined? The answer is, by default Csound interprets these values as seconds. An i-statement with a `p2` of 3, as shown above, will cause an event to begin precisely three seconds after the start of the score (or the start of the current section of the score).

For music that doesn't rely on a conventional structure of bars and beats, using seconds for `p2` and `p3` may work perfectly well. If your music is metrical in nature, though, you can change the default using a t-statement.

The t-statement

The t- in this score statement stands for "tempo." Each section of a Csound score (sections are terminated by s-statements, or by the e-statement that can optionally be used to end the entire score) can contain one t-statement. Using multiple t-statements within a section can cause Csound to get very confused, so don't do it.

A t-statement defines the tempo of a section in beats per minute. The tempo can remain fixed throughout the section, or it can speed up or slow down in whatever manner you like. The meanings of the p-fields in the t-statement are as follows:

- p1, which is implicitly the start time of the t-statement, must be 0, because the music has to have a tempo from the very start.

- p2 is the initial tempo in beats per minute (bpm).

- p3, p5, p7, and so on are times in beats. These numbers must be in non-decreasing order.

- p4, p6, p8, and so on are the tempi in bpm that Csound will adopt at the time noted in the preceding p-field.

If a section contains no t-statement, it is assumed to have an implicit t-statement of:

```
t 0 60
```

That is, the tempo is 60 bpm, or one beat per second. An s-statement, which ends a section, renders a preceding t-statement irrelevant: Each section needs its own t-statement.

The term "non-decreasing" in the list above is significant. Setting two odd-numbered p-fields in succession to the same value is often useful, as it produces a sudden tempo change. Consider this line, for instance:

```
t 0 180 2 180 2 60 4 60 4 180
```

The tempo is 180 bpm at the beginning of the section. At the end of two beats, it's still 180 bpm, but then it changes abruptly to 60 bpm. After two more beats it's still 60 bpm, but then, at beat 4, it changes abruptly back to 180 bpm. If we neglect to tell Csound that the tempo hasn't changed between beats 0 and 2 or between beats 2 and 4, it will produce a smooth ritard followed by a smooth accelerando:

```
t 0 180 2 60 4 180
```

Here, the music will start at 180 bpm, but it will immediately begin slowing down, so that it reaches 60 bpm at the end of two beats. During the next two beats it will speed up again gradually, until it reaches 180 bpm at beat 4.

It's important to understand that the value for p3 in an i-statement, when it is received by your instrument code, will have been adjusted by the preprocessor so that it is in seconds. In other words, p3 is in beats *only* while you're writing the score. Within the instrument, it's always a value in seconds. Except when the tempo is 60 bpm, the value of p3 will always be different from the value as stated in the score. This fact can have important consequences in programming envelope generators, for example.

The f-statement

The f-statement is one of the means of invoking Csound's GEN routines. See Chapter 7 for more on GEN routines, which can also be invoked using the `ftgen` family of opcodes from within the orchestra. The syntax of f-statements is similar to the syntax used with `ftgen`, except that the arguments to opcodes are separated by commas, while the p-fields of an f-statement are not. Here is a typical f-statement:

```
f 1  0  8192 10 1
```

The value for p1 is the number of the function-table that is created by the f-statement. p2 is the time at which the f-statement will run, p3 is the size of the table that will be created, and p4 is the number of the GEN routine that will be used to generate the table. The meanings of p5, p6, and so on are determined entirely by which GEN routine is being used.

Normally, p1 will be unique. That is, you might include half a dozen f-statements in your score—f1, f2, f3, f11, f12, and f101, for instance. If you reuse a value in p1, the new f-statement will override the old one. As a result, the data placed in the f-table by the first f-statement will be replaced by new data. This is sometimes useful. If you're creating a waveform in an f-table, for instance, you could create one waveform at the start of the score and a different waveform at a later point, by reusing the p1 value. The sound of any instrument that used this f-table would depend on whether the i-statement playing the instrument occurred before or after the second f-statement. For example:

```
f1 0 8192 10 1
f1 8 8192 10 1 2 3 4 5
```

For the first eight seconds of the section (or eight beats, if a t-statement is being used to set the tempo), f-table 1 contains a sine wave. After eight seconds, the table suddenly contains a rather thin-sounding waveform containing partials 1 through 5 in increasing amplitude. (For details on how the p-fields produce this waveform, look up GEN 10 in the manual.)

An f-statement with a p1 of 0 produces no f-table, but it can be useful in one specific situation: If you want the score to run for a while, even though the last i-statement has ended, you can enter an f0 statement. For instance:

```
f0 3600
```

This line will cause the score to remain active for 60 minutes (assuming the tempo is a default 60 bpm). If your instruments are responding to real-time MIDI input, such an f-statement will keep Csound running during your performance, even if there are no i-statements at all in the score. Another way to accomplish the same thing is with an e-statement that has a `p1` of 3600.

If the value in `p4` of the f-statement is positive, the data in the function-table will be rescaled to a range of ±1 after it is created. If the value is negative, however, rescaling is skipped. For more on this topic, see the "Post-Normalization" sidebar in Chapter 7.

Warping the Score with b- and v-

It's relatively easy to confuse yourself using b-statements and v-statements. They're useful mainly for organizing playback in complex scores. The b-statement resets the clock (either forward or backward) for subsequent i-statements, thus changing the meanings of `p2` in those i-statements. The v-statement warps both `p2` and `p3` of i-statements. The b- and v-statements each have only one p-field.

For a simple example of how to use a b-statement, imagine that you've written out a series of i-statements that define, perhaps, a complex two-bar bass line. You'd like the bass line to repeat every two bars. You could achieve this by block-copying the code and then editing all of the `p2` data in each pasted copy, but that would be time-consuming. Instead, you could simply make several copies of the data and then (assuming the bass riff is two bars of 4/4 time) separate them using b-statements. Rather than write out a series of notes, which would take up several pages when repeated, I'll substitute comment lines:

```
; ... the notes in the first riff, in which the first note presumably
; begins at time 0
b 8
; ... the same i-statements again, with the first note again beginning at
; time 0, except that "time 0" is now interpreted as "time 8"
b 16
; ... the same i-statements yet again
b 24
; ... and so forth
b 0
; ... and now the clock has been reset back to the start of the section,
; ready to receive the notes for another instrument ...
```

When you organize the score this way, the bass line will play several times in a row. Conversely, if you forget a b-statement, you'll hear two repetitions on top of one another, which will just make the bass line louder. The structure above can be used in combination with score macros, as discussed later in this chapter.

A b-statement can have a negative `p1`, thus setting the clock backward. (Notes that would fall before the beginning of the section are simply skipped.) A b-statement with a `p1` of 0 cancels a previous b-statement and returns the clock for the section to what it would normally be. That is, the `p2` of subsequent i-statements will be interpreted normally.

The `p1` in a v-statement must be positive. It is used as a multiplier for p2 and p3 in the following i-statements. For instance, consider this simple score:

```
;         dur   amp   pitch
i1 0   1      0.8   7.00
i1 1   1      0.8   7.02
i1 2   1      0.8   7.04
i1 3   1      0.8   7.05
v 0.5
i1 4   1      0.8   7.07
i1 5   1      0.8   7.09
i1 6   1      0.8   7.11
i1 7   1      0.8   8.00
```

In the absence of the v-statement, the eight notes would (assuming p5 is being processed by the `cpspch` opcode) play a C major scale with a steady rhythm. However, the v-statement warps p2 and p3 in the last four notes. What Csound plays, once the score has been processed, is this:

```
;         dur   amp    pitch
i1 0    1      0.8    7.00
i1 1    1      0.8    7.02
i1 2    1      0.8    7.04
i1 3    1      0.8    7.05
i1 2    0.5    0.8    7.07
i1 2.5  0.5    0.8    7.09
i1 3    0.5    0.8    7.11
i1 3.5  0.5    0.8    8.00
```

The fifth note event now starts at the same time as the third one (beat 2), and the seventh note event at the same time as the fourth one (beat 3). Don't forget—once the b- and v-statements have been processed, Csound doesn't much care what order events are written in in the score. You could write the score exactly as shown above if you like, but it looks a bit of a jumble. It will be sorted before it's played. After sorting, it will look like this:

```
i1 0    1      0.8   7.00
i1 1    1      0.8   7.02
i1 2    1      0.8   7.04
i1 2    0.5    0.8   7.07
i1 2.5  0.5    0.8   7.09
i1 3    1      0.8   7.05
i1 3    0.5    0.8   7.11
i1 3.5  0.5    0.8   8.00
```

The a- and x-statements

The a-statement and x-statement are likely to be most useful while you're developing a piece. The a-statement advances the playback by a given amount without producing any output, and the x-statement skips the remainder of a section. Suppose you're developing a longish piece and want to listen to your work starting two minutes in, without having to wait for two minutes each time playback starts. At the beginning of the score, assuming a tempo of 60 bpm, you could enter:

```
a 0 0 120
```

In an a-statement, p1 is meaningless. p2 is the time at which the advance is to begin (in this case it's 0, meaning the start of the piece), and p3 is the number of beats to advance.

In a similar way, an x-statement can be used to skip the rest of a section if you don't want to listen to it right now.

The s- and e-statements

In a score that includes several independent sections, each section can be terminated with an s-statement. The score as a whole can be terminated with an e-statement.

Csound will not output any sound that overlaps between one section and the next; the s-statement will always produce a brief moment of silence. I don't find this very satisfying musically, but in some circumstances it may not matter. The advantage of the s-statement is that each section keeps track of its own times (in p2 for each event), starting over at 0.

The e-statement seems, at first glance, even less useful. However, both the s-statement and the e-statement can include a p-field. This optional field is the number of beats after the end of the last event in the section or score during which Csound will continue to run. This p-field can be very useful if you've started an audio processing instrument, such as a reverb, in the orchestra header using the alwayson opcode. Normally you'll want the reverb to continue to run for a couple of seconds after the end of the last event. If the final event in the section ends at beat 200, for example, and you want the reverb to linger, you can end the section like this:

```
s 203
```

This will cause the section to last for three beats after the end of the last note. Using this p-field in an e-statement is especially useful when you're playing Csound live (using MIDI or some other performance input). A score can contain no events at all. If it ends like this:

```
e 600
```

then it will run for 10 minutes, waiting for performance input.

Score Entry Shortcuts

Let's face it: Writing out a musical score in the form of text, most of it consisting of long lines of numbers, is not fun and not a process that necessarily lends itself to an intuitive or inspirational way of working, at least not for more than a tiny segment of the populace. Fortunately, Csound provides some tools that can speed up score entry while also making your scores easier to read and more musically flexible.

Carry Symbols

The most useful shortcuts are probably the dot (.) and plus (+) symbols. These are both used in lists of note events that are all to be played by the same instrument. The dot tells Csound to use the same data you entered previously for that p-field. Here's a simple example. First, we'll write out all of the values by hand:

```
;      dur   amp    pitch
i1 0   1     0.7    7.00
i1 1   1     0.7    7.04
i1 2   1     0.7    7.07
i1 3   1     0.7    7.09
i1 4   1     0.7    8.00
```

Next, we'll replace the repeating values with dots:

```
;      dur   amp    pitch
i1 0   1     0.7    7.00
i1 1   .     .      7.04
i1 2   .     .      7.07
i1 3   .     .      7.09
i1 4   .     .      8.00
```

The dots tell Csound to repeat the previously stated values of 1 for p3 and 0.7 for p4. The result will be the same as before. One advantage of using dots, besides saving on typing keystrokes, is that if you later need to change the value of a p-field such as the amplitude value in the example above, you only need to retype it once.

The plus symbol can be used only in p2. It tells Csound, in effect, to create a legato line by adding the value of the previous p3 to the previous p2. Here is the previous example again, using plus symbols. The sound will be exactly the same as before, because the duration value in p3 is the same (one beat) as the amount by which each note follows the previous note.

```
;      dur   amp    pitch
i1 0   1     0.7    7.00
i1 +   .     .      7.04
i1 +   .     .      7.07
i1 +   .     .      7.09
i1 +   .     .      8.00
```

But what if we want a little separation between notes? In that case, a simple plus sign won't work, because the duration value of the first note will be too short. Instead, we can use the notation ^+x in p2, like this:

```
;       dur   amp    pitch
i1 0    0.3   0.7    7.00
i1 ^+1  .     .      7.04
i1 ^+1  .     .      7.07
i1 ^+1  .     .      7.09
i1 ^+1  .     .      8.00
```

The notation ^+1 tells the score preprocessor to take the value of the previous p2 and add 1 beat to it.

This type of shorthand is often useful when passages need to be block-copied. The code above could be copied and used in several passages, and only the p2 value of the first i-statement would need to be changed.

Note   The + symbol itself can be carried using a dot symbol. However, the ^+x shorthand cannot be carried.

When the values to be carried from one i-statement to the next are at the end of the text line, the dot can be omitted. Csound will understand that it's to carry the previously stated values for those p-fields. Let's add a few more p-fields to the example above to see how that looks:

```
;      dur  amp   pitch  atk   rel    pan
i1 0   1    0.7   7.00   0.01  0.05   0.6
i1 +   .    .     7.04
i1 +   .    .     7.07
i1 +   .    .     7.09
i1 +   .    .     8.00
```

In this example, we don't need to put dots in the last three columns for the attack, release, and pan p-fields because our musical concept calls for all of the values to be the same. Csound will pretend that it sees dots, translate the dots into numbers, and all will be well.

Ramping and Randomness

The symbol < can be used in a score to create an ascending or descending ramp between values. This symbol can also be carried using the dot symbol. Ramps are handy for programming crescendi and diminuendi, for example, and for moving a series of notes across the stereo field by changing a p-field that controls pan position. Here is a score that plays an ascending and descending scale while smoothly changing amplitude from loud to soft and back to loud:

```
;        dur   amp    pitch
i1 0     1     0.9    7.00
i1 +     .     <      7.02
i1 .     .     .      7.04
i1 .     .     .      7.05
i1 .     .     .      7.07
i1 .     .     .      7.09
i1 .     .     .      7.11
i1 .     .     0.05   8.00
i1 .     .     <      7.11
i1 .     .     .      7.09
i1 .     .     .      7.07
i1 .     .     .      7.05
i1 .     .     .      7.04
i1 .     .     .      7.02
i1 .     .     0.9    7.00
```

The tilde (~) symbol, used in a similar way, produces a random value between the two actual numbers given above and below it in the same p-field in the score. This is perhaps less useful than the ramp, because random values can easily be generated in the instrument itself.

Score Macros

A macro is an abbreviation. To use a macro in a score, you define the abbreviation and also the text that the abbreviation will be replaced with when the score is being processed. Macros are created using the #define symbol. The text that will be used to replace the macro as the score is processed is placed between # symbols. Here is a simple macro definition:

```
#define PLUCK #i11#
```

To call a macro within the score, use the symbol you've defined, preceded by the dollar sign ($). Having defined the macro above, we could replace this score line:

```
i11 0 2 0.8 7.00
```

with this one:

```
$PLUCK 0 2 0.8 7.00
```

These two lines will produce exactly the same processed score, because Csound will replace the text $PLUCK with the text i11. This hardly seems like an improvement, since we're doing more typing than before. But in a large score with dozens of instruments, it may be easier and less error-prone to define the names of the instruments than to remember their numbers.

As a side note, Csound also allows you to name your instruments in the orchestra and then refer to them in the score using double-quoted strings. The code above referred to `instr 11`. We could, instead, create this instrument using the line:

```
instr PLUCK
```

and then refer to it in the score like this:

```
"PLUCK" 0 2 0.8 7.00
```

In this case, no macro definition would be needed. Which system you prefer is a matter of taste. (For further details, see the page "Named Instruments" in the section of *The Canonical Csound Reference Manual* on "Syntax of the Orchestra.")

This type of basic replacement macro can also be useful if you have instruments that repeatedly use the same values for several p-fields. In place of this score code, which has repeating values for p5, p6, and p7, but different values for p8:

```
i1 0  1  8.00  0.6  2.5  0.7  3
i1 +  .  8.02  0.6  2.5  0.7  1
i1 +  .  8.04  0.6  2.5  0.7  1.4
i1 +  .  8.06  0.6  2.5  0.7  3
i1 +  .  8.07  0.6  2.5  0.7  0.9
```

we could use the following:

```
#define PARAMS # 0.6 2.5 0.7 #
i1 0  1  8.00  $PARAMS  3
i1 +  .  8.02  $PARAMS  1
i1 +  .  8.04  $PARAMS  1.4
i1 +  .  8.06  $PARAMS  3
i1 +  .  8.07  $PARAMS  0.9
```

If we later need to replace the values in p5, p6, and p7, we only need to do it once, by changing the macro definition, rather than dozens of times throughout the score.

A more useful macro is one that takes arguments. Up to five arguments can be used. The manual gives a simple example, which we may as well repeat here:

```
#define ARG(A) # 2.345 1.03 $A 234.9#
i1 0 1 8.00 1000 $ARG(2.0)
i1 + 1 8.01 1200 $ARG(3.0)
```

The macro called ARG has one argument, which is called A. This is referenced in the macro definition using the dollar-sign symbol ($). When the macro is used, the value of the argument A is added in parentheses. The preceding code is expanded by the score processor into this:

```
i1 0 1 8.00 1000 2.345 1.03 2.0 234.9
i1 + 1 8.01 1200 2.345 1.03 3.0 234.9
```

As you can see, the value symbolized by $A in the macro definition has been replaced by 2.0 in the first line and by 3.0 in the second line.

Computing Values in p-fields

The macro feature really comes into its own when combined with another handy shortcut. In place of a constant numerical value, a p-field in a score can contain an equation surrounded by square brackets. The "Evaluation of Expressions" page in the manual gives details.

By itself, the ability to evaluate equations in a score isn't much of a shortcut, though it can be useful if you're writing music in just intonation. Pitches in just intonation are defined using ratios of integers, so you could define a series of pitches (assuming your instrument is set up to use the data) using p-fields in this manner:

```
;      dur  octave  ratio
i21 0   1    3       [10/9]
i21 +   .    .       [6/5]
i21 +   .    .       [4/3]
```

Using a macro with an equation opens up new ways to handle the score while keeping it readable:

```
#define BASEDUR #2#
i21 0    [$BASEDUR + 0.3]
i21 ^+3  [$BASEDUR + 0.7]
i21 ^+3  [$BASEDUR]
```

Here, the p3 values of the three notes will evaluate to 2.3, 2.7, and 2.0. If we later decide that all of the notes in the passage need to be a little shorter, we can redefine BASEDUR to be 1.9 or 1.7, and all of the note durations will be adjusted accordingly.

This feature is well-nigh essential when the score contains looped phrases, as discussed in the section "Looping Score Sections," later in this chapter.

Using a Spreadsheet

The idea of using a spreadsheet program, such as Microsoft Excel or OpenOffice Calc, to create a piece of music may seem at first glance to be no more than a joke. But with certain types of Csound scores, a spreadsheet can be a definite improvement over a text editor as a user interface.

You're most likely to turn to a spreadsheet when your piece contains hundreds or even thousands of notes, and when each note event requires a large number of p-fields.

A spreadsheet offers at least two advantages in such cases. First, the p-fields are automatically aligned in vertical columns—no need to add or remove tab characters, as you would in a text editor, when you add extra digits to numbers or remove digits. This makes it easier to see what you're doing and to avoid mistakes. Second, in a spreadsheet you can easily edit vertical columns. If you need to subtract .1 from the amplitude p-fields in a long phrase, for instance, in order to avoid clipping, you can do it quickly with a few mouse-clicks, rather than having to type lots of numbers.

Once you've created a score in a spreadsheet, it's a trivial matter to select the cells containing your score, copy them, and paste them into your .csd or .sco file.

In a spreadsheet program, you can keep several versions of a score on separate sheets to keep backups and do quick comparisons. You can enter formulas into certain cells, and when you're ready to transfer the data to Csound the spreadsheet will write the result of the formula rather than the formula itself into the copy-paste buffer. This eliminates the need to use some of Csound's score language syntax.

Looping Score Sections

Music often contains phrases that repeat. Having to write out all of the score events for a repeated section can be tedious and error-prone, even if you use the copy/paste commands in your text editor. Csound defines a couple of different score statements with which sections can be repeated. The repetitions don't have to be identical; there are ways to introduce variations.

The r-statement

The r-statement is simple to use but has some limitations. The r-statement takes two arguments. The first is an integer that defines the number of repetitions that will be played. The second is in the form of text and defines a macro. The value of the macro will be incremented each time the loop repeats: It will be 1 on the first repetition, 2 on the second repetition, and so on.

The macro can be used in calculations of the values of p-fields, by enclosing the calculations in square brackets. The syntax for using a loop macro is the same as for any other Csound score macro: When the macro is referenced in the code, it is preceded by a dollar sign.

The repeating section that begins with an r-statement ends when an s-statement or e-statement is encountered.

Here is an example. In this example, p5 is being sent to one of the cpspch family of opcodes. The macro is named FERD. It is being used both to increase the pitches of the three notes by a chromatic half-step on each repetition and to increase the tempo on each repetition. The tempo will be 110 bpm the first time through the loop, 140 bpm the second time, and so on.

```
r 7 FERD
t 0 [80 + 30 * $FERD]
```

```
i1 0 1 0.4 [3.0 + 0.01 * $FERD]
i1 + . . [3.03 + 0.01 * $FERD]
i1 + 2 . [3.06 + 0.01 * $FERD]
s
```

The main limitation of the r-statement is that only one section of a Csound score can be running at any given time. A new section can begin only after the preceding section has ended. This fact makes it difficult (impossible, basically) to use r-statement loops in music where the loop is only one element in a polyphonic texture. It also has consequences if the instrument playing the last note in the loop has one or more envelopes defined with release segments: The loop can't begin its next iteration until the envelope release is complete, which will likely dislocate the rhythm.

The { and } Statements

Considerably more flexibility is provided by the {-statement and }-statement, but the syntax is not quite as simple as with the r-statement. The braces enclose a repeating loop. Like the r-statement, the {-statement has two parameters—an integer for the number of repetitions desired and a text macro that can be used to vary the repetitions.

Unlike the r-statement, the macro defined by the {-statement begins with a value of 0. It is incremented with each repetition, so with n repetitions, during the last repetition it has a value of $n - 1$.

The tricky bit about using this type of loop is that the p2 values of events between the { and } lines are not automatically advanced. It's up to you to advance them manually, using the macro. If you fail to do this, all of the repetitions of the loop will play at once!

This type of loop can run concurrently with other events in the score. Here is an example, similar to the previous one, in which two {} loops of different lengths run at the same time:

```
#define LOOPLEN1 #4#
{ 5 FERD
i1 [0 + $LOOPLEN1 * $FERD] 1 0.4 [3.0 + 0.01 * $FERD]
i1 [1 + $LOOPLEN1 * $FERD] . . [3.03 + 0.01 * $FERD]
i1 [2 + $LOOPLEN1 * $FERD] 2.3 . [3.06 + 0.01 * $FERD]
}

#define LOOPLEN2 #5#
{ 4 WIMP
i1 [0 + $LOOPLEN2 * $WIMP] 3 0.3 2.0
i1 [3 + $LOOPLEN2 * $WIMP] 0.5
i1 [3.5 + $LOOPLEN2 * $WIMP] .
i1 [4 + $LOOPLEN2 * $WIMP] 1.1 0.3 2.03
}
```

Notice the handling of p2. The rhythm within each loop is defined by the constants (0, 1, and 2 in the first loop; 0, 3, 3.5, and 4 in the second). These values have to be adjusted using the loop macros (FERD and WIMP) and the desired length of each loop.

The Sorting Hat

You thought you were going to get clear through this book without running into a single Harry Potter reference? Hah! Foolish muggle!

Before Csound can use a score to produce sound, the score has to be processed. This processing takes place in three phases, called Carry, Tempo, and Sort. The processing is well explained in the page of *The Canonical Csound Reference Manual* called "The Standard Numeric Score." In practice, the process is usually fairly transparent to the user, but if you don't know what's being done, you may occasionally find that your scores don't sound the way you expect them to.

Each section of the score is processed individually; sections don't overlap.

During the Carry phase, groups of consecutive i-statements whose p1 fields (the instrument numbers) correspond are processed. When a p-field contains a carry symbol, such as a dot or a plus sign, this symbol is replaced with an actual number. Likewise, when p-fields at the end of an i-statement have been left empty (an implicit carry operation), the missing data is added.

Macros created using #define statements are replaced with actual values during this phase.

During the Tempo phase, t-statements are considered. This operation converts p2 values from beats into actual values in seconds. With i-statements, the same operation is carried out on p3, so that the duration of the event is now defined in seconds rather than beats.

Finally, the Sort routine sorts all of the statements in the score into chronological order based on their p2. Sorting also "unfolds" any looped sections within the score, producing a list of discrete events, and macros whose values change during loop repetitions are turned into actual values at this time. When two events have the same p2 value, they are sorted so that their p1 values are in ascending order; this ensures that lower-numbered instruments will start before higher-numbered instruments.

The sorting process has an important implication: With certain restrictions if you're using carry symbols, -b and -v statements, or repeating loops using the {} loop syntax, it doesn't matter what order you place the events in within a given section. You can write out all of the events for instrument 2 from the beginning of the section to the end, and then below them write out phrases for instruments 1 and 3, intermingled. Csound will sort them all out and perform them in the proper sequence.

Legato Instruments

Up until this point in the book, we've been using Csound to play one detached note at a time. But as most musicians who use synthesizers are aware, most commercial synths can operate in a one-voice legato mode, sometimes called *mono* mode. When set to this mode, the synth responds to only one note at a time on the MIDI keyboard. When you press a new key before releasing the old one, the pitch will move up or down to the pitch dictated by the new key—but the tone will continue without interruption. In particular, the envelope generators won't retrigger (although in some instruments each envelope generator can be set to retrigger in legato mode, or not). Instead of hearing two discrete notes, you'll hear one sustaining note with a pitch change. And the pitch change need not be abrupt: The pitch may glide smoothly up or down from the old pitch to the new one.

Can Csound duplicate this trick? Certainly. Designing legato instruments is not as easy as pressing a Mono Mode button, however. In order to create a legato instrument in Csound, we'll have to unleash four or five new techniques and deploy them all at once. In this section we'll look at how to create legato lines from the Csound score; in Chapter 10 we'll return to the subject and show how to make a monophonic legato instrument that can be played from a MIDI keyboard.

The code examples, both here and in Chapter 10, will be a little more thorough than many of the examples in this book. Taking a few minutes to enter them into the text editor you're using for your Csound work will help you understand the concepts. A great deal more can be done with legato instruments than these examples demonstrate, but they will help get you on the right track.

The ideas in this section are adapted from the chapter "Designing Legato Instruments in Csound" by Richard Dobson in *The Csound Book* (MIT Press, 2000), and from Steven Yi's article "Exploring Tied Notes in Csound" in the Fall 2005 issue of *The Csound Journal*.

Let's look at the techniques one at a time.

First, the value for p3 in an i-statement in the score can be negative rather than positive. If it's negative, Csound assumes that the note will be tied to a following note that will use the same instrument (that is, the following note will have the same p1 value). Since p3 is reserved for the duration of a note event, setting a negative duration might seem odd, but the negative value is simply a flag that alerts Csound to what you have in mind. Having set a negative p3, of course, you can't simply use the symbol p3 in your orchestra code the way you normally would. A line opcode with a negative value for its duration argument, for example, wouldn't do anything, or at least it wouldn't do what you expected. In this situation, it's advisable to create, in the instrument, an i-time value for duration like this:

```
idur = abs(p3)
```

The abs opcode returns the absolute value of p3.

The final note in a string of notes that are to be played legato should be given a positive p3, as usual.

Buzzword   The absolute value of a number is the distance of the number from 0. The absolute value is either the same as the number (if the number is positive) or −1 times the number (if the original number is negative). Thus the absolute value of 3.7 is 3.7, and the absolute value of −6 is 6.

Second—and again, this may seem odd at first—the value for p1 in a score doesn't have to be an integer. Each instrument in the orchestra is defined using an integer as its identifier, but after defining instr 1 we can use values for p1 such as 1.1, 1.2, and so on. Csound will interpret these numbers as referring to distinct instances of the instrument. This distinction is of importance mainly if we're defining a legato instrument using a negative p3 value. For instance, if we do this:

```
i 1.1  0    -1
i 1.1  1    .
i 1.1  2    1
i 1.2  0.5  3
```

then Csound will understand that the first three i-statements are to be played by the same instance of instrument 1, while the last statement, even though it is to be played in the middle of the legato sequence, and by the same instrument, is not part of the legato note stream.

Third, the opcode tival returns 1 if a note is tied from a previous note, and 0 otherwise. In other words, tival lets us see whether the *previous* note had a negative p3. Also useful is the opcode tigoto. This is a goto statement (see the section "Logic and Flow Control" in Chapter 6) that passes control to the named label only when the note is tied from a previous note. In other words, tigoto is shorthand. This code:

```
tigoto slur
```

has the same result as this:

```
itie tival
if itie == 1 igoto slur
```

The label slur is an arbitrarily named label that you would use in your code.

Fourth, a good way to give a Csound instrument access to the data in p-fields for the previous and following notes in a legato line is to use the special symbols npx and ppx in the score, replacing x with the number of the desired p-field for the next i-statement (npx) or the previous i-statement (ppx). This is explained in the page in the manual called "Next-P and Previous-P Symbols."

In the example, we're going to use a nifty user-defined opcode (UDO) written by Steven Yi called tieStatus. This opcode senses the status of the current note. If the note is freestanding (not tied to a previous or following note), tieStatus returns –1. If the note is the first note in a legato group, tieStatus returns 0. If it's a middle note in a legato line, tieStatus returns 1. If it's the last note, tieStatus returns 2.

With that preamble, we're ready to take a look at the example. As usual, I've omitted the opening and closing tags from the .csd file.

```
sr = 44100
ksmps = 4
```

```
nchnls = 2
0dbfs = 1

opcode tieStatus,i,0
itie tival
if (itie == 0 && p3 < 0) then
   ; this is an initial note within a group of tied notes
   itiestatus = 0
elseif (p3 < 0 && itie == 1) then
   ; this is a middle note within a group of tied notes
   itiestatus = 1
elseif (p3 > 0 && itie == 1) then
   ; this is an end note out of a group of tied notes
   itiestatus = 2
elseif (p3 > 0 && itie == 0) then
   ; this note is a stand-alone note
   itiestatus = -1
endif
xout itiestatus
endop

instr 1
idur = abs(p3)
itiestatus tieStatus
ipitch = cpspch(p5)
iprevpitch = cpspch(p6)
ipitchramptime = p8
iamp = p4
inextamp = p7
iatk = 0.03

iphas = -1
tigoto slur
iphas = 0

slur:
if itiestatus == -1 then
   kamp linsegr 0, iatk, iamp, idur - iatk, iamp, iatk, 0
elseif itiestatus == 0 then
   kamp linseg 0, iatk, iamp, idur - iatk, inextamp
```

```
else
   kamp line iamp, idur, inextamp
endif

kpitch linseg iprevpitch, ipitchramptime, ipitch
asig oscili kamp, kpitch, 1, iphas
outs asig, asig
endin


</CsInstruments>
<CsScore>

; a waveform with a few low harmonics:
f1 0 8192 10 1 0.95 0.1 0.05
; a legato line:
;          dur    amp    pitch  prevpch  nextamp   glide time
i 1.1 0    -1     0.6    7.09   7.09     np4       0.1
i 1.1 +     .     0.3    8.00   pp5      np4       0.2
i 1.1 +     .     0.7    7.07   pp5      np4       0.1
i 1.1 +     2     0.2    7.10   pp5      0         0.3

; play some shorter non-legato notes in a lower octave:
i 1.2 0    0.3    0.2    5.09   5.09     0         0.01
i 1.2 0.5
i 1.2 1
i 1.2 1.5
i 1.2 2
i 1.2 2.5
i 1.2 3
i 1.2 3.5
```

The first four i-statements create a legato line using instrument 1. During each note, the amplitude of the tone glides smoothly up or down toward the amplitude of the next note thanks to the np4 symbol. At the beginning of each note, the pitch glides up or down from the previous pitch at a rate determined by p8.

At the same time, instrument 1 is playing a series of non-legato notes in a lower octave. One peculiarity of this implementation should be noted: Because linseg is being used to glide the pitch in the legato line, the value of p8 has to be non-zero even in the i-statements where p1 is 1.2. If p8 is 0, linseg will refuse to operate.

In the instrument code, the call to tieStatus is used to decide what kind of amplitude envelope to create. If we're playing an isolated, non-legato note, we'll use linsegr to generate a conventional envelope with an attack and a release. If this is the first note in the line, we'll start with an attack ramp up from 0. Otherwise, we'll ramp up or down from the current amplitude to the amplitude of the following note. The score defines p7 (inextamp) as 0 for the last note in the line, so it will fade out smoothly to silence.

The usage of tigoto is not strictly necessary, as the value of iphas could have been set in the if/then/else block. But this code is a little more concise.

The point of the value iphas—and this is a vital concept—is that it is needed as an argument to oscili. This argument is optional, and in most of the examples in this book it isn't used. But in a legato instrument it's needed. You would also need it if your legato instrument is using an LFO to create vibrato, and for the same reason. As the manual explains, a negative value for this argument causes the initialization of oscili to be skipped. When initialization is skipped, oscili will continue cycling through the waveform (which is created in the score by GEN 10) without resetting its phase to the start of the waveform. If you omit this argument, you will almost certainly hear a click at the beginning of the new note. The click will occur because there's a discontinuity in the waveform—a vertical jump from one audio value to another. If you comment out the final , iphas in the oscili line, you'll hear the clicks.

9 Front Ends

Csound was originally a program that was invoked by typing commands on the command line. The command-line version still works, and in some circumstances may be preferable—for example, if you're using Csound to do batch processing of sound files. In Windows, you can run Csound from a Command Prompt window (which emulates the functionality originally found in MS-DOS). In the Macintosh OS, you can run Csound from a Terminal window in much the same way. Today, however, most people prefer to run Csound from a front-end program. A front end is a second piece of software that provides a user interface, often with slick graphics and other features. After creating or loading a code file that contains one or more instruments and a score, you give a command that causes the front end to invoke Csound, thus producing sound.

Several developers have written front ends for Csound. Each of these programs has its own strengths. They generally reflect the desires and thought processes of one or two developers. Most of the front-end developers actively listen to feedback from their users and try to accommodate suggestions. Nonetheless, Csound front ends tend to be the result of individual effort, not of large development teams. Because of this, the available front ends don't always resemble commercial software. Some of them are, to be frank, a bit peculiar.

The fact that they're produced by individuals (unpaid or compensated only by voluntary contributions from users) has a second consequence: These programs are not always free of bugs. When you start using a front end, you may encounter things that don't work as expected, or things that you don't understand how to use because the documentation is sketchy. At that point, you will likely find yourself exchanging emails directly with the developer. Usually these folks are more than happy to help you, but courtesy pays dividends. You need to remember that you're dealing with someone who probably has many other demands on their time—a day job, a family, their own music-making, and their own list of things they would like to do to improve the front end. Sending a good, thorough bug report is helpful. Getting pissed off and complaining is not helpful.

CsoundQt (see Chapter 5) was chosen as the main front end to use and discuss in *Csound Power!* for several reasons—but it's not the only game in town. In this chapter we'll look at three other front ends for Csound, all of them mature and highly useful for certain types of music. Because space in this book is limited, none of them will be explored in as much detail as

CsoundQt. I'll focus on the most important features of each program and try to give you a clear idea of whether it might be right for you.

Not included in this chapter, but well worth exploring if you're adventurous, are athenaCL and IanniX. Neither is a Csound front end, but both can work with Csound to produce music.

athenaCL (www.flexatone.net/athena.html) is a deep, multi-dimensional music construction kit that can generate scores for Csound or SuperCollider, or even MIDI files. It runs as a module within the Python programming language and is invoked from Idle (the Python shell) using the command `from athenaCL import athenacl`. The documentation for athenaCL is extensive but not easy to grasp.

IanniX (www.iannix.org) is a system for generating OSC control messages from within an animated graphic environment. Scripts for Iannix can be written using JavaScript. Judging by the videos, the system looks powerful, and it's certainly intriguing, but at this point in time (summer 2011), the documentation is close to nonexistent.

blue

Wouldn't it be great if you could harness all the power of Csound within the mouse-operated graphic editing environment of a conventional multitrack sequencer/audio workstation? Thanks to blue, you can do exactly that, more or less—or rather, both more *and* less. blue (the name is always lowercase) will do some things that your favorite DAW won't do. On the other hand, some features commonly found in commercial software have no equivalent in blue.

blue is a Csound front end created and maintained by musician/programmer Steven Yi. It provides a multitrack timeline, a piano-roll note editor, a drum grid editor, a tracker-style editor, graphic editing of modulation envelopes, an audio mixer panel with effect sends, and a whole lot more. As amazing as blue is, however, it's a work in progress. It's a bit quirky and not as well documented as it could be. Because it depends on other software in your system, just getting blue to run is not always a transparent process. (When I've had problems, however, Yi has always been happy to help me troubleshoot them.)

Before tackling blue you'll need to understand Csound pretty thoroughly. blue doesn't eliminate the need to learn the nuts and bolts of Csound coding. Rather, it provides a suite of tools with which composers who are proficient in Csound can generate and manipulate complex scores far more quickly than would be possible with a text editor. You'll still be typing lots of little numbers, but the numbers will do more interesting things. Some tasks, such as editing tempo changes, can indeed be handled graphically in blue, without ever typing a line of code.

This section of *Csound Power!* makes no attempt to document every detail of the blue user interface. We'll talk about what you can do with blue, and I'll point out both the great features and some limitations, but without trying too hard to explain exactly what steps you'll need to take in order to carry out specific operations. As with other aspects of Csound, puzzling out the details on your own is just part of the process.

Downloading and Installing blue

The home page for blue is http://blue.kunstmusik.com. There you'll find links to the download page, the manual, and a library of user-built instruments. The download link takes you to the SourceForge repository, where both the latest version and older, archived versions are available.

To run blue, you need to have the Java Runtime Environment installed on your computer. (This is because blue is written in the Java programming language.) A version of the JRE is already installed on recent Macintosh operating systems. If you're using Windows or Linux, you'll need to download the JRE from www.java.com/en/download. Like blue, JRE is free.

After installing blue, you'll need to go to the Options/Preferences box and configure it for your system. In Mac OS, Preferences is found under the blue menu in the top menu bar; in Windows, Options is found in the Tools menu. Please don't be surprised if you have to try out various settings. Using blue 2.1.4 on my Mac, I had to set the path for the Csound Executable, which wasn't set properly by the default installation. In Windows, I had to uncheck the Use Csound API box to keep blue from crashing during real-time playback. Both of these issues have been reported and have been fixed in the latest version. I'm mentioning them here mainly as a way of suggesting that if you have a setup problem with blue, don't get discouraged: persevere.

If you're curious about blue, you might want to start by looking at the online wiki manual (http://blue.kunstmusik.com/wiki/index.php/Blue_User's_manual).

Overview

As Figure 9.1 should make clear, blue is designed to take full advantage of the multi-panel interface concept. Within the main window are three main work areas, each of which can assume a number of identities depending on which tab you click. The work areas can be closed when not needed, and the borders can be dragged to resize them. Tabs can also be "torn off" and docked in other parts of the main window if desired. Some of the work areas contain graphic objects; in others, you'll type Csound code.

Like Csound itself, blue divides the work of creating a project into two main areas—the score and the orchestra. When you're ready to listen to your work, blue will quietly generate a standard .csd file behind the scenes, but at the user interface level you'll be working in a much more modular fashion. (You can save the .csd to disk separately, so as to inspect it—a good educational experience.)

Each instrument in the orchestra has its own work areas for editing the code, and the score is similarly parceled out into numerous SoundObjects, which can be dragged around in a multi-track timeline. If you think of SoundObjects as being musical phrases, you won't be far wrong, but their functionality goes much further. I'll have more to say about SoundObjects below.

The main work area has eight tabs across the top, labeled Score, Orchestra, UDO, Tables, Global Orchestra, Global Score, Project Properties, and Blue Live. Just to make things a little more interesting, when you click on the Orchestra tab you'll find a subsidiary work area with more tabs for

Figure 9.1 The white-on-black text displays of blue seem to invite dim lighting and intense concentration. The central work area, which uses syntax coloring, shows the code for instrument 3. The orchestra browser is on the left and the Csound output display at the bottom. On the right is the properties panel for one of the SoundObjects in the score; the Note Processors list in the properties panel is an especially powerful feature of blue.

Global Orchestra, Global Score, and UDO, in addition to the Instrument Text tab and the Comments tab. In fact, each Instrument has its own windows for Global Orchestra, Global Score, and UDO. The point of such a multi-faceted design is this: After creating an instrument, you can save it to your Instrument Library. From the Library, you can load it into a different project by dragging it into the Orchestra list. If the instrument needs its own unique f-tables, global variables, or user-defined opcodes, you should enter them in the corresponding edit window for that instrument. The code will then be saved with the instrument when you store it in the Instrument Library. Conversely, code that you enter in the top-level work area for Global Orchestra, Global Score, or UDO will be saved with the project, but it *won't* be saved to the Instrument Library.

SoundObjects can also be saved to a Library, so you can swap musical phrases from one composition to another without having to cut and paste. Existing Csound .csd files (or .orc and .sco files) can also be imported.

Over on the right side are more work areas: the SoundObject Properties box, the SoundObject Library browser, the Scratch Pad, the Markers window, and the MIDI Input control panel.

Across the bottom of the main window you'll find the SoundObject editor, the mixer, and the Csound Output Console. If you're starting to think that blue might work best on a computer with a really large screen, I won't try to dissuade you. I've used it successfully on a laptop, but doing so entails quite a lot of opening and closing of work areas.

The Score

As Figure 9.2 shows, objects in blue's multitrack timeline interface look and behave quite a lot like the clips/parts/chunks (the terminology varies) found in commercial sequencers. The track lanes run horizontally, and each lane can be muted or soloed. Individual objects can be auditioned. An object of any type can be placed in any lane.

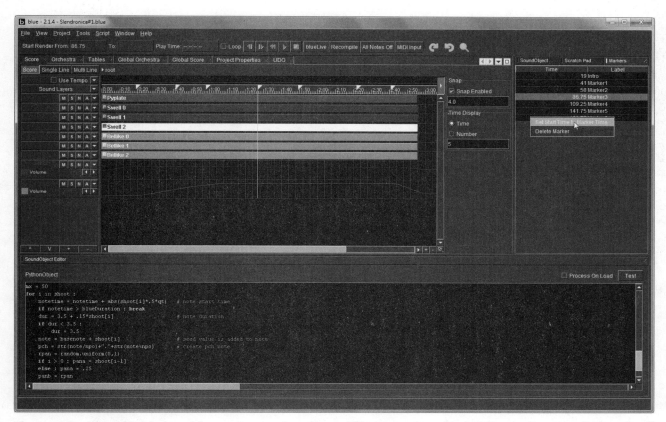

Figure 9.2   The objects in a blue score can be given different colors. Two automation envelopes are displayed (though they're hard to see in this image) below the objects, and the code for the Swell 2 object (highlighted in white in the track lane) is displayed in the lower panel. At right is the Markers window. Markers can be named, and the playback start point can be set to the location of any marker.

No fewer than 15 different types of objects can be inserted into a track—an AudioFile, a Comment, an External, a GenericScore, a Jmask, a LineObject, an ObjectBuilder, a PatternObject, a PianoRoll, a PythonObject, a RhinoObject, a Sound, a TrackerObject, a ZakLineObject, or a PolyObject.

Before we take a look at any of these individual object types, I should mention a few other properties of the Score itself. Across the top are a time ruler and a graphic editor for drawing a tempo envelope. Markers can be placed on the time ruler. Individual objects in the score can be stretched or shrunk with the mouse—and when you change an object's length in the track, the events in it will get longer or shorter and closer together or further apart in time. The object is plastic, in other words, with respect to time. (This behavior can be switched off if desired.) Objects can be named and given distinctive colors. They can be frozen as audio files, thus freeing up CPU power.

One of blue's more interesting and powerful features is the ability to apply Note Processors to objects in the score. If you've created a standard object that has dozens or hundreds of note events in it, and for some reason you feel the need to make adjustments to a given p-field in all of the events at once, there's no need to start typing numbers. Instead, apply a Note Processor to the object and use one of 17 different processes on all of the instances of that p-field at once. The processes include obvious choices, such as adding and multiplying; less obvious choices, such as rotating, inverting, and time-warping; and far-reaching possibilities, such as line-adding and line-multiplying. Note Processors are useful not only for quick edits but for adding variation to multiple copies of a given object. When repeating a phrase, you can change its loudness, pitch, or any other parameter defined by a p-field, altering it on each repetition.

Multiple score objects can be embedded in a single PolyObject. Essentially, you can have one entire score within another within another, all of them playing at once.

Score Objects

Explaining every feature of every type of score object in blue would take many pages. Certain types, such as the AudioFile and the Comment, are self-explanatory. Briefly:

Using a LineObject, you can create an arbitrary number of graphic envelopes, each of which can use an arbitrary number of breakpoints. You can set the minimum and maximum values of the envelope and give it a suitable name. blue will add the gk- prefix to the name, allowing you to use, for example, `gkline3` in your instrument code. To make this work, you need to use the `init` opcode in the orchestra header to let Csound know that the global k-rate variable exists. The same precaution applies to the ZakLineObject. This uses Csound's zak opcodes to send the data for the line to the instrument, so `zakinit` must be used, with an appropriate number of k-rate channels in order to use a ZakLineObject.

A PythonObject constructs the text for a score or a portion of a score using the Python programming language. Csound itself lets you embed Python code in your orchestra, but doing so requires a few special syntax wrinkles and the Python opcodes. To generate score events with Python in Csound itself, you'll need to use an opcode such as `event`, which generates score lines from within the orchestra. Using a PythonObject in blue is more straightforward: Just write some Python code that assembles a text string, and then assign this string to the `score` variable. For an example, look in the examples directory in your blue distribution. (You'll find the file pythonProcessor.blue in the noteProcessors sub-directory.) More complex examples of Python coding can be found in the projects feldman.blue and mikelsonPmask.blue, in the scripting sub-directory.

A RhinoObject operates in a similar manner but uses JavaScript in place of Python.

The PianoRoll object may appear at first glance (see Figure 9.3) to be a standard editing feature, but it is unique in its ability to display and edit microtonal scales, either based on Scala-format .scl files or in Csound's octave/pitch-class format, which can produce any number of steps per octave (and any definition you like of "octave"). Also available for editing notes in more familiar ways are the Pattern object, in which you can set up a drum grid, and the Tracker object, which borrows the layout and some of the functionality of tracker software. As with the graphic automation envelopes, the goal here is to let musicians use interface elements that they're familiar with, yet without sacrificing any of Csound's underlying power.

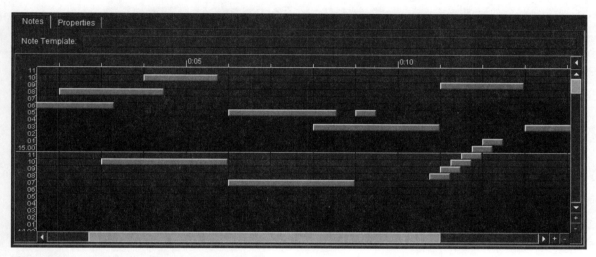

Figure 9.3 A piano-roll note editor in blue.

Score Automation

If you've created an instrument using BlueSynthBuilder (see Figure 9.4), or if you're routing the outputs of your instruments through the blue Mixer, you'll be able to edit graphic envelopes for all of the automatable parameters directly in the score. This feature goes a long way toward making blue operate more like a DAW. The main limitation, at the user interface level, is that you can't record automation data by grabbing the graphic knobs and sliders themselves with the mouse and fiddling with them while the music plays.

Internally, in the process of generating a .csd to send to Csound for playback, blue transforms automation data into new instruments and score events—hundreds of score events, each of which transmits one control value as a global variable.

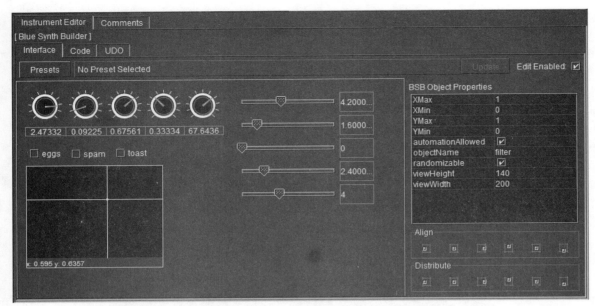

Figure 9.4 The graphic widgets that can be created with BlueSynthBuilder can transmit their values to your instrument either at the start of score playback (for sound design purposes) or via an automation envelope in the score (for musical expression). Instruments respond to live control movements while playing if the Csound API is enabled in the Options/Preferences box.

WinXound

In spite of its name, WinXound is not strictly a Windows program. It's cross-platform. Developed by Stefano Bonetti, it can be downloaded from http://winxound.codeplex.com.

WinXound (see Figure 9.5) is less ambitious than CsoundQt and far less ambitious than blue, but it has some strong features that will make it the right choice for some users. You can work on your .csd files in its text editor with user-configurable syntax coloring. The main edit window has multiple tabs for keeping several files open at once, and the view of a single file can be split horizontally or vertically. When your code contains errors, you'll find that WinXound is better than the current version of CsoundQt at finding and highlighting the lines where the errors are located.

The program has context-sensitive opcode help, auto-completion of code lines, a detachable help/output window, bookmarks for code lines, one-click font size zooming, the obligatory dialog box for running Csound's audio analysis tools, and a built-in display of the Csound manual. (Don't try switching to the frames version—that will crash WinXound.)

The entire Csound UDO code repository is bundled with WinXound. It opens up in its own pane in the help/output window, and you can drag opcodes out of it into your own code (or insert your own opcodes into the local copy of the repository).

WinXound has no dialog box tools for making settings. The program expects you to tell Csound what MIDI and audio devices (and related settings) to use, using the standard command-line flags. This can be done either in the <CsOptions> area of your .csd file or in a command-line field in the Settings box.

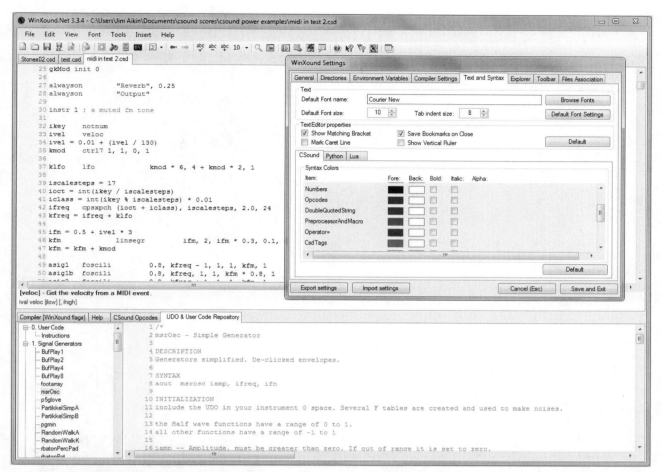

Figure 9.5 The WinXound front end features a multi-tabbed text editor with user-configurable syntax coloring, as shown in the Settings dialog box at right. The lower pane of the main window can display the Csound manual, output messages, an opcode directory, or the code repository (shown).

Cecilia 4.2

The user interface of Cecilia provides a clean, elegant environment for drawing automation curves. Several standard effects processors have already been implemented, and control panels for them are set up in the interface. At a basic level, you can load an audio file and process it in all sorts of ways without ever learning a thing about Csound. If you're willing to pop open the hood and get your fingers greasy, you'll find the full power of Csound waiting for you. You can add new sliders to the control panel and use them to control whatever you like.

The control panel window shown in Figure 9.6 is only half of the story. Cecilia also has a code-editing window with separate panes for editing interface, orchestra, and score code. Syntax coloring and line numbering are provided.

Cecilia's built-in processing modules, available from the File menu, include resonant filters, dynamics processors, a beautifully clean pitch and rhythm transposer, and much more. You can record automation moves of the sliders with the mouse during playback, and then capture the output as a new file to your hard drive.

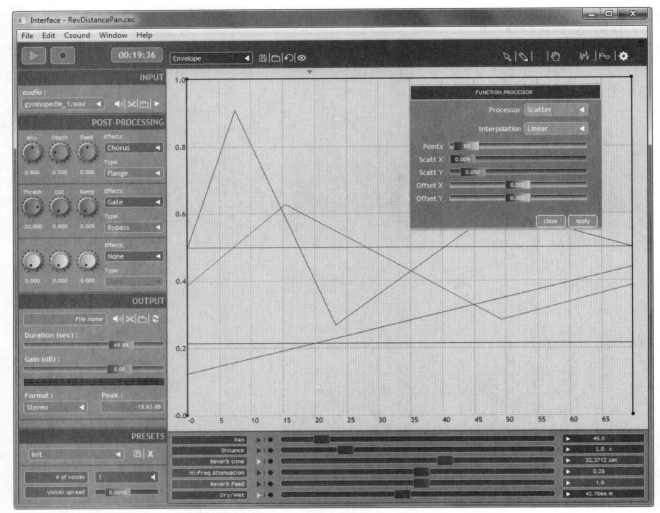

Figure 9.6 Cecilia's polished user interface includes built-in effects (the column on the left). The sliders on the bottom are coupled with lines in the graph and can be used for real-time modulation.

Cecilia was created by Jean Piché and Alexandre Burton at the University of Montreal in the late 1990s, and is currently maintained by Piché, Olivier Bélanger, and Dominic Thibault. Its main limitation, in my view, is that the documentation is less than forthcoming. The Help file supplied with the software has no table of contents, so finding information (assuming it's there to be found) is needlessly difficult. The tutorial pages available on the Web are badly out of date.

According to Bélanger, Cecilia 4.2 is the final version that will use Csound for audio generation. His plan, because the interface for Cecilia is already written in Python, is to generate audio directly in Python beginning with Cecilia 5.0.

Opinions about Cecilia are mixed. For some people, it has been the gateway to their interest in Csound. Other people, including some very knowledgeable Csound users, are put off by how mysterious its internal workings are. It seems to have been designed as an expert system, not for novices, as evidenced (for instance) by the fact that you won't always be warned if you quit without remembering to save your file.

While we don't have space for a full Cecilia tutorial here, two useful commands are worth mentioning. If you edit the code for the interface, nothing will change until you use File > Reset Interface. Also in the File menu, the command Show Computed .csd File will give you a great opportunity for study the underlying code. If you're diligent, you'll be able to figure out exactly how Cecilia is performing its magic.

10 Using Csound with MIDI, OSC, Pd, Python, and Live Audio

Although Csound was originally conceived as a freestanding, self-contained program for rendering audio files, it has been extended over the years to be compatible with various other software systems and can now be used very effectively in real time. In this chapter we'll look at several of the more common methods of extending Csound and using it live.

MIDI

For better or worse (and usually for the better), MIDI remains a vital tool for making music with any type of electronic technology. MIDI was introduced in 1982, so as I write this it is nearing its 30th anniversary. While the MIDI Specification has been extended in a number of ways over the years, the basics of the MIDI language haven't changed. (That's the "worse" part.) Nor will they. Given the huge installed base of MIDI devices, it's safe to say MIDI will never change in any fundamental way. It may eventually be replaced by OSC (Open Sound Control), which is a far more powerful communications protocol—but OSC remains poorly supported by commercial products. (A few tips on using OSC with Csound will be found later in this chapter.)

This book is not the place to provide a thorough explanation of the MIDI communications protocol or how it's used. If you're new to MIDI, you can find some helpful explanations online, but I have yet to see a good, complete discussion of the details on the Web. The MIDI Manufacturers Association (the official body that keeps the MIDI world in sync with itself) has a very decent, though short, tutorial at www.midi.org/aboutmidi/intromidi.pdf.

You're most likely to use MIDI in conjunction with Csound by sending MIDI messages to your computer from a hardware controller, such as a keyboard. Csound can also transmit MIDI messages, so it can be used to generate performances using hardware instruments or even MIDI-controlled light and video devices. Csound can also load and play Standard MIDI Files, so if you've created a composition in a conventional sequencing system you can port it over to Csound in order to make use of Csound's synthesis capabilities.

With respect to the ability to play Standard MIDI Files, the manual says this (lightly edited): "You can load a MIDI file using the -F or --midifile=FILE command-line flag. The MIDI file is read in real time, and behaves as if it were being performed or received in real time. The Csound program is not aware of whether MIDI input comes from a MIDI file or directly from a MIDI interface." So all of the information in this chapter about receiving MIDI messages in real time, other than the information about setting up a hardware MIDI system, should apply equally well to MIDI file playback.

Setting Up a MIDI System

The most common way to use MIDI (with Csound or with any other music software) is to connect a hardware MIDI controller of some sort to your computer. The controller could be a keyboard, a grid controller such as the Novation Launchpad, or something else. Some MIDI keyboards are also self-contained synthesizers, but we won't be concerned with that functionality here; we'll treat the keyboard strictly as a device that transmits MIDI data to your computer.

Many controllers can link directly to a computer using a USB cable. If your controller won't do this, you'll need a separate MIDI interface device. The interface will attach to the computer via USB or FireWire, and the controller will be connected to the interface using a standard five-pin MIDI cable.

Some MIDI interfaces are built into audio interfaces. This is a convenient type of device to have: It can handle both audio I/O and MIDI I/O for your computer.

Another way of using MIDI is to stream it from one program to another within the computer environment. In the Mac OS, this can be done with the IAC (inter-application control) bus, which is built into the system. Windows users can take advantage of MIDI Yoke (www.midiox. com), a free utility that provides eight separate software busses to link programs to one another. Users of 32-bit Windows 7 systems may also want to look at the Maple Virtual MIDI Cable (maplemidi.com).

This type of internal connection can be quite useful. For instance, if you would like to process the MIDI signals coming from your hardware controller with a program such as Pd before they're received by Csound, or if you would like to use Csound to generate MIDI and send it to Ableton Live, you'll need MIDI Yoke or Apple IAC.

There's no need for a Linux equivalent to these utilities, as ALSA MIDI contains routing and patching capabilities by default. However, the Csound implementation of ALSA MIDI uses the "raw" sequencer interface, so Linux users may need to load the vir-midi kernel module.

Tip The Mac OS IAC utility, with which two music applications can communicate via MIDI, is well hidden from the casual user. Go to the Applications > Utilities folder and launch the Audio MIDI Setup program. From the Window menu in this program, choose Show MIDI Window. Double-click the IAC Driver icon in the MIDI window and click the Device Is Online checkbox, as shown in Figure 10.1. This will give you an internal MIDI input/output bus.

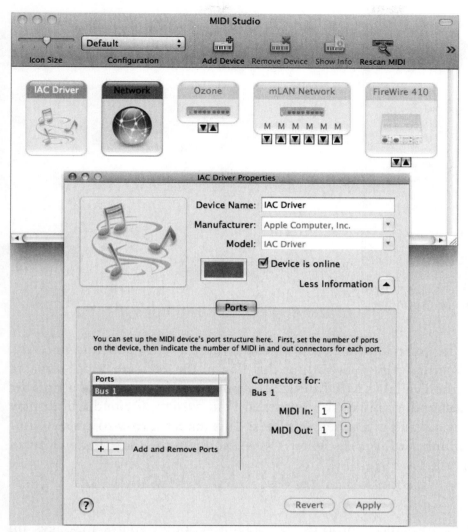

Figure 10.1 Switch on the IAC bus for internal MIDI communications in the Macintosh by opening up the MIDI window in the Audio MIDI Setup utility program.

Receiving MIDI Input

Once your MIDI hardware is set up, you can send MIDI messages into Csound in order to play your Csound instruments in real time. An assortment of opcodes is available for this purpose.

Before you start adding opcodes, you'll need to set up Csound so that it's looking for MIDI input. In CsoundQt, you can do this in the Run tab of the Configuration box, as shown in Figure 10.2. From the drop-down menu, select PortMidi as the RT MIDI Module. Then click on the box to the right of the Input Device (-M) field. The list of available input devices will be displayed. Click on the device you'd like to use, and you should be ready to go.

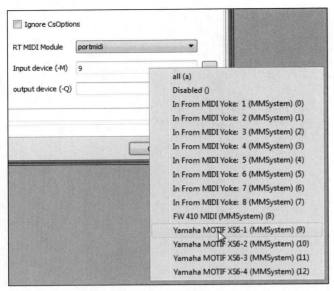

Figure 10.2 Choosing a MIDI input for CsoundQt.

If you're running Csound from the command line, you'll need to use the -M command-line flag, followed by a device number. Alternatively, you can put this flag in the <CsOptions> area of your .csd file. Csound refers to the available MIDI devices by number. If you choose a number for the -M flag that doesn't correspond to any of the devices in your system, Csound will display an error message that lists the devices and gives their numbers. This makes it easy to correct your choice. If you aren't sure what number to use, just enter -M999 and run the file. This will be an error, so you'll see the list displayed.

massign

MIDI defines 16 channels for performance purposes. By default, Csound routes messages on these 16 channels to the instruments in your orchestra that are numbered from 1 to 16. As a side benefit, Csound automatically interprets sustain pedal messages (Control Change 64) and keeps notes sounding until the pedal is lifted.

Using the first 16 instruments for the 16 channels is convenient, but it may not always be what you want. If you need to route channels to different instruments, put one or more calls to the massign opcode in your orchestra header. For instance, to get messages on channel 1 to instrument 101, you would write:

```
massign 1, 101
```

This opcode is also useful if you want to prevent MIDI messages from triggering your instruments. An input value of 0 means "all input channels," and an output value of 0 means "disable the response to note triggers on this channel." To prevent MIDI triggering, do this:

```
massign 0, 0
```

Using `massign` in this manner doesn't shut off the MIDI message pipeline entirely; it simply prevents MIDI note-ons from triggering new events. You can still create instruments that respond to other kinds of MIDI messages.

MIDI Note Messages   Each MIDI note message contains three pieces of information—the channel (from 1 to 16), the note number (from 0 to 127), and the velocity (from 0 to 127). The keys on a standard five-octave MIDI keyboard transmit note numbers 36 through 96, and Middle C is note 60.

The note-on and note-off messages are separate types. A note-on is transmitted when a key is pressed, and a note-off when the key is lifted. However, for technical reasons having to do with data transmission speed in early MIDI systems, a note-on message with a velocity of 0 is interpreted as a note-off. (If you're curious about the reasons for this odd design choice, enter the term "MIDI running status" into your favorite search engine.) If you're writing code to test what sort of MIDI message your Csound instrument is receiving, it's essential to understand this point. You may not know whether your MIDI keyboard is sending note-offs when keys are lifted, or note-ons with velocity 0, so your code should be written so as to handle both possibilities.

As a result of this design, when a new note starts, its velocity will be between 1 and 127. The velocity value is a measure of how fast the key was traveling when (or just before) it struck the keybed. Many explanations of MIDI velocity incorrectly use phrases such as "how hard the key was pressed." Pressure (also called *aftertouch*) is a separate type of MIDI data—in fact, it's two different types, channel pressure and polyphonic pressure. Pressure has nothing to do with velocity, although in some hardware both pressure and velocity are sensed using the same physical mechanism.

cpsmidi, veloc, and notnum

When an instrument is being triggered using MIDI note-on messages (and terminated via note-off messages), the `cpsmidi` opcode can be used to get the frequency value that corresponds to a MIDI note in 12-note-per-octave equal temperament. Here is some setup code for an instrument that uses `cpsmidi` as well as `veloc` (to get the MIDI note-on velocity value) and `ctrl7` (to get modulation wheel movements):

```
ifreq cpsmidi
ivel veloc
ivel = 0.01 + (ivel / 130)
kmod ctrl7 1, 1, 0, 1
```

MIDI note-on velocities have a range from 1 to 127. The third line of the above code scales the value of `ivel` so that it is approximately in the range between 0.01 and 1.0, as that range will probably be easier to use in your other Csound code. Other velocity scaling methods are easy enough to set up. You can even use the raw velocity value as an index into a table so as to implement a velocity response curve.

If you want to play some other type of tuning from your MIDI keyboard, you can get the MIDI note number directly using `notnum`. The lines below produce exactly the same output as `cpsmidi`, but the process is easier to customize:

```
ikey notnum
ioct = int(ikey / 12) + 3
iclass = int(ikey % 12) * 0.01
ifreq = cpspch (ioct + iclass)
```

Here, the raw note number (`ikey`) is being transformed into octave/pitch-class data, as explained in the "Pitch Converters" section of Chapter 7. If we want the keyboard to play in 17-note equal temperament, for instance, we can edit the above slightly so as to be able to use `cpsxpch`:

```
iscalesteps = 17
ibasepitch = 30
ioct = int(ikey / iscalesteps)
iclass = int(ikey % iscalesteps) * 0.01
ifreq cpsxpch (ioct + iclass), iscalesteps, 2.0, ibasepitch
```

pgmassign

If you need to route your keyboard performance to a different instrument while playing the music, you can do it by switching the hardware controller's MIDI output to a different channel, but this may not always be convenient in the heat of performance, and in any case it limits you to a maximum of 16 playable instruments. Another method is to use `pgmassign`. With this opcode in play, MIDI program change messages can be used to switch instruments. To do this, you would first create a named program-switching instrument, like this:

```
instr ProgSwitch ; a program switcher
pgmassign 1, 1, 1
pgmassign 2, 21, 1
endin
```

This instrument would then be made active using `alwayson` in the orchestra header:

```
alwayson "ProgSwitch"
```

In this example, the keyboard is transmitting on channel 1 (the third argument to `pgmassign`). Program change 1 routes notes on channel 1 to instrument 1. Program change 2 routes them instead to instrument 21. It appears in my experiments that `pgmassign` offsets the actual transmitted values by 1. That is, MIDI program changes are numbered 0–127 but are interpreted by pgmassign as having values from 1 to 128. (This is not as unusual as it may sound. The 16 MIDI channels are actually numbered 0–15, but they are universally referred to as being in the range 1–16.)

midiin

The most generic way to get MIDI data from an active input port is to use midiin. The prototype is:

```
kstatus, kchan, kdata1, kdata2 midiin
```

This opcode has four outputs: The status byte, the channel (1–16), and the two data bytes associated with the message. The status byte defines the type of message being received. The values, as listed in the manual, are:

- 128 (note off)
- 144 (note on)
- 160 (polyphonic aftertouch)
- 176 (control change)
- 192 (program change)
- 208 (channel aftertouch)
- 224 (pitch-bend)

If no MIDI message is in the input buffer, the value of kstatus will be zero. This enables us to write a simple but useful always-on MIDI data monitor, which will display MIDI messages to the Output Console:

```
instr MidiMonitor
kstatus, kchan, kdata1, kdata2 midiin
if kstatus != 0 then
    printks "Status %d, channel %d, data %d, %d.\n", 0, kstatus, \
    kchan, kdata1, kdata2
endif
endin
```

If you're not familiar with MIDI, a few points about this may be less than transparent:

- Depending on what your keyboard is transmitting, you may see a note-on message (status 144) rather than a note-off each time you lift a finger. See the "MIDI Note Messages" sidebar earlier in this chapter for further details.
- Channel aftertouch messages have only one data byte, so the value of kdata2 will always be zero when channel aftertouch is being received.

- Control change messages use the first data byte to indicate which controller is being moved (in a range from 0 to 127) and the second data byte to indicate the current value of the controller. The MIDI modulation wheel, for example, is controller 1.

- Pitch-bend messages have two data bytes, giving them a theoretical resolution of 14 bits. (MIDI uses up one bit in each byte, leaving seven bits to contain data.) But some hardware controllers don't take advantage of this high resolution, so the second data byte may always be 0 or 64.

Other MIDI Input Opcodes

Numerous opcodes are available for grabbing MIDI messages from the input buffer: aftouch, chanctrl, polyaft, pchbend, midictrl, ctrl7, and so forth. Some of these are meant to be used within an instrument that is being triggered by a MIDI note-on message, so they assume the value of the MIDI channel. Others let you specify the desired channel as an argument, so you can use them even in instruments that are not responding to MIDI note triggers.

You may want to set the initial value of a MIDI control change message, so that it will be something other than zero when your MIDI performance starts. This might be especially useful if you're using CC7 or CC11 messages to control instruments' volume, because a default of 0 will cause an instrument to be silent until you move your hardware controller device. For this purpose, you can use ctrlinit in the orchestra header. For example, this line:

```
ctrlinit 1, 7, 100
```

will cause CC7 on channel 1 to be set to an initial value of 100 each time the file starts playing.

The ctrl14, ctrl21, midic14, and midic21 opcodes are described in the manual as producing 14-bit or 21-bit floating-point values from two or three MIDI control change messages. This is a non-standard use of MIDI control change messages, and some work would be required to set up your controller hardware to transmit data in the correct form (if it could do so at all). MIDI has a mechanism for transmitting 14-bit control values using two separate control change messages, one for the MSB and one for the LSB, but if your hardware will transmit using this format at all (not guaranteed), it will almost certainly assume that you want to transmit 14-bit integers, not 14-bit floating-point values. So this Csound feature is likely to be of limited utility.

In my experiments, in Csound version 5.13 aftouch produces a maximum output value (default 127) until it receives the first channel aftertouch message. This is a bug in Csound. The workaround is to use midiin instead:

```
kaft init 0
kstatus, kchan, kdata1, kdata2 midiin
if kstatus == 208 && kchan == 1 then
    kaft = kdata1
endif
```

Performance Considerations

When playing Csound instruments in real time via MIDI, you may hear glitches in the audio output. This can happen for two reasons—CPU overload and output clipping distortion. CPU overload tends to sound like dropouts. Clipping tends to sound like popping, clicking, and grinding, or in extreme cases like nasty buzzing. In this section we'll look at how to prevent these problems.

Also worth noting: In real-time performance, Csound doesn't know how long your notes are going to be, so its normal envelope generators (`linseg`, for example) can't calculate an amplitude envelope that tapers nicely to 0 at the end of the note. The solution is to use the versions of envelope opcodes whose names end with -r: `linsegr`, `expsegr`, and so on. (You might expect to be able to use `adsr` in this situation, to take advantage of its classic approach to enveloping, but `adsr` is not an -r opcde. Use `madsr` instead.) MIDI-triggered notes will go into the release portion of the -r envelope when a note-off message or a note-on with velocity 0 is received.

CPU Overloads

CPU overloads happen when you're asking the computer's main microprocessor to do more work per second than it's capable of doing. It can't keep up, so there will be a brief gap during which it has no data to send to the output. This is also called a *buffer underrun*, because the driver for the audio hardware is trying to get new data from the buffer in order to send the data on to the hardware, but the CPU hasn't had time to put new data in the buffer yet, so the buffer is empty.

Four or five strategies are available for handling buffer underruns.

First, you can simplify your performance itself by requesting fewer simultaneous notes. If you're playing an instrument whose amplitude envelopes have long release segments, for instance, you'll have overlaps. Notes that are dying away and no longer important musically will still be using computer resources, because each note you play starts a new instance of an instrument. Shortening the release segments of the notes' envelopes will reduce the number of overlaps, thereby reducing the total number of notes being generated at once.

Second, you can simplify your instrument code. If you can replace a k-rate argument to an opcode with an i-time argument, the opcode may run more efficiently. Multiplications are slightly more efficient than divisions, so look for places where you can replace something like this:

```
kresult = kdata / 5
```

with this:

```
kresult = kdata * 0.2
```

Changing one division to a multiplication isn't likely to make any perceptible difference, but if your code has dozens of divisions per k-period, you may see some improvement when you make this change.

If you can get rid of an LFO without changing the timbre in an undesirable way, or replace data that's being calculated on the fly with data stored in a table, you'll see an improvement.

You may be wondering, how much of my CPU power does this or that opcode use? Detailed figures haven't been published—and given the sheer number of opcodes, doing the research to answer this question would be a large undertaking. In some cases, there may not be a definite answer, because the CPU load will depend on the arguments sent to the opcode. As Oeyvind Brandtsegg pointed out in a discussion of this topic on the Csound mailing list, the granular synthesis opcodes will use more CPU when large amounts of grain overlaps are being requested.

Third, you can increase the value of `ksmps`. For rendering high-quality audio, a value of `ksmps=1` is ideal, but for live work, you may find that you need `ksmps=100`. The tradeoff is that k-rate envelopes that are being used to modulate the audio will start to sound a bit grainy.

Fourth, you can increase the buffer settings. There's a tradeoff here: Doubling the size of the software and hardware buffers doubles the latency—the amount of time that passes between when you press a MIDI key or button and when you hear the result.

I find that I can set `-b` to 512 and `-B` to 1024 and generally get acceptable low-latency performance from my computer with an ASIO driver. (The ASIO output driver in my Windows 7 computer is ASIO4ALL v2.) The same values with a non-ASIO driver, such as the Windows MME driver, won't work acceptably. The settings given above will work under ASIO when I play six or eight notes at once on a three-oscillator, two-envelope instrument with a global reverb; more complex instruments and more polyphony might require higher settings to avoid problems. Needless to say, you should check your entire music set before going onstage to make sure the settings you've chosen won't cause your system to choke in the middle of a concert! Values of 128, 256, 384, 512, 768, and 1024 would be typical for `-b`, and `-B` should probably be twice or four times as high.

Fifth, if some portions of your music won't change from one gig or concert to another—if they're backing tracks, for instance—you can render them to the hard drive ahead of time and substitute a sample playback instrument to stream the audio from the hard drive. This is not practical with music that's entirely improvised or being generated by algorithmic processes, of course, but if you can pre-record some parts of the music, you should see a huge improvement in the CPU performance.

Finally, it should be noted that modern computers are typically running many processes in the background, without your necessarily being aware of them. Such processes "wake up" periodically and grab some CPU cycles. Streamlining your operating system by shutting off background processes can help prevent buffer underruns.

Avoiding Clipping

When you're developing a score that won't be performed onstage, you can easily avoid clipping just by lowering the output amplitudes of all the instruments in your orchestra. In live work, you can't do this. By the time you hear the clipping, it's too late.

I've had good luck using the compress opcode. With the proper settings, this seems to tame high output levels without introducing any artifacts. For more information, see the section on compress in Chapter 7.

The audio produced by Csound is of such high quality that you should be able to lower the overall output level of the orchestra somewhat and compensate by turning up your amplification system. The amount of background noise introduced by doing this will almost always be masked by the ambient noise of the club or concert hall.

Keeping Csound Running

The normal behavior of Csound is to keep running until it has finished rendering a score (either to a disk file or to the audio output) and then stop. Using Csound for a MIDI performance, we obviously need it to keep running in the background, doing nothing, until it receives a suitable MIDI input. There are three more or less interchangeable ways to do this.

The old-fashioned method was to create a score with a dummy f-statement set to some arbitrary time:

```
f0    3600
```

If the score is running at the default rate (one beat per second), this statement will cause Csound to keep running for an hour and then stop. Instead, you can use a p-field with an e-statement. The e-statement ends the score. This line does the same thing as the dummy f-statement:

```
e    3600
```

A more practical method is to use the alwayson opcode in the orchestra header, most likely in conjunction with an instrument such as a global reverb processor, which you want to continue to be active throughout the performance:

```
alwayson "Reverb"
```

This will cause Csound to run until you terminate it manually, for instance by clicking the Stop button in the CsoundQt interface.

A Monophonic Legato MIDI Instrument

Each time you press a MIDI key, Csound starts a new instance of the corresponding instrument—by default, the instrument whose number corresponds to the MIDI channel. This is fine if you're planning to play chords. But what if you want a monophonic instrument that will produce legato lines? This is a standard feature of commercial MIDI instruments.

Producing the same effect in Csound requires a little trickery. The example below is adapted from a code example provided by Victor Lazzarini. Almost nothing of Victor's work remains except the basic idea, which is this: Instrument 1, which we'll assume is responding to MIDI channel 1, does nothing but derive the pitch from the MIDI note number. The tone is generated by an always-on instrument (instrument 11). The latter counts the number of instances of instrument 1 that are currently playing, using the active opcode. If active returns zero, instrument 11 knows that no keys are pressed, so it ramps the amplitude of the output down to zero.

The comments in the code will explain what's going on.

```
sr = 44100
ksmps = 4
nchnls = 2
0dbfs = 1


alwayson "ToneGenerator"
giSaw ftgen 0, 0, 8192, 10, 1, 1, 1, 1, 1, 1, 1, 1, 1, 1, 1, 1, 1, 1
gkCheck init 0
gkPitch init 260


instr 1 ; activated from MIDI channel 1, tracks the pitch
gkPitch cpsmidib 2
gkCheck = 1
endin


instr ToneGenerator

; check whether any instances of instr 1 are active
kon active 1
; velocity sensing -- only accept a new velocity input if
; there's no note overlap (if kon == 1) -- get the velocity
; and scale it to an 0.2 - 1.0 range
kvel init 0
kstatus kchan kdata1 kdata2 midiin
if kstatus == 144 && kdata2 != 0 && kon == 1 then
    kvel = kdata2 * 0.006 + 0.2
endif


; amplitude control
kampraw init 0
if kon != 0 then
    kampraw = 0.5 * kvel
    ; fast attack:
    kenvramp = 50
else
    kampraw = 0
    ; slow release;
```

```
    kenvramp = 1
endif
kamp tonek kampraw, kenvramp

; pitch glide -- higher numbers cause faster glide
ipitchglide = 4
kpitch tonek gkPitch, ipitchglide

; oscillators
idetune = 0.3
asig1 oscil kamp, kpitch + idetune, giSaw
asig2 oscil kamp, kpitch, giSaw
asig3 oscil kamp, kpitch - idetune, giSaw
asig = asig1 + asig2 + asig3

; if no MIDI keys are pressed, reinitialize the filter envelope
if gkCheck == 1 && kon == 0 then
    reinit filtenv
endif

ifiltdec1 = 1.5
ifiltdec2 = 3
filtenv:
kfilt expseg 500, 0.01, 8000, ifiltdec1, 2000, ifiltdec2, 500, 1, 500
rireturn

; smooth the filter envelope so a reinit won't cause it to jump --
; also have the cutoff track the keyboard and velocity
kfilt tonek (kfilt * (0.6 + kvel * 0.5)) + kpitch, kenvramp
afilt lpf18 asig, kfilt, 0.3, 0.1

outs afilt, afilt
endin

</CsInstruments>
<CsScore>
e 3600
```

Csound and VST

In theory, Csound is capable of loading and running third-party plug-ins in the VST format. Given the number of high-quality commercial and freeware VST instruments, this feature makes it easier to produce evocative sounds with a minimum of effort.

The vstinit, vstnote, vstedit, and related opcodes enable you to load and use VST plug-ins. These opcodes require the file vst4cs.dll, which is not distributed with Csound. It is, however, readily available. If you post a polite message to the Csound mailing list, most likely someone will be happy to send you a copy or point you to a download link. It should be copied into your Csound > plugins64 directory.

My experiences with vst4cs.dll have been decidedly mixed. Some plug-in instruments work well. Some of them produce sound but display blank edit windows. Some of them crash Csound. However, this book is being written in the summer of 2011. If you're reading it a couple of years from now, the situation may have improved. Or you may find that the current version works well with the particular VSTi you want to use. As they say, your mileage may vary.

It's also possible that Windows users may be able to figure out how to run Csound itself as a VST plug-in within a host program. This is done using files called CsoundVST.dll and vst4cs.dll. These files are, again, not included with the standard Csound distribution, apparently due to licensing issues, but a version of Csound that includes them can be downloaded from http://michael-gogins.com.

I've never had any luck getting CsoundVST to run, and the instructions in the manual are sketchy to the point of being nearly useless. If you have enough patience and determination, you may be able to get it running, but you'll probably find it easier to download MIDI Yoke and simply send MIDI data from your sequencer to Csound with Csound running as a separate program.

A better alternative, if you want to run your Csound instruments within a VST host, may be to download and learn to use Cabbage (http://code.google.com/p/cabbage). Cabbage is a toolkit (available for Windows only at this writing, but Linux and Mac OS versions are in the works) with which you can turn Csound instruments into standard VST plug-ins.

OSC

Open Sound Control (OSC) is a powerful, open-ended communications protocol for sending data from one piece of music software or hardware to another. Two programs can be linked using OSC even if they're running on different computers. It could be argued that OSC requires a bit more expertise to set up than a MIDI communications system—or it could be argued that OSC is actually easier to use than MIDI, because you're not limited to MIDI's fixed set of message types and control value ranges. With OSC, you can define messages in whatever way you need, so once you learn the syntax, the path to musical satisfaction will be smoother.

Although it has been in existence for more than a decade, OSC remains poorly supported by the major hardware manufacturers. It has made some inroads in the software world, however. Renoise, Apple Logic Audio, Csound, Pd, SuperCollider, Native Instruments Reaktor, and some Linux programs work with OSC.

Andres Cabrera has uploaded an excellent five-minute video to YouTube (www.youtube.com/watch?v=JX1C3TqP_9Y&list=PL3EE3219702D17FD3&index=12&feature=plpp) showing how to use OSC for communications between Csound and Pd. The setup is entirely different from running Csound as an object within Pd, a topic that will be covered later in this chapter. The musical results might or might not be similar; that's up to you. Pd is used in the video, and we'll use it here, entirely as a matter of convenience. It's readily available and arguably easier for a newcomer to work with than SuperCollider.

 Caution The Pd objects sendOSC and dumpOSC, which are used in the tutorial video, are now deprecated. They may work for you, but I'm told that they're not free of bugs. In the discussion in this section, we'll use Pd's newer udpsend and udpreceive objects. The Pd objects that work with them, such as packOSC and unpackOSC, are distributed with Pd-Extended 0.42.5, which is the latest version at this writing, but they are not loaded automatically when Pd starts. To load them, you must create an object box whose text reads import mrpeach, as shown in Figure 10.3. Oddly enough, this object doesn't even need to be connected to a bang or loadbang to do its job; however, you may need to save your patch, close it, and reopen it in order for the import command to take effect.

To begin experimenting with OSC, launch Pd and create the patch shown in Figure 10.3. The horizontal slider should be given a range from 0 to 1.0. This slider will be used to send amplitude data to Csound, so an upper limit of 1.0 is a good idea, assuming you're running Csound with 0dbfs=1. The range of the vertical slider, which will control oscillator frequency, is less crucial; a range from 100 to 400 might be good.

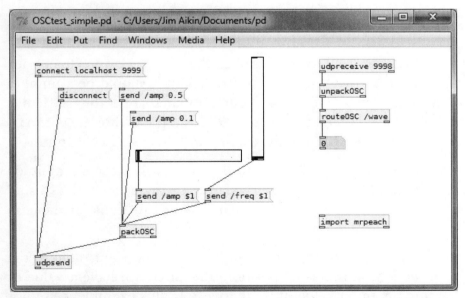

Figure 10.3 A simple patch in Pd with which to try out the OSC features of Csound. The objects on the left side will transmit OSC values to Csound; the objects on the right will receive from Csound.

In Csound, create the following .csd file:

```
sr = 44100
ksmps = 4
nchnls = 2
0dbfs = 1

giSine ftgen 0, 0, 8192, 10, 1
giOSC OSCinit 9999

instr 1 ; receive from OSC
kamp init 0
kfreq init 200
ktrig1 OSClisten giOSC, "/amp", "f", kamp
ktrig2 OSClisten giOSC, "/freq", "f", kfreq
asig foscil kamp, kfreq, 1, 1, 1, giSine
outs asig, asig
endin

instr 2 ; send to OSC
kosc oscil 100, 0.2, giSine
OSCsend kosc, "localhost", 9998, "/wave", "f", kosc
endin

</CsInstruments>
<CsScore>
i1 0 60
```

In order for Csound to transmit to OSC, you need to put a call to the OSCinit opcode in your orchestra header, as shown. The argument to this opcode is arbitrary, but it should be a number higher than 1024, as the lower-numbered ports are reserved. Your computer's operating system is probably using some of them, though most will remain unused. 9999 is a good choice. OSCinit is not needed if Csound is not receiving from OSC but only sending to OSC using OSCsend.

Looking at instrument 1, you'll see two calls to OSClisten. The first will receive amplitude values from Pd using the /amp destination, and the second will receive frequency values using the /freq destination. These same items are used in the Pd patch; you can think of them as named channels if you like.

OSClisten is a rare example of a Csound opcode whose output is on the right, among the arguments. It also has an output on the left, in the usual position; the latter will have a value of 1 when OSClisten has just received data and a value of 0 otherwise. In this example we're not using this output. We're only using the outputs kamp (in the first line) and kfreq (in the second). These variables have to be declared before they can be used; hence the uses of init in the preceding two lines.

The rest of the code for instrument 1 is straightforward. If you've been reading *Csound Power!* attentively, you should have no trouble understanding it.

Start this file by clicking CsoundQt's Run button. (The first time you do this, your computer's operating system may ask you whether you would like to allow the communication. This is a security feature. Just click OK.) You won't hear anything, because kamp has been initialized to zero. Bring up the Pd window, hit Ctrl+E if necessary to take it out of edit mode, and click the connect localhost 9999 message. This will make the OSC connection active. Then click on the send /amp 0.1 or send /amp 0.5 message box. This message will be sent to the packOSC object, and thence to udpsend. You should now hear the sound of the Csound instrument. You can adjust its volume with the horizontal slider and its pitch with the vertical slider, which also send messages.

When you click Pd's disconnect message box, the communications port will be closed, but Csound's output will continue. You can shut it off in the normal way, by clicking the Stop button.

Let's look at the syntax for OSClisten in more detail. Here is the prototype:

```
kans OSClisten ihandle, idest, itype [, xdata1, xdata2, ...]
```

The left-side output (kans) has already been explained. We've set ihandle using the handle returned by the call to OSCinit, which is giOSC. (The name is arbitrary, but it should be a global init-time value.) The argument corresponding to idest is a string: "/amp" or "/freq". This string is, again, arbitrary—we can put whatever we like here, beginning with a slash character—but it must correspond to the message being transmitted by the other device.

The argument to itype is, again, a string. This tells the OSC port what type of data we expect to receive. As the Csound manual explains, "The string can contain the characters 'cdfhis', which stand [respectively] for character, double, float, 64-bit integer, 32-bit integer, and string. All types other than 's' require a k-rate variable, while 's' requires a string variable." In the example above, we're expecting to receive a floating-point number from Pd, so we use "f". Finally, we tell OSClisten what variable to put the data in (kamp or kfreq, as the case may be).

To try sending OSC messages from Csound, replace the call to instrument 1 in the score with a call to instrument 2 and then click the Run button. When you look at the Pd window, you should see the number object on the right side scrolling up and down from –100 to 100 as the output of the control-rate oscillator in instrument 2 is sent over OSC.

Instrument 2 uses OSCsend. Here is the prototype:

```
OSCsend kwhen, ihost, iport, idestination, itype [, kdata1, kdata2,
    ...]
```

The first argument, kwhen, triggers the sending of a new OSC message each time it changes. In the example above, we want each change in the output of the oscillator to be sent, so we use kosc for this argument as well as for the data argument.

Assuming that both Csound and Pd are running on the same computer, ihost should be set to "localhost". The port argument is 9998, corresponding to the argument to Pd's dumpOSC object. The value for idestination is "/wave", which matches the argument to Pd's OSCroute object. As with the use of OSClisten, explained earlier, the argument itype is "f" because we're planning to send a single floating-point number. The number itself, in this case kosc, is the final argument.

Sending and Receiving Longer Messages

As you might already have inferred from looking at the prototypes of OSClisten and OSCsend, an OSC message can contain more than one data value. To see this functionality in action, edit your Pd patch as shown in Figure 10.4. The new patch sends values using the /data identifier and receives them using the /mods identifier. To see the received values, you'll need to keep Pd's console window open.

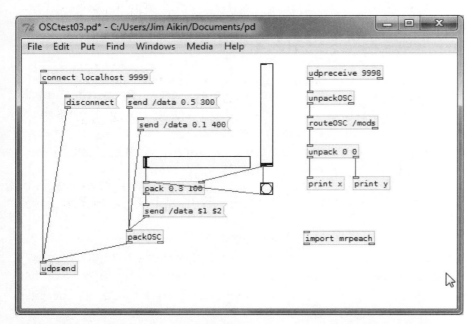

Figure 10.4 A Pd patch that can send and receive OSC messages, each message containing two floating-point numbers. The message boxes in the upper center send two data values each, and the sliders can be used to change one data value at a time. The two print boxes send the values received over OSC to Pd's console window.

The revised Csound instruments look like this:

```
instr 1 ; receive multiply from OSC
kamp init 0
```

```
kfreq init 200
ktrig1 OSClisten giOSC, "/data", "ff", kamp, kfreq
asig foscil kamp, kfreq, 1, 1, 1, giSine
outs asig, asig
endin
instr 2 ; send multiply to OSC
kosc oscil 100, 0.2, giSine
ksig line 0, p3, 1
OSCsend kosc, "localhost", 9998, "/mods", "ff", kosc, ksig
endin
```

The `itype` arguments to `OSClisten` and `OSCsend` now say `"ff"`, because we're sending and receiving messages with two floating-point numbers in each message.

Data Buffering

In a thread on the Csound mailing list, Lou Cohen pointed out that OSC messages can potentially arrive faster than Csound can process them. This is especially likely if you're using a high value of `ksmps` in order to prevent CPU overload in live performance. If several messages are in the input buffer, strange things can happen.

Note You may want to do the same kind of input processing with MIDI messages, because they're buffered in the same way. However, MIDI messages being sent from MIDI hardware are limited to a lower bandwidth than OSC, so the likelihood of losing messages is lower.

Here is a UDO that Lou reports using to filter the OSC input so that a Csound instrument only has to deal with one message per k-period. This opcode discards everything but the last message of some specified type in the input buffer.

```
opcode getosc, k,Sk ; reads OSC message, emptying input buffer
Smsg,kvalue xin
kcount = 0
getmore:
    kk OSClisten giport, Smsg, "f", kvalue
    if (kk>0) then
        kcount = kcount + 1
        kgoto getmore
    endif
xout kvalue
endop
```

Here, according to Lou, is a typical call to this UDO:

```
gkpitchval getosc "/wii/1/accel/pry/0", gkpitchval
```

Connecting Two Computers Using OSC

I haven't yet tried this, but I'm told it should be fairly easy to set up. A router (wireless or wired) is a good choice for setting up a local network. You'll also need to know the IP address of each computer. In Windows, you can get this information by running the program ipconfig from the Command Prompt. From the Mac OS Terminal, you can run ifconfig, which will display the same information. You would then use the IP address of the receiving machine in place of "localhost" in the call to OSCsend.

Connecting two computers over the Internet using OSC should also be possible, but the latency will inevitably be somewhat higher and also somewhat unpredictable. In order to do this, you'll also need to configure your router properly and deal with your computer's firewall.

Real-Time Audio Processing

Setting up Csound to receive external audio and process it in real time could hardly be easier. Assuming you've chosen the correct audio inputs in the Run tab of CsoundQt's Configuration box and that you've hooked up the left and right stereo input signals to your computer's audio hardware, you can receive the incoming signals like this:

```
aL, aR inch 1, 2
```

Ideally, you'll be using a low-latency audio driver, such as ASIO, but that's really all there is to it. The inch will grab the signals from channels 1 and 2 of your audio interface, after which you can process them in whatever manner you desire.

Below is a simple example—a stereo delay with filtering. Before trying out this example, please note: It uses a bandpass filter in a delay loop. This makes it *extremely* sensitive to small changes in parameter values. Runaway feedback can occur if the parameters stray even slightly too far in one direction or another, so please be careful when entering and editing this code. Ear damage is forever.

```
giSine ftgen 0, 0, 8192, 10, 1
alwayson "DelayProcessor", 0.5, 0.9

instr DelayProcessor
itime = p4 * 2
itimeR = itime * 1.5
iLfdbk = p5 * 0.025
iRfdbk = iLfdbk ; * 0.8

aL, aR inch 1, 2
```

```
klfo oscil 0.002, 0.4, giSine
kfiltLFO oscil 400, 0.13, giSine

adelL delayr itime
aLtap deltapi (itime * 0.5) + klfo
aLfilt resonr aLtap, 700 + kfiltLFO, 300
delayw aL + aLfilt * iLfdbk

adelR delayr itimeR
aRtap deltapi (itimeR * 0.5) - klfo
aRfilt resonr aRtap, 700 - kfiltLFO, 300
delayw aR + aRfilt * iRfdbk

aoutL = aL * 0.7 + adelL * 0.7
aoutR = aR * 0.7 + adelR * 0.7
outs aoutL, aoutR
endin

</CsInstruments>
<CsScore>

e 3600
```

Using Csound with Pd

As noted in Chapter 1, Pd (http://puredata.info) is a powerful, free, cross-platform-compatible programming language for music. The user interface of Pd is almost entirely graphical; it could hardly be more different from Csound conceptually. Graphical programming is appealing to many musicians.

There's no denying, however, that Csound has more synthesis opcodes than Pd. (Also, if you have issues with tendinitis or carpal tunnel syndrome, Csound may be a better choice simply because Pd requires far more extensive use of the mouse.) Fortunately, you don't have to choose one or the other. If you've chosen to install the Pd front end, which is an option in the Csound installer dialog, you'll find a file called csoundapi~.dll in your Csound > bin folder. Copy this into Pd's "extra" folder, which will be found in the root folder for Pd, wherever you have installed that.

On the Macintosh, Pd needs to see a file called csoundapi~.pd_darwin. You'll find this in /Library/Frameworks/CsoundLib.framework/Versions/5.2/Resources/PD/. (Note that this is the Library folder on the root of the hard drive, not the Library folder in your own user directory.) This file needs to be copied to a directory that is in Pd's search path. In my Mac, this is jimaikin > Library > Pd.

Once you've copied and pasted the file, you can launch Pd and create a Csound object by typing `csoundapi~` in a new object box. If the installation is correct, you'll see a standard Pd object box, as shown in Figure 10.5. If you haven't put the .dll in the right place, Pd will send an error message to its Console window. By itself, the csoundapi~ object isn't much use, however. It needs to receive an argument that tells it what .csd file you want to run. For instance, if you want to run a file called vocaltones.csd, you would leave a space after `csoundapi~` and type `vocaltones.csd`.

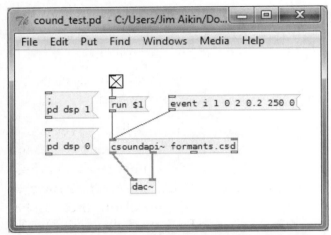

Figure 10.5 The csoundapi~ object in Pd has one inlet and four outlets. The two outlets on the left transmit stereo audio from Csound, which can be sent to the Pd dac~ audio output object. After attaching a toggle to the "run $1" message box, as shown, and turning on Pd's audio by clicking the "; pd dsp 1" message, click an event message box to send a real-time score event to Csound.

The csoundapi~ object can receive control, MIDI, and audio signals from Pd, and can transmit control and audio outputs to Pd. You can send new score events to Csound by sending a Pd message beginning with the word "event". A good article describing the details of the process is available online in the Csound Floss manual (http://en.flossmanuals.net/csound/ch052_csound-in-pd). There's little need to repeat the content of that article here.

Using Python within Csound

One of the more powerful and open-ended features of Csound is its compatibility with the Python programming language. Python code can be embedded in your Csound orchestra—or, going the other direction, you can invoke Csound itself from within Python.

Csound is, among other things, a computer programming language. It might seem odd to want to embed code in a second programming language within your Csound code. Why not just write everything you need using Csound's orchestra code syntax and avoid the hassle of learning an entirely new language?

In some cases, the answer may be, "Yes, that's right. Just use plain Csound." In other cases, using Python will offer some advantages, especially for the high-end user:

- Python provides various ways to manipulate text strings. If your orchestra relies on being able to assemble strings on the fly, in order to pass them to the scoreline opcode, you may find that using Python will make your life easier. (Note: Starting with version 5.0, Csound includes a greatly expanded set of string manipulation opcodes, so Python loses some of its competitive edge in this area.)

- Python implements lists and arrays. Csound has no equivalent of these data types; to get the same functionality without Python, you would have to resort to some fairly awkward workarounds using groups of tables. (Note, however, that Csound 5.14, released just before this book went to press, implements arrays as local data within instruments.)

- Python comes with an extensive library of math functions, as well as a wealth of external modules, any of which may be useful for some sophisticated types of instruments.

For the *Csound Journal*, Issue 6 (May 2007), Andrés Cabrera wrote an excellent introduction to the use of Python within Csound. This article is available online (at www.csounds.com/journal/issue6/pythonOpcodes.html). If you want to learn the basics, it's a must-read. The final section of the article provides an excellent example of how to use Python to create strings of notes using the logic of Markov chains. With Markov chains, you can control the precise likelihood that a note of any given pitch will be followed by a note of another given pitch. The results can be much more musically sensible than if each new pitch is chosen entirely at random.

 More Ways to Code   By the time you read this, Csound will probably have been expanded to allow the use of embedded code in the Lua programming language. The chief advantage of Lua, according to Michael Gogins, is that Lua runs much faster than Python. He also commented, "Lua is slightly more concise than Python, but because of some minor quirks, Python is slightly easier to write. Python currently has many more third-party libraries than Lua, but Lua has plenty and will get more. Lua is more elegant than Python, which is saying a lot, because Python is already very elegant."

Python is one of the easier programming languages to learn. Its syntax is fairly straightforward, and excellent tutorials are available online. Another advantage for the newcomer is that Python is an interpreted language. Your code needn't be compiled before it will run; you can experiment with it in real time, either from your computer's command prompt or using the Python Shell, which is called IDLE. (Yes, the name is a reference to *Monty Python's Flying Circus*.)

To get started, you'll need to download Python from www.python.org. A number of versions are available. Csound 5.13 is compatible with Python 2.7, but not with more recent versions. If you're using a later version of Csound, check the documentation or post a query to the Csound mailing list to find out which version of Python to install.

> **Tip** Unlike Csound, Python makes strict use of indentation (via the Tab key) as a way to structure blocks of code. If you forget an indent, your code won't run.

Your next task will be to learn Python. That process is not covered in *Csound Power!*

When installing Csound, you were asked whether to install the Python interface. This option is listed among the interfaces in the installer dialog. If you neglected to do that, you'll need to run the installer again.

The Python Opcodes

There are a lot of Python opcodes. Fortunately, they're named using a consistent syntax, so figuring out which one you need is easy. As *The Canonical Csound Reference Manual* explains, rather tersely, the syntax is:

```
"py" + [optional context prefix] + [action name] + [optional x-time suffix]
```

What this means is as follows:

All python opcodes start with the letters "py". Next, you may or may not need a lower-case "l". If present, this causes any Python variables defined within the instrument to be local—specific to the current note event, and not carried over. In the absence of an "l", Python variables are global. If they're global, changes made by a variable in one Python function will be reflected in other functions that reference the same variable, even if those functions are running in other Csound instruments.

The action names for Python opcodes include `init`, `eval`, `call`, `assign`, `exec`, and `run`. The optional x-time suffix, "i", tells Csound whether you want the Python opcode to run at init-time (if the "i" is present) or on every k-rate pass (if there's no "i").

The `call` opcodes have an added wrinkle. They call Python functions, and a function can return (output) from zero to eight values. A number appended to `call` tells Csound how many output values to expect. For example, after defining a Python function called `get_note`, you might write this:

```
kp4, kp5, kp6 pycall3 "get_note", kdata1, kdata2
```

This code would pass the values in `kdata1` and `kdata2` to the Python `get_note` function and put the three return values of the function into `kp4`, `kp5`, and `kp6`. Presumably, your code would then use these values with an `event` opcode to start a Csound note.

The Python opcodes can also be used in triggered form (suffix "t"). Triggered opcodes take an additional argument, the k-rate trigger, before the name of the function, file, or variable that the Python opcode will use. This is a k-rate trigger, so the suffixes "t" and "i" are mutually exclusive. The opcode will be triggered whenever the value of the trigger is not 0.

To use Python within Csound, you should call the `pyinit` opcode in your orchestra header. (`pyinit` is no longer needed in the most recent builds of Csound, but may still be needed in older versions.) Once you've done this, you can use `pyruni` in the header to set up an arbitrarily complex set of functions in Python.

 Note   Most Python code takes up more than one line. The Csound compiler will be able to cope with this structure if you surround the code with double curly braces. Use { { at the beginning of the code and } } at the end.

Extending Csound Using Scripting Languages

Csound orchestras and scores are in the form of pure ASCII text files. Thus it's relatively easy to generate either separate .orc and .sco files or, more likely, unified .csd files, using another programming language. The other language may also be able to invoke Csound directly, causing the generated file to play. Using Csound in this way is, of necessity, more complex than using Csound by itself, as you'll have to master two separate programming languages. The main reason to use this approach is because you can generate massive scores that would be impractical to produce by entering one note at a time in a text editor.

A granular synthesis texture, for instance, could be produced in which each sound grain was a separate event in the score, each event making use of a dozen or more p-fields. Thousands of score events might be needed for each minute of sound output. Music requiring complex, precisely calculated polyrhythms would also be a good candidate for this approach.

Various scripting languages can be used for this purpose. In Issue 5 of the *Csound Journal*, in an article on using Perl with Csound, Jacob Joaquin mentions, in passing, that JavaScript, Lisp, PHP, Python, and Ruby are all options. "I recommend avoiding using languages such as C and Java," Joaquin adds, "as they are particularly unwieldy in processing and managing text compared to the languages I've just mentioned."

Csound in Ableton Live

...and now for something completely different.

As this book was being prepared for publication, a new way of using Csound was released. CsoundForLive (www.csoundforlive.com) is designed specifically to work within Ableton Live—specifically within the Max For Live environment. Max For Live embeds Cycling '74 Max/MSP within Live and is not a free component, so not all Live users will be able to take advantage of CsoundForLive.

Some of the CsoundForLive modules are free, while others are available for sale.

When a CsoundForLive plug-in is loaded into Live (see Figure 10.6), the Csound code itself can be edited using your default Csound editor: In my system, clicking on a button in the plug-in's

Figure 10.6 Two CsoundForLive plug-ins running in Ableton Live.

panel opens CsoundQt. If you need to add new knobs or sliders, you'll find that the plug-in panel itself can be edited using the Max For Live programming interface.

Both effects and synthesizers are available in various CsoundForLive packages. A few of the plug-ins in the initial release are very nice. Others are quite simple in design and may not compare favorably with Live's existing instrument and effect suite. The point of using CsoundForLive is that once you're proficient in writing Csound code, you'll be able to customize the plug-ins to meet your own needs, which you can't do with Live's own plug-ins.

Index

Like the Book?

Let us know on Facebook or Twitter!

facebook.com/courseptr

twitter.com/courseptr

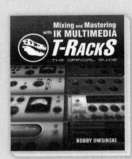
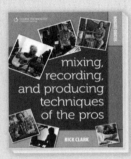